IRONY AND MISREADING
IN THE *ANNALS* OF TACITUS

This book examines Tacitus' *Annals* as an ironic portrayal of
Julio-Claudian Rome, through close analysis of passages in
which characters engage in interpretation and misreading. By
representing the misreading of signifying systems – such as
speech, gesture, writing, social structures and natural phenomena
– Tacitus obliquely comments upon the perversion of Rome's
republican structure in the new principate. Furthermore, this
study argues that the distinctively obscure style of the *Annals* is
used by Tacitus to draw his reader into the ambiguities and
compromises of the political regime it represents. The strain on
language and meaning both portrayed and enacted by the *Annals*
in this way gives voice to a form of political protest to which the
reader must respond in the course of interpreting the narrative.

ELLEN O'GORMAN is Lecturer in Classics in the University of
Bristol.

Irony and misreading
in the
Annals of Tacitus

ELLEN O'GORMAN

University of Bristol

PUBLISHED BY THE PRESS SYNDICATE OF THE UNIVERSITY OF CAMBRIDGE
The Pitt Building, Trumpington Street, Cambridge, United Kingdom

CAMBRIDGE UNIVERSITY PRESS
The Edinburgh Building, Cambridge CB2 2RU, UK   http://www.cup.cam.ac.uk
40 West 20th Street, New York, NY 10011–4211, USA   http://www.cup.org
10 Stamford Road, Oakleigh, Melbourne 3166, Australia

First published 2000

Printed in the United Kingdom at the University Press, Cambridge

Typeset in Monotype Bembo 11/13pt in QuarkXPress® [SE]

A catalogue record for this book is available from the British Library

Library of Congress cataloguing in publication data
O'Gorman, Ellen.
Irony and misreading in the Annals of Tacitus / Ellen O'Gorman.
    p.   cm.
Includes bibliographical references.
ISBN 0 521 66056 4 (hardback)
    1. Tacitus, Cornelius – Technique.   2. Tacitus, Cornelius.
Annales.   3. Rome – Historiography.   4. Rhetoric, Ancient.   5. Irony.
I. Title.
PA6705.A9035   1999
878'.0109–dc21   99-26462
                                                                      CIP

ISBN 0 521 66056 4 hardback

Contents

To study adequately any breakdown in communications we must first understand the nature and structure of the particular mode of communication that
has ceased to function . . . language in operation, language in drift, language in
the nascent state, and language in dissolution.

Roman Jakobson

*quid scribam . . . aut quo modo scribam aut quid omnino non scribam hoc tempore, di me
deaeque peius perdant quam perire me cotidie sentio, si scio.*

Tiberius Caesar

Preface

The editions of Tacitus' works used throughout this work are: R. M. Ogilvie and I. Richmond, *Agricola*, Oxford 1967; H. Heubner, *Annals*, Stuttgart 1983; K. Wellesley, *Historiae*, Leipzig 1989. All translations are my own unless otherwise indicated.

I have used the terms 'princeps' and 'emperor' interchangeably according to the rhythms of individual sentences rather than as precise analytical terms. Similarly (though perhaps less noticeably for the classicist reader) I have conflated 'Tacitus' and 'the narrator'.

This is a revised version of a PhD dissertation completed at the University of Bristol, Department of Classics and Ancient History, under the supervision of Catharine Edwards; the comments of my examiners, Charles Martindale and John Moles, and of the CUP readers contributed significantly to the transformation from thesis to book. Two years of graduate research were aided by a fees-only award from the British Academy; during this time I received further financial aid from the University Access Fund and held a teaching fellowship in the Department itself. I would also like to thank the University Alumni Foundation for funding attendance at overseas conferences. In the course of writing and rewriting I have benefited enormously from the intellectual engagement, careful reading, computer support, collegiality and friendship of many people: Duncan Barker, John Betts, Mark Buchan, Catríona Cannon, Louise Charkham, Ray Clare, Howard Duncan, Geoff Foote, Bob Fowler, Chris Hall, Debra Hershkowitz, Al Judge, Duncan Kennedy, Earl McQueen, Charles Martindale, Neville Morley, Lin Pountney, Christopher Rowe, Patrick Sinclair, Gideon Tearle, Neil Titman, Sharon Watson, Thomas Wiedemann, Phil Young and Vanda Zajko. I am also extremely grateful for the advice of Pauline Hire at Cambridge University Press, and for the scrupulous copy-editing of Susan Moore. Finally, I would like to thank my family, Matty and Peggy Fox, Duncan Kennedy and Synnøva O'Gorman, and especially my mother, Pauline O'Gorman, to whom this book is dedicated.

Introduction:
irony, history, reading

> The ironist aspires to be somebody who gets in on some redescription,
> who manages to change some parts of the vocabularies being used. The
> ironist wants to be a strong poet.
>
> Michael Roth, *The Ironist's Cage*

SENTENCE STRUCTURE AND HISTORICAL INTERPRETATION

Tacitus is a notoriously difficult writer; the central theme of this study is
what the difficulty of Tacitus means and what are the possible ways a
reader can respond to this difficulty. Examining what a difficulty *means* is
a rather different action to examining what a difficulty *is*: in the latter
case, we identify difficulty, overcome and disregard it; in the former case
we bring it with us, as it were, entering into an ongoing relationship with
difficulty. I will argue in this study that what is difficult and obscure in
Tacitus' style of writing, what seems to call out for clarification, is central
to Tacitus' modality of historical and political thought. In other words,
Tacitus conveys to his readers his conception of imperial politics by
enmeshing them in ambiguous and complicated Latin sentences. If we
decode these sentences and translate Tacitus into clear prose, therefore,
we lose the historical representation and analysis of which Tacitus'
writing is the vehicle. To overcome the difficulty of Tacitus is ultimately
to disregard him; instead we must bring Tacitus' difficult style along with
us and examine how that style informs not only what we read but *how* we
read.

This argument depends upon an association between Tacitus' subject
(Roman history at the time of the Julio-Claudian emperors) and Tacitus'
writing. In other words, it assumes that when we read Tacitus' *Annals* we
do so not exclusively either to find out about first-century Rome or to
examine Tacitean style, but for a combination of both purposes, however

I

much we may emphasise one over the other as the object of our study. If we conceive of the two as fully separable we will discard either Tacitean style (in favour of a more realistic narrative of the past) or Tacitean politics (in favour of a more formalist analysis of the text's structure). If, as I hope to do here, we conceive of the two as not entirely separable, we can approach a position where the formal structures of Tacitus' prose embody a political judgement of the principate. Tacitean style can be seen as the manifestation in narrative of a particular historical understanding, one which is integrally linked to a senatorial view of the principate. Sir Ronald Syme, in an article entitled 'The senator as historian', stressed the extent to which historiography, in this tradition, embodied the perspectives of the ruling class.

> In the beginning, history was written by senators (first a Fabius, and Cato was the first to use the Latin language); it remained for a long time the monopoly of the governing order; and it kept the firm imprint of its origins ever after. The senator came to his task in mature years, with a proper knowledge of men and government, a sharp and merciless insight. Taking up the pen, he fought again the old battles of Forum and Curia. Exacerbated by failure or not mollified by worldly success, he asserted a personal claim to glory and survival; and, if he wrote in retirement from affairs, it was not always with tranquillity of mind.[1]

The senator's history is informed by his 'proper knowledge', knowledge acquired through practice in government. Syme goes on to inscribe Tacitus in this tradition, yet Tacitus wrote under the principate, at a time when the senate continued to act out its function while watching the encroachment of the imperial household onto its executive power. The position of the senatorial historian in relation to the history of the principate is inevitably sceptical, not only about the new mode of administration but also about the place of the senator in this new political world.

Syme, in the passage quoted above, writes a history of historiography, situating Tacitus' writing in a tradition which starts with Fabius and Cato. Another version of literary history (constructed by Syme elsewhere, as we shall see) places Tacitus' historical perspective and the style which embodies it into a tradition of sceptical historiography which stretches back to Thucydides in the fifth century BC. If we detach the notion of the sceptical historian from any specific historical period (such

---

[1] Syme (1970) 1–2.

as fifth-century Athens or Imperial Rome) we can sketch in generally universal terms what denotes the sceptical historian: one who expresses suspicion at evident causes or pretexts, preferring instead to represent himself as scrutinising the appearance of things (presumed to be false) in order to penetrate to the less evident or hidden causes (presumed to be true). Most importantly, the sceptical historian presents his reader with *both* false appearance *and* hidden truth, as well as the scrutiny which led him to characterise things in such a manner. For such a historian language becomes important both as the means and the object of enquiry. False appearances for the most part are held in place by lying words and euphemisms; the historian in turn uses his own language to suggest where words are used as a veil to obscure the truth and where words directly and transparently represent the truth. For a sceptical historian such as Tacitus, however, false appearances are just as important as, if not more important than, hidden truth. To represent a political regime as one sustained on façade and deception is to make a significant judgement about it, and an understanding of that regime will in part be founded on the logic and structure of the façade.

In other words, scepticism towards, say, Augustus' claim to have restored the republic would be articulated by suggesting that 'restoration of the republic' is a euphemism masking the hidden truth, which could be 'establishment of a principate' or 'restitution of monarchy'. But although 'restoration of the republic' is thereby characterised as a false appearance, its role as a powerful ideological claim is not diminished; the phrase evokes the complexity of Augustus' hold not only on contemporary power but also on history. It offers a historian and her readers a way of understanding the Augustan regime which does not depend upon the truth value of the phrase 'restoration of the republic'.

Central to sceptical history, therefore, and central to Tacitus is the practice of analysing events by representing an appearance as false and unearthing something claimed to be truth, which is sometimes at odds with the appearance. Most importantly, however, the sceptical historian does not replace falsehood with truth, thereby erasing the façade, but rather sets the two in conjunction. Nor is the truth necessarily the dominant feature of the historian's thought, as I have argued above. Historical understanding in Tacitus' writing, therefore, resides in the continual interplay of these sometimes incompatible features, false appearance and hidden truth.

This modality of historical understanding is expressed in Tacitus'

3

distinctive sentence structure; three elements in particular contribute to this expression. The first is the relationship and respective weight of main clauses and subordinate clauses. The Tacitean sentence notoriously displaces emphasis from the main clause onto subordinate clauses, which carry the weight of the sentence's meaning but remain syntactically dependent, not self-sufficient. Ronald Martin introduced the issue in this way.

> (Tacitus) makes use, far more than any other Latin writer, of sentences in which the main clause is completed early and the centre of gravity is displaced to appended, syntactically subordinate, elements. But the restructuring of the sentence is not simply a mannered anti-classical reaction; rather it reflects a different attitude towards history.[2]

As an example of this, we can consider a sentence from early in book 2 of the *Annals*, where Tiberius' reaction to disturbances in Parthia and Armenia is presented, along with an interpretation of this reaction.

> But it did not seem unpleasing to Tiberius that the East was in turmoil, since on this pretext he could remove Germanicus from his customary legions and put him in the way of deceit and disaster when he was placed in charge of new provinces.
>
> *ceterum Tiberio haud ingratum accidit turbari res Orientis, ut ea specie Germanicum suetis legionibus abstraheret novisque provinciis impositum dolo simul et casibus obiectaret.* (2.5.1)

Although the main clause, occupying a strong position, opens the chapter, the subordinate clause governed by *ut* first makes Tiberius' reaction understandable to the reader, and also forms the crucial transition from the Eastern provinces to the German campaigns, the subject of the ensuing narrative. The subordinate clause, therefore, is the predominant feature of both narrative and historical explanation. As well as explaining Tiberius' reaction, the subordinate clause sets up the Eastern mission as a 'pretext' for the subversion of Germanicus; the telling word *species*, by implying that Tiberius' provincial policy is a cloak for a deeper purpose, enhances the explanatory authority of the subordinate clause.

At other times the Tacitean sentence is structured in the following ways: external evidence is the matter of the main clause, while interpretation, usually of hidden causes, makes up the subordinate clauses; or a fact is stated in the main clause while two subordinate clauses, compris-

---

[2] Martin (1981) 221.

4

ing the false apparent cause and the true hidden cause, are placed in apposition to each other. The hidden truth uncovered by the historian, therefore, depends upon the false appearance, which as the main clause or a balancing subordinate clause supports grammatically what it is claimed to obscure politically. This syntactical interdependence is not meaningless, but rather reflects the necessity for keeping falsehood and truth in interplay for historical understanding.

An example of this is the striking conclusion to book 1, to which I will return in a number of the following chapters. The generalised statement about freedom with which Tacitus ends this book seems to be provoked by the ambiguity of Tiberius' comments about the candidates for the consulship.

> Often he said that he had only passed on to the consuls the names of those who had proposed themselves as candidates; but others could propose themselves, if they had confidence in their influence or merit: plausible in words, in matter empty or deceitful, and the more they were cloaked in the mask of liberty, the more they were bound to break out in more dangerous servitude.

> *plerumque eos tantum apud se professos disseruit, quorum nomina consulibus edidisset; posse et alios profiteri, si gratiae aut meritis confiderent: speciosa verbis, re inania aut subdola, quantoque maiore libertatis imagine tegebantur, tanto eruptura ad infensius servitium.* (1.81.3)

The interpretation of Tiberius' speech is structured around the contrast between appearance (words) and reality (matter), highlighted, as F. R. D. Goodyear remarked, by the chiastic arrangement of the contrasting terms.[3] But the stark contrast between appearance and reality here is glossed by a comparative construction which creates syntactical interdependence between the two. The correlation of false appearances to outbreaks of truth conveyed by the structure *quanto . . . tanto* suggests that truth can only be understood in relation to its indicator, falsehood. This suggestion once more strengthens the status of falsehood in the process of historical understanding.

The second element of the Tacitean sentence, associated with the first, is the shift from one kind of syntactical construction to another between clauses which in classical Latin would appear under the same construction. Friedrich Klingner summed up the effect as follows:

---

[3] Goodyear (1981) 186.

A syntactical system is scarcely indicated before it is already overtaken by a second, and so on. At no point in the course of the sentence is one able to anticipate the overall direction in thought or form.[4]

This syntactical diversification (*variatio*), as Klingner has observed, not only creates a lively style, but also makes a requirement of the reader to read closely. It suggests that clauses, like appearances, are not equally balanced in experienced reality. Most importantly, when false appearance and hidden truth are presented in this way, the imbalance between clauses actively discourages simple replacement of falsehood with truth. In other words, the Tacitean sentence represents truth and falsehood in language which is not transferable between clauses.

A rather oblique instance of this could be seen to be the opening of the account of Tiberius' withdrawal from Rome in book 4. The narrative of this occurrence diverges almost immediately into a consideration of several, not mutually exclusive, reasons for the emperor's self-exile. But the opening sentence presents the occurrence itself in terms of appearance and reality.

> Meanwhile after having long considered and often deferred his plan Caesar finally travelled into Campania, on the pretext of dedicating temples, one to Jove at Capua, another to Augustus at Nola, but determined to live far away from the city.

> *inter quae diu meditato prolatoque saepius consilio tandem Caesar in Campaniam, specie dedicandi templa apud Capuam Iovi, apud Nolam Augusto, sed certus procul urbe degere.* (4.57.1)

As with the previous example from book 2, the term 'pretext' (*species*) implies some deeper purpose which the opening ablative absolute clause has also hinted at in referring to a 'long considered plan'. The reality which this pretext masks is represented in the emphatic participle phrase at the end of the sentence. Although this conclusion 'reveals' Tiberius' determination masked by the pretext, the switch from ablative noun (*specie*) to nominative participle (*certus*) creates a disjunction between the two clauses. The adverbial *specie*, denoting the manner or means of Tiberius' movements, is not straightforwardly balanced by the adjectival *certus*, which qualifies Tiberius by indicating his state of mind. Indeed, the opening of the participle phrase with *sed certus* momentarily suggests that certain knowledge about Tiberius' real intentions is about to be

---

[4] Klingner (1955) 193.

revealed.[5] Hence the term *certus* intensifies the sense that the final phrase is revealing the truth, while at the same time that sense is undermined by awareness that it depends upon a partial misreading of the words.

The final element of sentence structure is asyndeton, the juxtaposition of clauses without explicit conjunctions. Here the effect is not so much of imbalance or variety as of vivid concentration. The relationship between clauses, rather than being unexpected, remains to be determined. Again the reader is required to look closely, and to interpret the sentence in part by assigning a relationship from clause to clause. Syme, referring to this asyndetic practice, expressed confidence in the process of interpretation.

> The omission of words and connectives goes to ruthless extremes for the sake of speed, concentration, and antithesis; and stages in a sequence of thought or action are suppressed, baffling translation (but not hard to understand).[6]

When Syme separates 'translation' and 'understanding' in this way he glosses over the difficulty of assigning unspoken conjunctions to a Tacitean sentence, and thereby he replicates the dilemma in which readers find themselves, faced both with the difficult text and with the expectations of the community of readers. We can consider this in relation to perhaps the most infamous example of Tacitean compression: the opening paragraph of the *Annals*, which sketches the history of power at Rome in a succession of brief sentences. In the absence of conjunctions which would make explicit the interpretation of this history, the reader's attention is directed instead to the densely packed terms of power and power-holders in the passage, and is required to invent a progression between them.

> The city of Rome from the beginning was ruled by kings; Lucius Brutus established freedom and the consulship. Dictatorships were taken up when the time required it; neither was decemviral power valid beyond two years, nor did the consular jurisdiction of military tribunes last long. The despotisms of Cinna and Sulla were not of long duration; and the strength of Pompey and Crassus quickly passed to Caesar, as did the armed force of Lepidus and Antony to Augustus, who accepted everything, worn out with civil discord, under his command in the name of princeps.

---

[5] *TLL certus* III A/B.   [6] Syme (1958) 347.

urbem Romam a principio reges habuere; libertatem et consulatum L. Brutus institituit. dictaturae ad tempus sumebantur; neque decemviralis potestas ultra biennium, neque tribunorum militum consulare ius diu valuit. non Cinnae, non Sullae longa dominatio; et Pompei Crassique potentia cito in Caesarem, Lepidi atque Antonii arma in Augustum cessere, qui cuncta discordiis civilibus fessa nomine principis sub imperium accepit. (1.1.1)

The concluding relative clause about Augustus serves to slow down the narrative as the turbulence of the old Republic gives way to the stability of the new status quo. This is in contrast to the opening sentences, a series of independent main clauses, each describing a different aspect of power at Rome. The extreme variety of words for power (*potestas, ius, dominatio, potentia, arma, imperium*) suggests at first that this constitutes a precise description of different aspects of rule, or a studied avoidance of synonyms.[7] But the extreme disjunction between the independent clauses can be provoking to the reader of history, who expects more than a simple temporal progression from the kings of early Rome to the civil wars of the first century BC. What we seem to be presented with in this passage is a naïve chronicle, but the implicit temporal progression appears to us as the false appearance beneath which we must probe.[8] Precisely the disjunction between the different statements, the absence of explicit links, evokes the idea of a hidden reality, a true relationship between these different aspects of power.

One series of relationships we could invent depends upon the notion of time, which is also explicit in the passage. The different aspects of power here seem to be differentiated in part by their duration, and terms recur which convey the time-bound nature of power (*ad tempus, ultra biennium, neque diu, non longa, cito*). The three modes of rule which are not explicitly time-bound are monarchy in the first sentence, 'liberty and the consulship' (*libertas et consulatus*) in the second, and 'command in the name of princeps' (*imperium nomine principis*) at the end. While we can

---

[7] Koestermann (1963) 58, for example, regards Tacitus' practice here as an avoidance of the same terms on stylistic grounds. The politics of judging whether terms are synonymous, oppositional or 'mere' variety is discussed further in the next section of this chapter.

[8] White (1978) 93 discusses such reliance on 'mere' temporal progression as 'the ironic denial that historical series have any kind of larger significance or describe any imaginable plot structure . . . [w]e could conceive such accounts of history as intending to serve as antidotes to their false or overemplotted counterparts and could represent them as an ironic return to mere chronicle as constituting the only sense which any cognitively responsible history could take'.

8

read the institution of liberty and the consulship as putting an end to monarchy, the most pressing question for the reader is whether we see liberty and the consulship as ending with the establishment of Augustus' *imperium*. The over-riding sense of types of power giving way one to another, which is conveyed by the insistence on their temporality, suggests that this is the case. But the absence of explicit conjunctions means that the responsibility for this interpretation rests upon the reader, who could equally decide to read liberty and the consulship as continuing to exist under Augustus' command.[9]

Moreover, any interpretation of the relationship between Brutus' institution and Augustus' *imperium* will affect and be affected by the relationship implied between the early kings of Rome and the new princeps. If these three types of rule (monarchy, oligarchy, principate) delineate and replace one another, what precise relationship does the reader invent between monarchy and principate? Tacitus leaves the historical interpretation here very much up to the reader by his opening statement 'the city of Rome from the beginning was ruled by kings', where no abstract noun for power is used, and even the verb 'to rule' can be translated in terms of possession, as 'to have' or 'to hold'. The reader is left to judge what the rule of kings would be called, to 'translate' this sentence as *imperium* or *dominatio* or whatever.

Tacitus' opening paragraph lacks a plot, reacting to the over-determination of Roman history by an ironic return to simple chronology as a means of understanding the past. But the irony of this chronicle is that it imposes on the reader the responsibility to create a plot in order to make 'full' sense of the passage. Whether they read the successive modes of power as progress, decline or cycle, they are implicated from the very outset of the narrative in the process and politics of historical interpretation.

In this way the process of scrutiny which the historian enacts in setting up false appearance against hidden truth continually invites the reader to join in, to scrutinise the text and decode its hidden meanings. As I stated at the outset of this section, a final decoding of Tacitus would ultimately be a different, a non-Tacitean work. On the other hand, a simple acceptance of what Tacitus says would seem also to be a singularly non-

---

[9] One interpretation which could be made from this passage is that, if liberty is bound up in the office of consul, the continuation of consulships in the principate stands as a sign of liberty under Augustus. Another interpretation would be to read this association of liberty and consulship alongside the conclusion to book I (quoted above), where Tiberius' ambiguous control over the candidate list is read as a sign that liberty is dead.

Tacitean activity. (I find it difficult to believe that the ideal reader of Tacitus is not a sceptical reader.) A reading practice that would more effectively mirror Tacitus' own sceptical enquiry would involve scrutiny of the text for what it says and how it says it, but would not aim to privilege one over the other so much as acknowledge their ongoing dynamic relationship.

THE IRONIC TRADITION

The term which above all others shapes this way of thinking about history is the term 'irony', which places an unquantifiable distinction between a statement and 'its' meaning. Hayden White, whose analyses of history-writing have been enormously influential over the last thirty years, characterises the ironic historian as follows:

> Anyone who originally encodes the world in the mode of metaphor, will be inclined to decode it – that is, narratively 'explicate' and discursively analyze it – as a congeries of individualities. To those for whom there is no real resemblance in the world, decodation must take the form of a disclosure, either of the simple *contiguity* of things (the mode of metonymy) or of the *contrast* that lies hidden within every resemblance or unity (the mode of irony).[10]

If we take the example I used earlier, that of Augustus' claim to have restored the republic, we can see how this claim encodes Augustus' acts in the metaphor of return to the past, and how this claim enforces a particular attitude not only to Augustus' acts but also to the past, as something worth returning to. A sceptical historian, disclosing a contrast between that claim and what he calls the truth (perhaps Augustus' establishment of the principate), is operating within the mode of irony in his representation of Augustus' acts, but his analysis too depends upon a representation of the past as something worth restoring. The difference is that the historian, unlike Augustus, maintains that the restoration does not *really* take place.

Tacitus' unmasking of the realities of power operating in the principate could be described as 'a disclosure ... of the contrast that lies hidden within every resemblance or unity'. But disclosure and decoding, as we have already seen, are processes which inherently value the disclosed or decoded phenomenon at the expense of that which obscures or encodes; since the obscurity is an important part of reading Tacitus we need to be

[10] White (1978) 128.

suspicious of terms such as 'decoding' which implicitly return us to a reading practice which we rejected for the reasons outlined above. The mode of 'irony', which White describes here as a process of decoding metaphor, potentially allows for a more Tacitean reading practice when it operates within language.

I have already defined irony as a mode of speaking which establishes an unquantifiable distinction between a statement and 'its' meaning. The word 'unquantifiable' is crucial here; the ironic statement does not mean what it says, yet it has a meaning which is both separate from and associated with the statement (hence my use of scare quotes in the phrase 'a statement and "its" meaning'). A crude definition of an ironic statement would define the meaning as *opposite to* what is said, but it is better to conceive of the meaning of an ironic statement as *different from* what is said, not exclusively or even necessarily its opposite. The ancient Roman definitions of irony, in the rhetorical handbooks of Cicero and Quintilian, use the term 'otherwise' or 'other than' to denote the difference between meaning and statement. Cicero in particular, referring to the mode of irony as 'dissimulation', says,

> Sophisticated dissimulation is when you think things other than what are said (*cum alia dicuntur ac sentias*), not, in that manner I spoke about earlier, when you say the opposite (*contraria*), as Crassus did to Lamia, but when in your whole manner of speaking you are at play seriously (*severe ludas*), when you think otherwise from what you say (*cum aliter sentias ac loquare*). (Cic. *De Orat.* 2.269)

Irony depends upon the divergence in sense between utterance (*quae dicuntur*) and the unsaid (*quae sentias*). But the nature of the unsaid is indeterminable; all we know about it is that it is *aliud* – *other than* what is uttered.[11]

---

[11] Quintilian's position of irony is (ironically) more difficult to pin down. At times he suggests that irony is a statement which conveys the opposite of its ostensible meaning, as at 9.2.44 and 9.2.65, in both of which he uses the term *contrarium*. But in the first of these two passages he goes on to characterise irony (both trope and figure) in more plural terms: 'that which is a trope is more blatant, and although it means other than what it says (*aliud dicit et sentit*) it does not pretend to be otherwise ... but in the figure the veiling of intention is apparent rather than explicit, and just as in the trope words diverge from words (*verba sint verbis diversa*), so in the figure the meaning diverges from the speech and tone of voice and the whole aspect of the case' (Quint. *Inst. Orat.* 9.2.46). I am not sure that Quintilian propounds a particularly 'neat theory' of irony, and am more interested here in the echoes of Cicero, in particular the reliance on the more ambiguous *aliud* to characterise the unsaid meanings of the ironic statement.

How then are we to read something which means other than what it says? If the difference between meaning and statement is not one of opposition, we cannot decode irony simply by appending 'not' to the end of every sentence. Linda Hutcheon suggests that this uncertainty entangles the reader in the dynamics of irony:

> With irony, there are ... dynamic and plural relations among the text or utterance (and its context), the so-called ironist, the interpreter, and the circumstances surrounding the discursive situation; it is these that mess up neat theories of irony that see the task of the interpreter simply as one of decoding or reconstructing some 'real' meaning (usually named as the 'ironic' one) ..., a meaning that is hidden, but deemed accessible, behind the stated one.[12]

So, for example, if we make the ironic statement, 'Augustus, of course, claimed to have effected a restoration of the republic', we are not only stating a surface meaning which is arguably true, we are also evoking the unsaid, that what Augustus was effecting was something other than a restoration of the republic. It is up to the reader to decide what precisely Augustus is said, or rather *not* said, to have effected (establishment of principate, restitution of monarchy, suppression of freedom, institution of tyranny, death-blow to the oligarchy ...), since any of these is potentially what the ironic statement *really* means. But since the choice of meaning is left to the reader, making that choice entails taking up a position, making a political judgement about Augustus' regime. Hence it could be argued that irony, and Tacitean irony in particular, is mobilised in relation not only to the principate but also to its critics, suggesting that they examine closely the nature of the principate they criticise *and* the nature of their criticism. The ironical statement therefore not only embodies a particular, sceptical attitude on the part of the writer, but also compels the reader to take her own political stance in relation to the past; taking that stance is part of the act of reading. Also, and most importantly, the ironical statement cannot simply be reduced to one precise political judgement any more than it can be expanded to cover *all* political judgements; readers will variously argue for what they believe is the real meaning of the ironical statement, but it will for the most part be read

---

[12] Hutcheon (1994) 11. Consequently the term 'irony' can be seen to allow more plurality of meaning than the recently employed term 'doublespeak', on which see Bartsch (1994). Doublespeak inherently brings the reader down to a dual or double meaning in any statement, leading back to the crude notion of oppositional meaning which I am attempting to leave behind in the discussion above.

ironically (the telling 'of course' makes it difficult to preclude irony) and therefore will not be read as an acceptance or verification of Augustus' claim.

Given all of this, it is hardly surprising that Klingner characterised reading Tacitus as follows:

> Each new clause appears before the reader like an uncanny encounter with a hidden thing, an ambush for a wayfarer. In this way the reader is drawn into the drama of the history, a drama which remains unknown from moment to moment, which changes its direction constantly and is oppressingly dangerous. He feels that he is in the middle of the torment of events; he witnesses with consternation the dramatic reversals of circumstance like one present, not with the detachment and superiority of the analytic observer but like, for example, the reader of Caesar.[13]

Those parts of Tacitus' text which perhaps most explicitly invite reflection upon the role of Tacitus' reader are the episodes in which characters within the text themselves engage in acts of reading and interpretation. Tacitus' reader follows the characters (sometimes the narrator) in the act of reading, not always coming to the same conclusion; the differences as well as the parallels are suggestive. In particular, Tacitus continually represents his characters in the act of *misreading*; the failure of interpretative skills seems to be a dominant feature of Tacitus' Imperial Rome. This makes an important political point. The logic of communication depends upon a shared range of meanings, which are usually constituted by the society in which the communication takes place.

> [I]n the optimal exchange of information the speaker and the listener have at their disposal more or less the same 'filing cabinet of *prefabricated* representations' ... Thus the efficiency of a speech event demands the use of a common code by its participants.[14]

The 'prefabricated representations' on which the aristocracy of Julio-Claudian Rome draw are republican, senatorial rhetorical tropes, but the nature of the principate is such that these representations are insufficient in their new environment. Sign systems such as physiognomy, architecture, astrology and both written and spoken language, all of which are instrumental in the organisation of Roman culture, are evoked in order to point up their failure to convey meaning in the new world of

---

[13] Klingner (1955) 193.   [14] Jakobson (1971) 241.

the principate. In other words, the principate is portrayed as breaking with tradition not only politically but in hermeneutic, interpretative terms as well; its 'semantic relevance' is called into question. The disjunctive sign system can thus be mobilised as a metaphor, employed ironically, for the political regime at which the narrative protests.

STASIS AND STATUS

Tacitus, then, represents Imperial Rome as a place and a time where social communication breaks down to a certain extent, resulting in misunderstandings, pretence and perhaps aporia. Not only does pervasive misunderstanding serve as a powerful metaphor for the perversion of the political system from senatorial to imperial rule, it also operates as the means by which Tacitus situates himself in a tradition of sceptical historiography, reaching back through his Roman predecessor Sallust to the Greek historian Thucydides. In all three historians (as well as elsewhere in ancient writing) the perversion of language and of its capacity to convey meaning is presented as a symptom of a society in the midst of social and moral upheaval. The emblematic passage from Thucydides' history is his account of revolution (*stasis*) spreading from Corcyra through the Greek cities in 427 BC.

> Then the other cities revolted, and those who revolted later, hearing of past actions, greatly increased the excess (ὑπερβολήν) of innovating (καινοῦσθαι) their ideas (διανοίας) by the cunning art (περιτεχνήσει) of their attacks and the novelties (ἀτοπίαι) of their revenge. And the customary names of things were exchanged (ἀντήλλαξαν) according to their judgement. For unreasonable recklessness was called loyal courage (τόλμα μὲν γὰρ ἀλόγιστος ἀνδρεία φιλέταιρος ἐνομίσθη), and cautious delay was timidity veiled under a fine name (εὐπρεπής), and wisdom was a cloak (πρόσχημα) for cowardice, and understanding of the whole picture was inactivity in all things; thoughtless vehemence was considered (προσετέθη) the mark of a man, and to plot desertion was a fair reason for steadfastness. (Thuc. 3.82.3–4)

Thucydides here uses the perversion of language, words wrenched from their customary meanings and misapplied elsewhere, to illustrate most vividly the perversion of political and social norms during *stasis*. He has already narrated how such social constraints as family relationships or religious respect have ceased to have any force; now he demonstrates how the very language used to evaluate human actions is strained. When the actions and words of the revolutionaries (στασιῶται) are represented as unnatural and uncustomary, nature and custom are assumed to utilise language which has a transparent, unforced correspondence to reality. In other words, language is 'normally' clear and *appropriate*; it is customary to use the *proper* words for things. When Thucydides records the perversion of language he also restates its proper usage: 'unreasonable recklessness was called loyal courage' is a statement which not only charts the application of the term 'loyal courage' but also grounds the narrative in the assumption that the action so called is *properly* named 'unreasonable recklessness'. The judgements of the στασιῶται, how they evaluated their actions, are viewed through the filter of Thucydides' assertion of the proper value of these actions. This could be seen as ironic history *par excellence*, as the latent contrast between revolutionary word (loyal courage) and deed (unreasonable recklessness) is made manifest in Thucydides' narrative.

But this irony, too, is what draws the reader into a complex relationship with Thucydides' text. It achieves this by three strategies. The first is the demonstration by the text that language, and its capacity to mean or to mislead, works at all levels. The so-called 'false terms', the terms which are 'misapplied' in *stasis*, are themselves seemingly used in a self-consciously rhetorical fashion. So the στασιῶται represent themselves as unmasking misapplied language when they rename 'cautious delay' as 'timidity veiled under a fine name' (εὐπρεπής), and 'wisdom' as 'a cloak for cowardice' (πρόσχημα). While the narrative itself sets up the vocabulary of *stasis* as 'false', the false vocabulary which it cites in turn questions the idea of a natural language before *stasis*, a natural language which must be assumed if the force of the narrative's condemnation is to be maintained.[15] Furthermore, the Thucydidean text at first seems to offer a reassuring control over the difficult question of meaning by presenting it as a metaphor; the passage conveys the extremes of violence and sacrilege perpetrated during this period through a change in language use: words as a metaphor for acts. Colin Macleod represented this as circumstances shaping behaviour and belief, and *subsequently* language.[16] But language is not so easily confined to the role of metaphor or symptom of *stasis*. The sentence preceding the language-change 'metaphor' arguably represents

---

[15] Macleod (1983) 133: 'the *stasiotai* not only modified language, but in doing so, believed themselves to be unmasking falsehood'.   [16] Macleod (1983) 125.

the change in behaviour and belief which (supposedly) precedes the change in language. But this first sentence is itself charged with rhetorical and quasi-rhetorical terms.

> Those who revolted later, hearing of past actions, greatly increased the excess/hyperbole (ὑπερβολήν) of innovating (καινοῦσθαι) their ideas/meanings (διανοίας) by the cunning art (περιτεχνήσει) of their attacks and the novelties (ἀτοπίαι) of their revenge.

Stasis, like war, is presented as a form of perverted art in Thucydides' history; here the acquisition of *stasis* as art or skill (τέχνη) appears as 'a kind of sophistic instruction'.[17] The actions of the στασιῶται are hyperbolic; they strain *topoi* unnaturally, and form meanings which depend overmuch upon novelty for effect: the στασιῶται are already Silver Latin. This sentence of Thucydides problematises the characterisation of the rest of the passage as 'just' metaphor; language and its perversion does not simply 'stand for' the perversions of non-linguistic actions. Rather, *stasis* and language are implicated throughout; the challenge that the text presents to the reader to 'decode' its vocabulary induces the very confusion that Thucydides is representing as having afflicted the Greek states in 427 BC.

This is particularly to be noted in the second strategy of the ironic text. This has to do with how we read the relationship between the 'true' term and the 'false' term in this passage. The apparent syntactical simplicity of the final sentence in the passage is achieved by the balancing of various substantival phrases around the verbs 'was called' (ἐνομίσθη) and 'was considered' (προσετέθη). This structure draws the reader into an interpretation of the text which depends upon polarity, whereby a word either means *exactly* what it says or *exactly the opposite* of what it says. This would seem to be backed up by Thucydides' statement that 'the customary names of things were *exchanged*' (ἀντήλλαξαν).[18] But the contrast between, for example, 'unreasonable recklessness' and 'loyal courage' does not simply happen, nor does it remain uncontested. One reading of the passage, that of Dionysius of Halicarnassus, by evaluating the adjectives 'unreasonable' and 'loyal' as superfluous, presented 'recklessness' (τόλμα) and 'courage' (ἀνδρεία) as 'natural', unquestioned opposites (Dion. Hal. *De Thuc.* 29). Macleod, addressing Dionysius' criticisms, maintained that '[s]ince *tolma* and *andreia* . . . could be all but synony-

---

[17] Macleod (1983) 125.   [18] Macleod (1983) 132; Wilson (1982) 20.

16

mous, the adjectives serve to show exactly what was the confusion that the *stasiotai* brought about by their use of language'.[19] In other words, Macleod's reading presents the nouns not as 'natural' opposites but as 'natural' synonyms; the adjectives, the *real* 'natural' opposites, serve to demarcate the shift of meaning. Yet again, the commentator A.W. Gomme considered the nouns to be opposites when he marked as 'clearly wrong' the interpretation of τόλμα and ἀνδρεία as *variatio* rather than contrast,[20] and John Wilson (arguing against the view that words in *stasis* 'change their meanings') put forward the view that 'there are aspects or *species* of phenomena normally called τόλμα ἀλόγιστος . . . which could reasonably be called ἀνδρεία'.[21] These readings demonstrate that, even among those (such as Gomme, Macleod and Dionysius) who subscribe to the view that direct contrast is here represented, there is no agreement as to exactly where the contrast resides, whether it is between the adjectives or the nouns. The authority for interpretation cannot depend upon an appeal to the 'real meaning' of words, or the 'natural structure' of clauses. The redefinitions enforced by the στασιῶται, therefore, demonstrably represent the same process as Thucydides' own narrativising of these events. To a great extent the reader is responsible for *inventing* the ironies of the Thucydidean text, which interrogates each reader in turn by its presentation of these questionable 'opposites'.

The third strategy which draws the reader into a dynamic relationship with the text has to do with the harshness or difficulty of Thucydidean style. Not only is it difficult to establish where the exact force of the ironic contrasts between words resides, but also the very structure of the sentences creates unease in the reader. Dionysius of Halicarnassus, whose comments on Thucydides' adjectives I have noted above, subjects this particular passage to an extended close reading, seeing in it an example of *inappropriate* language. Dionysius in effect rewrites the passage in a more direct (κυριώτερον), clear (σαφές) and unpretentious (οὔτε θεατρικόν) language. In one respect Dionysius can be seen as missing the point by not appreciating Thucydides' style here, but in another respect he can be seen as subjecting Thucydides to a similar sort of analysis to the one brought to bear upon the στασιῶται by Thucydides himself. In short,

---

[19] Macleod (1983) 133.
[20] Gomme (1956) *ad loc.*, citing Jan Ros (1938) *Die* ΜΕΤΑΒΟΛΗ *(Variatio) als Stilprinzip des Thukydides*, Paderborn.   [21] Wilson (1982) 19.

Dionysius indicts Thucydides for the improper use and excessive innovation of language. Thus he introduces his discussion of Thucydidean
style by promising to delineate the stylistic aspects in which Thucydides
was the first to innovate (ἐκαίνωσεν), using the same verb as Thucydides
himself did of the innovations in revolutionary action (καινοῦσθαι). In
his detailed discussion of the constituents of Thucydidean style, moreover, Dionysius continually reasserts the proper, normal, or natural use of
language: 'of the nouns themselves he inverts (ἀναστρέφων) their use . . .
he alters the natural uses (φύσεις) of singular and plural . . . and violates
the natural (κατὰ φύσιν) agreement of gender' (Dion. Hal. *De Thuc.* 24).
Among Thucydides' faults Dionysius singles out 'a failure to observe
throughout the whole of his history in what way strange and artificial
language should be used, and how far he should go before stopping'.
Thucydidean excess, wrenching words from their proper place, seems
very close to the excess of *stasis*, but then *stasis* is for us always a very
Thucydidean phenomenon. The difficulty of language is an integral
feature of inhabiting *stasis*, and the Thucydidean representation ensures
that a reader experiences *stasis* as interpretation. Revolution is experienced as linguistic play, but it is a deadly serious game; as Cicero says,
irony is when you play seriously (*cum severe ludas*).

　　This passage of Thucydides is, as I have said, emblematic for the tradition in which some Roman historians situated themselves. In the first
century BC the ex-senator Sallust produced two monographs and a
history in this Thucydidean mode. Sir Ronald Syme, in his study of
Sallust, traces two possible reasons for Sallust's turn to Thucydides. The
first evokes the context of the contemporary Roman debate on Attic
versus Asiatic style; Sallust's turn to Thucydides is thereby interpreted in
terms of Sallust's anti-Ciceronianism. The second seeks to explain
Sallust's Thucydideanism in the context of the political situation.

> [F]or Sallust, Thucydides may have been a late and sudden discovery.
> Less perhaps from literary polemics than as a result of civil war, disillu
> sion, and the impulsion towards history.[22]

Syme here makes of Thucydides an appropriate voice for the last generations of the Roman republic, suggesting perhaps that Thucydidean style
was adopted by Sallust because it could most accurately and properly
represent the events which Sallust wished to record. This suggestion of

---

[22] Syme (1964) 54.

18

Syme's follows Sallust's own implicit claim that his representation has a particularly privileged relationship to the truth. But very strong historical interpretations are being made when Thucydidean style is represented as appropriate for writing a history of events nearly three centuries later. The events described and experienced by Thucydides in the fifth century BC are called up as a parallel, a type in relation to which the first-century BC Roman events will make sense. The differences between the two sets of events are, perhaps, played down.

This situation is exacerbated when we bring Tacitus back into the picture. We have now three historians, one Greek, two Roman, whose lives span five centuries, but who are seen to be united by a tradition of writing ironic history. The style of writing glosses over the immense temporal differences between these histories. Although a historian mobilises all the power of a tradition when he situates himself within it, tradition also threatens to undo the historical specificity which is also claimed when writing about particular events at a particular time. In other words, when Tacitus, in very Thucydidean terms, raises his voice in protest against the principate by focusing on the perversion of language, he risks subverting his specific political point by evoking a sense of timelessness for the phenomenon.

One way in which Tacitus calls attention to the difference between himself and Thucydides allows him to retain the historical specificity of his attack on the emperors. When Augustus by gradual encroachment transformed the oligarchy of Rome into an autocracy, one of the most potent justifications for his continued supremacy was achieved by pointing to the alternative, what he represented as the *inevitable* alternative: civil war. In his list of achievements Augustus refers to the period 'after I had extinguished the civil wars and by universal consent was in charge of everything' (*Res Gestae Divi Augusti* 34.1). Tacitus, as we have already seen, rewords this as 'Augustus, who accepted everything, worn out with civil discord, under his rule with the name of princeps' (*Ann.* 1.1.1). The threat of civil war enforces compliance with the rule of one man, but when Tacitus, describing this regime, reworks the style of writing which was seen as appropriate not only for describing revolution in the Greek states but also for Sallust's history of a Roman civil war, he is implicitly challenging the imperial claim that the principate is a better alternative to a civil war. The principate, Tacitus claims, is most properly represented in a style which evokes its similarities to, rather than its differences from, civil war. I will return to this in my analysis of book 1.

At the end of his three-chapter summary of Augustus' rise to power, Tacitus describes the new Roman state, comprising men who have experienced only civil war and autocracy, in terms which question Augustus' claim to have restored the republic: 'How many individuals were left who had seen the republic?' or 'How few individuals were left who had seen the republic!' (1.3.7).[23] The fourth chapter, embarking on the account of Augustus' death, epitomises Augustan Rome in Thucydidean terms: 'Therefore, with the state revolutionised (*verso civitatis statu*), there was nothing left anywhere of ancient, decent morality' (1.4.1). The two words *versus status* render in Latin the combination of unchanging *static* and transforming, *inverted* elements which is covered by the single Greek word *stasis*.[24] Tacitus points up his translation of Thucydidean *stasis* here by amplifying *versus status* with the words 'there was nothing left anywhere of ancient, decent morality': precisely the qualities of innovation and wickedness which marked the actions of Thucydides' revolutionaries. Moreover, the use of *versus status* self-consciously gestures towards itself as translation; since *vertere*, 'to turn' or 'to invert', can also mean 'to translate' (OLD 24a), *versus status* can be read as meaning 'translated *stasis*'. Syme referred to this Thucydidean line of Tacitus' as 'highly relevant to the phraseology of the revolutionary age',[25] and himself took on the trope when he entitled his history of Augustus 'The Roman Revolution', arguably an English translation of Tacitus' phrase.

The words *versus status*, therefore, signal both the tradition of ironic history and the difference from that tradition. This is not a simple repetition of *stasis*, collapsing Tacitus' and Thucydides' texts into a timeless irony, undifferentiated in its political application. Rather, *versus status* is both the same as *stasis*, by explicating its contradictory elements, and a new twist (or turn) on *stasis*, making its own particular representations. If under the new regime the accustomed evaluations of words change, this is potentially so of the phrase *versus status* itself; the question of whether and to what extent it *means* 'stasis' both draws attention to and enacts the strain upon language. This reflects in microcosm a considerable risk taken by ironic history, which is that the writing of history itself is potentially circumscribed by the loss of meaning it describes. Tacitus portrays a new state from which the old values are absent and in which the vocabu-

---

[23] *quotus quisque reliquus, qui rem publicam vidisset?* How 'rhetorical' is this rhetorical question? Cf. O'Gorman (1995b) 104–8 for an extensive examination of this phrase.
[24] See Liddell & Scott *stasis* B.I.1 (stationariness) and B.I.3 (state of affairs) vs. B.III.2 (sedition, discord) and B.III.3 (division, dissent). [25] Syme (1958) 196 n. 4.

lary of the republic is perverted to a new use. How then can his reinstatement of republican values have any meaning? The profound discontinuity to which his history gives voice forecloses on the possibility of that history effecting any intervention into the political corruption of the principate; Tacitus potentially denies to his own writing the meaning which would enable it, as a senatorial history, to reclaim administrative power. As Michael Roth has put it, 'ironist critics present a landscape of the possibilities absent for them as well as for us'.[26] From this position the act of writing history might appear to be pointless from the outset. The very existence of Tacitus' history, however, could be said to rescue it from this extreme of meaninglessness, retaining partial (but only partial) control over signification. In particular, the existence of Tacitus' history may testify to an ironic hope for political redemption in some distant future.[27] Moreover, the multiple ironies of Tacitus' text could be seen to direct themselves to the eternal present of the reader. Misreading and meaninglessness are mobilised as political interpretation in the *Annals*, as I have argued above, but they could also be seen to have an immediate didactic purpose. The difficulty of Tacitus' text exhorts the reader to try harder, and to fight for the legitimation of her reading.

The evocation of meaninglessness in order to make a specific political point, therefore, tends to create an oscillating movement between extreme discontinuity and the restoration of some meaning or meanings. The reader of Tacitus, having learnt from his text, needs to position herself within this movement, to present her reading and her learning process as legitimate within a given community of readers. In keeping with the tradition of ironic history which I sketched above, most of the readings in this study are focused on specific terms in Tacitus which cover a contradictory range of meanings. So, for example, in my brief examination of the term *versus status* above, I explicated a number of possible meanings for the word *versus*, from 'overturned' and 'revolutionised' to 'translated'. The aim of such readings is not to establish one final meaning for the word under analysis, but to allow a multiplicity of meanings to interact at the level of the individual sentence, within the passage as a whole, and across the entire text, where the repetition of words and phrases offers the opportunity to re-read and re-invent the meaning at any particular point. Clearly the multiple meanings of a sentence or a

---

[26] Roth (1995) 156.
[27] I will return to this possibility at the end of the next chapter.

phrase are not organised without hierarchy; some meanings will be more 'self-evident' while others will strain against what seems to be the overall trend of the sentence. But, as I have argued throughout this introduction, language under strain is the representation of ironic history; the ironic reader, according to my position, gains much from engaging in a sort of creative misreading.

Imperium sine fine: problems of definition in *Annals* I

Every narrative, however seemingly 'full', is constructed on the basis of a set of events that might have been included but were left out ... And this consideration permits us to ask what kind of notion of reality authorizes construction of a narrative account of reality in which continuity rather than discontinuity governs the articulation of the discourse.

Hayden White, *The Content of the Form*

boundlessness ... *See also* continuity

Deborah Roberts, Francis Dunn and Don Fowler, index to
Classical Closure

In the introductory chapter I had already started to examine how Tacitus' designation of the Augustan regime as a *versus status* potentially draws a line of continuity between the principate and the civil wars which that regime claims to have resolved. Tacitus' use of the phrase, therefore, can be seen to dissent from the totalising claims of the principate: claims to order, stability, and continuity with a pre-civil war (republican) past. In contrast, Tacitus offers a different totalising claim about the principate: that it manifests the very same destructive elements of disorder within its regime. Thereby he counters the claim to continuity (totalising boundlessness) by redescribing it as a chaotic (totalising) boundlessness achieved by the collapse of definitions. This entails, most importantly, the collapse of the boundary between principate and civil war. I have gestured towards this ironic redescription by deploying the Virgilian phrase *imperium sine fine*, 'empire without end', in this Tacitean context where, I would argue, it becomes 'empire without definition'.[1]

[1] Virgil's Jupiter (*Aen.* 1.279) is here 'promising' the Augustan regime. My ironic perspective on this phrase necessarily simplifies Virgil; I will discuss in the conclusion how irony constructs a non-ironic past against which to define itself.

This chaotic boundlessness also infects the Tiberian regime, with which most of *Annals* I is concerned. In the difficult transmission of power from Augustus to his adopted son (the first transmission of its kind since the early kings of Rome), claims to continuity, to the 'mere' following of precedent, play an important role. Hence Tiberius repeatedly sets his decisions in relation to the acts of his predecessor, stressing at all times that he is not an innovator in the process of autocratic rule. Although Tiberius in citing Augustan precedent uses imagery of limitation, suggesting that continuity with the previous regime confines him to a predetermined set of actions, Tacitus' own insistent representation of Augustan precedent as excessive and disorderly works against the official depiction of the continuity between present and precedent as ordered and controlled. This is particularly in evidence towards the end of book I, where the princeps and senate attempt to curb theatrical disorder by demarcating the proper places for actors, limiting the contact with the senatorial class, and subjecting their bodies to disciplinary control.

> Many things were decreed on the limit of their pay and against the irresponsibility of their supporters, among which the most significant were that no senator may enter the house of a pantomime actor, that Roman knights should not surround them as they go out in public, or look at them anywhere other than in the theatre, and that the praetors should have power to punish with exile any excessive behaviour of the spectators. (77.4)[2]

These legislative attempts fail because they lack continuity with the Augustan precedent of immunity of actors, indulgence towards plebeian theatrical enthusiasms, and countenancing of a close relationship between aristocrat and actor on one notable occasion.

> Augustus had indulged them in this entertainment, when he was complying with Maecenas' passion for Bathyllus; nor did the emperor shrink from such enthusiasms, and he thought it was civil to mix with popular pleasures. (54.2)

Augustus appears here as the authority for what in the Tiberian regime is transgressive and disorderly.

Such dual and frequently competing representations of Augustus as both limit and transgression are evoked by the terms *finis* ('limit', 'end')

---

[2] Unless otherwise indicated, all quotations in this chapter are from the first book of the *Annals*. Reference numbers will denote chapter and paragraph number only.

and *excessus* ('going out', 'excess'). When, for example, Tiberius invokes Augustus as a limiting precedent for the number of candidates to be proposed for the praetorship, he uses this imagery: 'when the senate encouraged Tiberius to increase (*ut augeret*) the number, by swearing an oath he bound (*obstrinxit*) himself not to exceed it (*non excessurum*)' (14.4). This restriction, which hedges Tiberius in and which characterises Augustus as a limit, is undermined by the indications elsewhere of Augustan precedents for excess, most notably in the example of theatrical discord. How does one swear 'not to exceed' (*non excessurum*) in relation to 'excess' (*excessus*)? This poses a serious question not only to Tiberius but to Tacitus himself, who claims to start his *Annals* 'from the death (*excessus*) of the god Augustus'. One possible response to an excessive precedent is to exclude it; but although Tacitus starts firmly enough with the exclusion of Augustus from his narrative, as a historian seeking to explain events by setting them in context he is continually driven to re-invoke the deceased emperor in order to make sense within his narrative. Augustus, therefore, represents a boundary and the transgression of that boundary in terms of historical narrative as well as of social order. His death, which marks the beginning of Tacitus' *Annals*, is referred to as the *finis*, end or limit, and as the *excessus*, transgression or excess.

The problem of setting, oversetting, recognising or refusing to recognise limits pervades book 1, and threatens to unravel the book's own defining qualities as the start of a new work. *Annals* 1 is a particularly dense and complex book, so I will confine myself in this chapter largely to a reading of the mutiny episodes, chapters 16–30 set in Pannonia, and 31–49 in Germany. Although I have just sworn not to exceed these limits, I must nevertheless start by pointing out that although these chapters appear to be clearly demarcated from the surrounding narrative,[3] the elements of chaos, disorder and potential civil war which emerge in the mutiny episodes are discernibly present in the German campaign and back at Rome. In particular, the theatrical disorder against which the senate legislates at the end of book 1 is described by Tacitus in terms reminiscent of the mutinies, reminding us that in the German mutiny the instigators are called 'a native crowd, from a recent conscription in the city, accustomed to irresponsible play and unable to bear labour' (31.4: a characteristic delineation of the urban mob), while the instigator in

---

[3] Rome 1–15; Pannonian mutiny 16–30; German mutiny 31–49; German campaign 50–71 (with interruptions); Rome 72–81.

Pannonia, Percennius, is introduced as 'once the leader of a theatrical faction … and learned, because of his histrionic enthusiasm, in the confusion of a gathering' (16.3). The difficulty for a reader of limiting her interpretation to one section of the book replicates the issues of exclusion and control which beset the narrator and his characters.

I will return to the problematic limits of the mutiny episodes below. The episodes themselves seem to be set in parallel, with many scenes seemingly echoing or providing variations on each other. The Pannonian mutiny is calmed by Drusus, the son of Tiberius, while the German mutiny is put down by Tiberius' adopted son, Germanicus. This has suggested to many readers that the episodes invite comparative judgement of the two young Caesars,[4] or that the episodes are elaborated in order to provide further characterisation of Germanicus. I will be looking at Germanicus in the next chapter; my analysis of the mutinies takes a different tack. Reading across these two episodes, I want to focus on how they stage a series of attempts by the various army commanders to control the mutinous armies through the use of definition. In short, I intend to examine how the commanders seek to define the mutiny *as* mutiny, sedition, disorder, almost-civil war. In addition, I will examine how the commanders' definitions are resisted by the mutineers, who seek to impose and promulgate their own meanings of their actions. The analogy with Thucydides' στασιῶται (discussed in the introductory chapter), who use different names for things, is strikingly clear.

What the mutinies enact, however, which differentiates them from Thucydidean *stasis*, is a process of *teaching* definition. In effect, what the commanders are doing is trying to teach the mutineers how to read *correctly*, that is, correctly according to the requirements of the ruling class. The reader of Tacitus is confronted, therefore, with competing readings, some of which are given the added weight of narrative assent, while others are left ambiguous. The authority of particular readings is not always quite as expected, so that Tacitus' reader can experience the unsettling feeling of having just condemned what seems subsequently to be validated by the narrative. The process of reading the mutinies thus becomes a process of learning to read, for Tacitus' audience as much as for the characters within the narrative itself.

---

[4] Drusus and Germanicus are explicitly compared in an episode in book 2, focalised through the Roman people.

Central to this question of reading is the question of metaphor and its limits. Another reader of Tacitus, for example, may well respond to my last paragraph by saying that the mutiny episodes are 'really' about the mutinies, which doesn't necessarily preclude me from reading them as a metaphor for reading. The question then arises, when and by what means do we move from an account of mutiny as mutiny to an account of mutiny as metaphor? Take mutiny as civil war, for example: when is mutiny *like* a civil war and when *is* it a civil war? Since the events of the era are always mediated through narrative, the distinction between metaphor and reality is somewhat arbitrarily drawn. Or, rather, distinguishing between events which are *like* civil war and events which *are* civil war itself constitutes one specific mode of historical understanding. This limit (if it is seen as a limit) between metaphorical and non-metaphorical is one that I will be probing more or less explicitly throughout this chapter.

The mutinies, with their hard military equipment, invite readings which respond to their realism, but they have often failed to give satisfaction as windows into the world of the Roman army, since Tacitus neglects to supply important details which the military historian needs to make sense of the account. A metaphorical reading, focused on the same military details, is not precluded by the text, and may yield more interpretations where the narrative becomes a challenge rather than a disappointment.

Much of the imagery of the mutiny episodes is concerned with the rival manipulation of signs in order to convey and enforce meaning. For the most part the commanders are concerned to emphasise distinction and rank, while the mutineers represent their resistance to this by stressing their unity as an indiscriminate mass. Language of separation and conglomeration is frequent throughout; a representative example is the exchange between Germanicus and the legions of upper Germany soon after his arrival at their camp.

> He ordered the assembly standing there to disperse into maniples, since they seemed to be all mixed up: the response was they could hear better as they were; then let them bring forward the banners, so that this would distinguish the cohorts right away; slowly they obeyed.

adsistentem contionem, quia permixta videbatur, discedere in manipulos iubet: sic melius audituros responsum; vexilla praeferri, ut id saltem discerneret cohortes: tarde obtemperavere. (34.3)

The commander makes two demands before he will address the army, first that the soldiers should separate themselves into their individual troops. The refusal to do so constitutes a refusal to accept the hierarchical structuring of the military body. Germanicus' second demand is that the banners which signify individual troops be brought to the front, so that he is able to make distinctions between different cohorts. The banners here come to stand (in) for the military distinctions which the soldiers themselves refuse to acknowledge. The extent to which their obedience is significant depends on how significant the banners are to them or to Germanicus – or to Tacitus' reader. Are the banners 'merely' a metaphor for military order or do they 'stand for' military order in a more 'real' sense? We will reconsider this question when looking at some of the other banners (*vexilla*), eagles (*aquilae*) and standards (*signa*) which litter these episodes.

The narrative of this exchange between Germanicus and the legions mirrors these attempted and resisted divisions by repeated use of the separative (*dis-*) and conjunctive (*con-*) prefixes. This too is a pervasive feature of the mutiny episodes, which echo with competing and opposing *dis-* and *con-* compounds, with the additional separative prefix *se-* operating occasionally. So in the passage quoted above Germanicus' two commands have the associated aims to disperse (*discedere*) and to distinguish (*discernere*). The resistance to these commands is conveyed when, after Germanicus' speech, he is overwhelmed by 'indistinguishable voices (*indiscretis vocibus*)'. This use of language associates separation with order, but in the same episode *dis-* prefixes are applied to terms which denote not distinction and control but turbulence and disorder. So just before Germanicus issues his commands he is greeted with 'dissonant complaints (*dissoni questus*)', and in his speech, he implicitly reproaches the soldiers by contrasting them with Italy and Gaul, where there is 'consensus, not at all discordant (*consensum, nil . . . discors*)'. The narrator, by juxtaposing similar sounds with divergent meanings, has the narrative enacting the very conflict of definitions which is at issue in the mutiny itself.

The predominant effect of this passage, however, seems to uphold the commanders' definitions over those of the mutineers. This is because, although there is manifestly a conflict of the application of the *dis-*prefixes in Tacitus' narrative and Germanicus' speech, the *con-* prefixes are firmly on the side of the status quo. That is to say, the mutineers do not here lay claim to any *con-* term in order to describe their unified opposition to command. While Germanicus uses *consensus* to denote universal assent to Tiberius' principate among the other armies, and both Tacitus and Germanicus evoke the unity of the well-regulated army, with its proper divisions, through the use of *contio* and *cohors*, the mutineers in this passage do not appropriate any such terms of unity to counter the commander's mode of description. Indeed the indiscriminate mass of the mutinous army is called by Germanicus *permixta*, 'all mixed up', a term of mingling or confusion which reflects anxiety about definition and which also recurs throughout the mutiny episodes as a pejorative term of chaos, madness and civil war.

Hence it is arguable that in this particular passage the commander, with Tacitus' help, offers us a stronger reading than the mutineers, albeit a reading with many inner contradictions. This passage presents fewer challenges to the expertise of Tacitus' reader (beyond the question of how metaphorical the banners are), but this is not always the case in the mutinies.

Let us turn to an early example which mirrors many of the elements I have already outlined. In the Pannonian mutiny, the first of the two episodes, the army responds turbulently to an inflammatory speech by Percennius. The climax is a revolutionary suggestion: 'and finally they reached such a pitch of madness (*furoris*) that they agitated to merge three legions into one (*tres legiones miscere in unam*)' (18.2). The word *miscere*, 'to mix, mingle or merge', is used here, and again conveys the sense of a chaotic overwriting or transgression of boundaries into one indiscriminate mass. As when Germanicus saw the German legions 'all mixed up (*permixta*)' the sense here is not so much of unity as of a lack of definition. The mutineers' attempted merger, however, does not succeed: 'driven back by rivalry, since each soldier sought the honour for his own legion'. Loyalty to the title of the individual legion makes the soldiers reluctant to abandon that identity; the divisions of the status quo seem to be upheld. Tacitus links their subsequent action to this failed attempt in the following way.

> They turned to another thing / in another direction and put in one place the three eagles and standards of the cohorts (*una tres aquilas et*

signa cohortium locant); at the same time they piled up *(congerunt)* earth
and built a tribunal from which their position would be more conspicuous *(conspicua)*. (18.2)

The juxtaposition of *una tres* enacts at the level of word order the congre-
gation of the standards, and underscores the mutineers' success in a
merger which they had earlier failed to achieve (the failure also, perhaps,
reflected in the word order of *tres legiones miscere in unam*). More than this,
the unity of the three standards is emphasised by the repeated *con-*
prefixes of *congerunt* and *conspicua*. The construction of a tribunal mirrors
the collection of the three standards, but also, as an organised project,
manifests the unity of the mutineers, countering descriptions of them as
a disorderly mass.[5]

At the end of the Pannonian mutiny the soldiers 'returned the standards, congregated in one place at the beginning of the sedition, to their
proper positions *(signa unum in locum principio seditionis congregata suas in
sedes referunt)*' (28.6).[6] This action reflects their acceptance of the commanders' definition of them as disorderly. Their earlier unity is recalled
by the designation of the standards as *congregata*, but here the narrative
agrees more with the definitions of the status quo. Whereas at the height
of the mutiny the standards were collected in a conspicuous position
(conspicua sedes), at the end they are returned to their own positions *(suas
in sedes)*. Their own, proper, natural positions are the positions designated
for them by the status quo. The return of the standards to their proper
positions in the camp mirrors the soldiers' return to their proper positions in the military order.

The standards by the end of the mutiny seem to stand as symbols or
signs *(signa)* for the mutineers' actions. But it is worth returning to the
first collection of the standards to look more closely at the relationship
between sign and action. The moving of the standards is explicitly characterised by Tacitus as 'another thing *(alio)*', a diversion from the failed
merger of the legions: 'they turned to another thing / in another direc-

---

[5] Later in the account the mutineers inexplicably abandon this construction, which
appears as a sign of their disorder. Their later abandonment of the project creates a
discord with the account at 18.2, where the construction of the mound and the tribunal is narrated in perfect tense, denoting a completed action.
[6] The juxtaposition of <u>seditio</u> <u>congregata</u> points up the process by which the unity of the
group, figured by *con-*, is potentially redescribable as schism from the military body,
figured by *se-*. The motion implicit in *seditio* (glossed elsewhere as *motus*) is also contrasted with the stationary implications of *sedes*.

tion (*in alio vertunt*)'. When the relocation of the standards is characterised as other than the merger of the legions, at the same time as the
similarity of the two acts is highlighted, the narrator points up the relationship of metaphor which could be seen to operate here. Metaphor as
the representation of one thing by another perhaps suggests that the standards are to be translated into another event (*in alio vertunt*). If we remember that *vertere* can mean 'to translate' as well as 'to divert', we could read
the standards as a metaphor operating at the level both of action and of
narrative. But how can the standards be a metaphor for something that
doesn't take place? This is why it could be said that what they do is 'stand
in for' (as a diversion) rather than 'stand for' (as a metaphor).

The process by which the soldiers arrive at an acceptance of military
distinctions and an associated acceptance of their actions as disorderly is
represented as an act of interpreting the natural world. Chance, Tacitus
tells us, provides an eclipse of the moon, which the soldiers interpret as
both a reflection and a result of their own activities.

> Chance alleviated a threatening night, which was about to break out in
> crime. For in a clear sky the moon was suddenly seen to fade. The
> soldier, ignorant of reason, took it as an omen of present affairs, assimi-
> lating the defection of the light to his own toils, and believed that what
> he was doing would end well if brightness and clarity were returned to
> the goddess. So they roared with the sound of bronze, the harmony of
> trumpets and horns; as the moon became brighter or darker they
> rejoiced and grieved; and after rising clouds had obscured it from view
> and they believed it buried in darkness, since minds once struck are
> prone to superstition, they lamented that this portended eternal strug-
> gles for themselves, and that the gods were angry at their deeds.

> *noctem minacem et in scelus erupturam fors lenivit. nam luna claro repente caelo*
> *visa languescere. id miles rationis ignarus omen praesentium accepit, suis*
> *laboribus defectionem sideris adsimulans, prospereque cessura <ad> quae perg-*
> *erent, si fulgor et claritudo deae redderetur. igitur aeris sono, tubarum cornu-*
> *umque concentu strepere; prout splendidior obscuriorve, laetari aut maerere; et*
> *postquam ortae nubes offecere visui creditumque conditam tenebris, ut sunt*
> *mobiles ad superstitionem perculsae semel mentes, sibi aeternum laborem*
> *po<r>tendi, sua facinora aversari deos lamentantur. (28.1–2)*

'Proper' military order is assimilated to the laws of the cosmos; the
natural and divine world turns away in revulsion from the unnatural acts
of the mutineers. Despite this powerful claim on behalf of the status quo,

validating military command with the law of the gods and of the universe, Tacitus emphatically asserts that the soldier who interprets in this way is 'ignorant of (the) reason (*rationis ignarus*)'. Thus the interpretation which, more than any other in the Pannonian mutiny, returns the mutineers to correct and orderly behaviour, is prejudged as both unlearned and irrational. Here seems to be a moment where the narrator denies the authority of a reading offered from within the text. This is certainly how G.O. Hutchinson has taken it.

> We must stress, once more, however, the great importance to Tacitus of exhibiting caution, sobriety, and intelligence. He reinforces this appearance, like the Elder Pliny, by cool or pungent disdain for the ready belief of the unenlightened. So at *Ann.* i. 28. 1–3, when ignorant soldiers see divine significance in an eclipse, Tacitus presents their theology and behaviour as grotesque and almost exotic; this also fits his whole depiction of the mutinous soldiers, which is marked both by perception and by hauteur.[7]

The discrediting of the ignorant soldier's reading implicitly elevates the interpretative authority of the narrator, who then appears to the reader as a perceptive interpreter. Yet the judgement of the soldier as ignorant is undermined by the way in which his interpretation fits with the narrative of the mutiny as a whole. The soldier 'assimilates' the waning of the moon to the army's neglect of military duties, arguably a plausible recognition of one similarity between the two events. One of the first signs of military neglect to an observer is the unpolished or discarded insignia of the soldiers. This is what Drusus sees when he first arrives in the camp: 'the legions, not rejoicing as is customary, nor bright with insignia (*neque insignibus fulgentes*)' (24.3). When the same term for 'brightness' (*fulgor*) is used for the moon four chapters later, it would seem that the narrator is implicitly backing up the soldier's interpretation of a similarity between neglect and eclipse. Indeed, it is arguable that Tacitus stacks the cards against his explicit judgement of the soldier as ignorant by the semantic subtlety with which the 'ignorant' interpretation is represented. The assimilation of the eclipse (*defectio* in the soldier's words) to the mutiny (*seditio* in the commanders' words) could be seen as a 'correct' reading of the two terms, which are practically synonymous. Similarly, the use of the word *labores* to denote the soldier's activities (orderly or disorderly) hints

---

[7] Hutchinson (1993) 243.

at its associated use to denote the natural waning or unnatural eclipsing of the moon. Hence the whole phrase 'assimilating the defection of the light to his own struggles (*suis laboribus defectionem sideris adsimulans*)' promotes the assimilation of mutiny and eclipse and belies the ignorance of the soldier. Indeed, this interpretation of the eclipse is a well-read one, not only because an eclipse frequently stands for civil war, but also because Tacitus' phrase echoes earlier representations of eclipse, such as Virgil's 'the various defections of the sun and the toils of the moon (*defectus solis varios lunaeque labores*)' (*Geo.* 2.478).

The eclipse, therefore, problematises the simple progression from incorrect to correct reading across the Pannonian mutiny. The reader of Tacitus becomes implicated in the difficulties and responsibilities of interpretation. Is the soldier's reading to be despised? Then how do we account for the fact that this is what restores order? Why does Tacitus tell us that the soldier is ignorant while demonstrating the range and complexity of his interpretation? Most importantly, do we discount what Tacitus tells us about this interpreter's expertise, and what judgement are we thereby making about Tacitus' own interpretative authority? Is this the sort of scepticism Tacitus teaches?

Although the Pannonian eclipse shakes our sense of how to read correctly, the initial parallels between the two mutinies suggest that our exercise in reading the Pannonian mutiny will enable us also to understand the German mutiny, which, we are told, occurs 'at almost the same time and for the same reasons (*isdem ferme diebus isdem causis*)' (31.1). The comparison between Drusus and Germanicus, which I mentioned earlier, is drawn to the reader's attention by the strong verbal parallels in the accounts of each prince entering the mutinous camp, Drusus in chapter 25 and Germanicus in chapter 34. Such parallels and comparisons suggest that the reader who embarks on the account of the German mutiny has already acquired some expertise in reading with which to deal with this longer piece of narrative. The first explicit comparison with Pannonia organises our perceptions of the German mutiny in relation to the 'earlier' mutiny: 'this was not one, like Percennius among the Pannonian legions . . . but many faces and voices of sedition (*non unus haec . . . sed multa seditionis ora vocesque*)' (31.5). Our understanding of the German mutiny, it seems, is organised not around similarity but around contrast.

Despite the disorderly appearance of the German mutiny in this first statement, the many voices of sedition given in indirect speech are strikingly univocal in substance. Unlike the clamour of the Pannonian army, which overwhelms Drusus with a barrage of rhetorical questions and ironical asides, the voice of sedition in Germany presents a balanced and unvaried assertion of power: 'in their hand was the Roman state, by their victories the republic was increased, from them the generals' titles were received (*sua in manu sitam rem Romanam, suis victoriis augeri rem publicam, in suum cognomentum adscisci imperatores*)' (31.5).[8] The juxtaposition of a unified statement in indirect speech with a narrative judgement of that speech as multivocal once more presents the reader with a choice of interpretations. Is the German mutiny unlike the Pannonian in the content of its speech (the contrast I have just drawn) or in the origin of that speech (the contrast pointed out by Tacitus)? Or are the two mutinies more alike? Do we discount Tacitus' differentiation of the two here in favour of his earlier statement about their similarity?

The difficulty in reading the German mutiny seems in part to derive from the strong display of unity put on by the soldiers. As I pointed out earlier, the conflict between the soldiers and their commanders is played out through competing definitions of what is going on. While the commanders' aim is to impose recognition of these actions as disorderly and transgressive, the soldiers seek to represent their actions as unified opposition to injustice. At the start of the German mutiny the self-representation of the soldiers presents a challenge to the readers of and within the narrative.

> To those interpreting more deeply the minds of soldiers, this was the particular sign of great and implacable emotion, that they were inflamed, not in scattered groups nor by the inspiration of a few men, but unanimously; they were silent unanimously; with such equality and constancy, that you would believe they were being ruled.

> *id militares animos altius coniectantibus praecipuum indicium magni atque implacabilis motus, quod neque disiecti nec paucorum instinctu, sed pariter ardescerent, pariter silerent, tanta aequalitate et constantia, ut regi crederes.* (32.3)

---

[8] Cf. Goodyear (1972) 245. The repetition of *sua . . . suis . . . suum* echoes the movement of the Pannonian standards from their transgressive 'one place (*unum in locum*)' to their 'proper position (*suas sedes*)'. The structure of the word pattern in the German mutiny inverts that of Pannonia: *unam . . . una . . . unum in locum . . . suas sedes / non unus . . . sua . . . suis . . . suum.* Implicit here is the mutineers' claim that self-determination *is* the proper place of the German soldier.

This sentence asserts again the distinctive univocality of the mutineers, noticed in their indirect speech in chapter 31. Their unity is such, however, that *you* would be inclined to misread: 'you would believe they were being ruled'. The direct address to the reader brings home vividly the extent to which the signs of mutiny at this point in the narrative are signs too of the status quo. Tacitus challenges the expertise of his reader, who would see behind these signs a regulating force. He does so by juxtaposing with *your* supposed interpretation one made by real experts, 'those interpreting more deeply the minds of soldiers'. What these experts see behind the signs is not the regulation imposed by the status quo, but 'great emotion (*motus*)' or 'great disturbance'. The term *motus* appears as the opposite to *status*, but the signs for both here are the same.

So we are presented here with two readers of the same set of signs: those who look deeply and make connections (*coniectantes*); and one credulous reader who 'misunderstands' the signs. There is an implicit suggestion that the expert readers here are engaging in historical inquiry, since *coniectare* is a historian's term for his own activity, and looking deeply into events is a standard historical activity since Thucydides. The expertise of interpretation is founded upon drawing connections (*coniectare*) between signs and their meanings. The 'proper' connection to draw in this instance, according to Tacitus, is to see the constancy (*constantia*, standing together) of the soldiers as a sign of disturbance (*motus*, movement), or *in other words* to invalidate the intelligibility of the word *constantia* in this context. But if the conjunctive prefix in *constantia* is denied significance by these expert interpreters, this very denial threatens to unravel the significance of the word *coniectare*, which relies on the *conjunction* of sign and meaning. It may lead us to ask on what grounds these interpreters make a connection between inner disturbance and outward constancy, and on what grounds Tacitus invalidates your belief that constancy here is a sign of order. It may also lead us to reflect on how the various readers in and of this narrative use connective and separative conjunctions not only to describe what is going on in the mutinies but also to assert its meaning. Significance is created by connections, while meaninglessness is characterised by disjunction. But an excess of connections collapses into meaninglessness; if *constantia* is a sign both of disturbance and of order it undermines the need for, as well as the meaning of, hierarchy and rule.

The soldiers' appropriation of the signs for order here destabilises the limit of definition between order and disorder. This is mirrored at the ends of both mutinies, where the re-imposition of proper military order and the quelling of mutiny takes on the chaotic signs of disorder: men running in all directions and random killings narrated with the emotive words 'to slaughter' (*trucidare*) and 'massacre' (*caedis*). The paradox that what is set in motion to quell disturbance effectively extends that disturbance is what strikingly represents the difficulty of sharp definition, and is particularly in evidence in the longer account of the German mutiny, where the punishment of mutineers is in two phases. In the first punishment scene at chapter 44 Tacitus represents a parody of order rather than 'actual' disorder: 'the legions stood with drawn swords in front of the assembly (*pro contione*)' (44.2). One commentator on this passage, Henry Furneaux, suggests that *pro contione* here could be translated 'after the fashion of an assembly'.[9] This translation emphasises that the assembly was self-constituted, a point made explicitly in the following sentence: 'the cruelty of the deed and the hatred was the responsibility of the soldiers'. Moreover *pro contione* could also have the sense of 'fulfilling the function of' or 'as a substitute for' an assembly, since it is clear from the earlier narrative that any assembly summoned at this stage would have to be concerned with the punishment of individual mutineers. The exact meaning of *pro contione* then depends on the notion of metaphor; are the 'repenting' mutineers *like* an assembly, or *are* they an assembly? And how does their appearance in the execution of justice 'with drawn swords' affect the status of the assembly, when it recalls their maddened state at the beginning of the mutiny: 'suddenly maddened they attacked their centurions with drawn swords (*destrictis gladiis*)' (32.1)?

The problem of definition, which is also the problem of finishing the mutiny, is even more urgently stated in the second scene which 'closes' the German account. The commander in this scene is Aulus Caecina, whose efforts to end the mutiny in the upper camp are also attempts to avoid the sort of disorderly punishment that has already been imposed on the legions of the lower camp. Germanicus writes to Caecina warning of 'indiscriminate massacre (*promisca caedes*)'[10] if the punishment of scapegoats is not effected before his arrival (48.1). As we have already seen in the accounts of both mutinies, *miscere* is a frequent term to connote the indiscriminate groupings of discord, while *caedis* is used both for the

---

[9] Furneaux (1884) 212.

[10] As Goodyear (1972) 309 comments, Tacitus arguably adopted the usage *promiscus* rather than *promiscuus* consistently throughout the *Histories* and *Annals*; clearly the resonances with *miscere* are pointed up by this usage.

slaughter of officers by the mutineers and for the executions of scape-goats after the supposed restoration of order. What Germanicus threat-ens, therefore, bears more resemblance to the chaos of sedition than to some sort of limiting disciplinary action. Caecina picks up on the sense of *promisca* when he warns his assistants that 'innocent and guilty alike (*iuxta*) perish' (48.3): in indiscriminate massacre the status of the victims becomes meaningless. In an attempt to pre-empt chaotic killing Caecina calls in the various standard-bearers of the army, officers responsible for these symbols which we have already seen operating as 'signs' of mutiny. This use of the standard-bearers could thus be seen to symbolise an attempt to fix definitions, preserve distinctions (such as the one between innocent and guilty) and impose meaning.

Within the group of Caecina's picked men, the standard-bearers and loyal soldiers, the definitions are upheld which keep punishment within limits. They begin the punishment with a signal or sign (the same term as for 'standard') given amongst themselves (*signo inter se dato*), but the limits of the punishment, and its associated meaning, remain significant only within this particular group, who do not succeed in conveying this meaning to other soldiers. The chapter ends, therefore, with a descrip-tion of the kind of slaughter which some, at least, find indiscriminate.

> Then, with the signal given amongst themselves, they burst into the mess-tents, they slaughtered the unaware men, with no-one, except for those in the know, recognising what was the beginning of the massacre, what the end.
>
> *tunc signo inter se dato inrumpunt contubernia, trucidant ignaros, nullo nisi consciis noscente quod caedis initium, quis finis.* (48.3)

Here again we are presented with two types of reader, in this case knowl-edgeable (*consciis*) and ignorant (*ignaros, nullo . . . noscente*). The knowl-edgeable reader, the standard-bearer, is aware of the limits of his action, while the ignorant is caught up in an event which he cannot apprehend, unable to recognise its outline or structure. The surrounding narrative, however, undermines the knowledge of the 'conscious' reader in two ways. First, by calling this event a 'massacre (*caedis*)' Tacitus reminds us that these actions are being taken in order to prevent an 'indiscriminate massacre (*promisca caedes*)' in which innocent and guilty alike will suffer. While the standard-bearers seem to be imposing a more 'discriminate' massacre on the guilty soldiers, the narrative continues by describing how some soldiers became aware of what was going on. The result is the massacre of good as well as bad soldiers: 'and some good men were massacred (*caesi*) after the worst men also took up arms, having understood (*intellecto*) against whom this cruelty was directed' (49.1). Innocent and guilty die together, as opponents in battle rather than as victims of the same punishment. I will return to this distinction later.

The second way in which the narrative undermines the authority of a knowledgeable reader here is by the term 'unaware/ignorant (*ignari*)' applied to those soldiers not in the know. We have already seen how, in the account of the eclipse, Tacitus' characterisation of soldiers as ignorant (of rationality) is set against a sophisticated and literate interpretation of the eclipse by these same ignorant soldiers. This potentially triggers the reader's suspicion about the validity of judging the soldier to be ignorant. The soldiers at the end of the German mutiny are ignorant of their own deaths, having been slaughtered before they know that they are being attacked. But Tacitus seems to be expanding on the term *ignari* when he adds 'with no-one recognising what was the beginning of the massacre, what the end'. The ablative absolute *nullo . . . noscente* appears almost to be a gloss on *ignaros*; those who cannot recognise the limits of the event are lacking knowledge, unknowing. But how is this ignorance upheld by the narrative in the face of the superior knowledge of the standard-bearers?

One answer would be that the inability to recognise limits in the discourse of mutiny and disorder constitutes correct perception of the state of affairs. I have already noted how the signs of mutiny and of military order are continually interchanged, so that representations of disorder and of the status quo become disturbingly similar. I have also noted, at the outset of this section, that the qualities of disorder which might seem to be contained in the mutiny episodes spill out into the surrounding narrative, infiltrating Germany and Rome with the signs of chaos. In addition, we have seen how the roots of civil disorder are traced back in the narrative, time and again, to Augustus, the supposed remedy for civil war. Disorder leaks out through time, space and narrative, with no-one recognising its beginning or its end. The ignorant soldier again, perhaps, offers us an interpretation of *Annals* I which seems more plausible than the narrator would explicitly allow.

Such an interpretation, which calls into question the validity of maintaining distinctions, is countered by the knowledgeable standard-bearer, who opposes the collapse of all distinctions with a specifically local knowledge, knowledge shared among a few. According to this knowledge, you do not so much discover distinctions or definitions as invent them. The standard-bearers do not seek definitions in their chaotic world; they give a sign among themselves and then they fight for the maintenance of that sign. It could be argued that the standard-bearer is responding with action to a reading of the world as meaningless chaos. Distinctions may well dissolve, indiscriminate massacre may well be inevitable, but the gesture of giving a sign, fixing a limit, must still be made. One distinction is held by the end of this episode, that between the good and the bad, as I have pointed out above. Moreover, this distinction is recognised by both sides, as the mutineers come to understand who is targeted in the attack. The term *intellecto,* 'having understood', points to a correct reading by the previously unaware soldiers; the distinction which they recognise here is upheld also by their opponents. It is, however, the distinction which enables them to prolong the killing. Despite this one stable meaning, despite the gesture of giving a sign, the outcome is disastrous for all participants, good and bad alike. Germanicus, arriving at the camp, utters the 'concluding' definition: 'not a remedy but a calamity (*non medicinam illud sed cladem)*'.[11]

MAKING A DIFFERENCE

As I mentioned at the start of this chapter, the theatrical disorder in Rome at the end of *Annals* I can be traced in a line of continuity to the mutinies, and is explicitly given the precedent of Augustan sanction.

> Augustus had indulged them in this entertainment, when he was complying with Maecenas' passion for Bathyllus; nor did the emperor shrink from such enthusiasms, and he thought it was civil to mix with popular pleasures. (54.2)

This line of continuity problematises the various attempts within and by the narrative to delimit discord. The problem is evidenced not merely by the theatrical element in the city; the business in the senate which precedes the accounts of the mutinies seems to be sharply differentiated from the mutinies by space, subject matter, and modes of description. We

---

[11] Germanicus and his legions continue past this definition to project discord and disaster onto the German tribes: in order, as Germanicus says, 'to wipe out (the memory of) the sedition (*oblitterandae seditionis)*' (51.3). This echoes the original reason given by Tacitus for the continuation of a German war: 'in order to wipe out the infamy (*abolendae infamiae*) of the loss of Varus' army' (3.6). I will examine the relationship between Varus' legions and the army of Germanicus in the next chapter.

move from Rome to the provinces, from senatorial discussion to military action, from non-violent to violent transmission of power. Tacitus begins the mutinies accounts thus: 'this was the state of affairs (*status*) in the city, when sedition (*seditio*) took over the Pannonian legions' (16.1). The distinction seems validated by the terms applied to each sphere; urban *status* as against provincial *seditio*, a term which denotes both turmoil and, etymologically, divergence. Distinction here is an effect of definition; the term *seditio*, formed from separative *se-* and *eo*, 'to go', is associated with moving away rather than standing still, *stare, status*.[12] In addition, *seditio* is glossed in Tacitus' narrative as 'dissent (*dissensio*)' and 'disturbance (*motus*)'; the last term in particular seems quite distinct from *status* in the city. But the state of affairs in the city, when it is called *status*, becomes coloured by the 'revolutionised state (*versus status*)' that is Imperial Rome, a state that is not only 'displaced' but 'translated' (as I have argued in the introduction) from Thucydidean *stasis* or sedition.

When *status* is translated it becomes *seditio*, and the sharp distinction collapses between city and province, order and disorder. This collapse could be said to be articulated by the beginning of the mutiny account and arguably it diminishes our ability to call this piece of narrative 'the beginning of the mutiny account'. But by whom is *status* thus translated? One answer would be 'by the reader who recognises neither the beginning nor the end' (a reader both ignorant and sophisticated, as we have already seen). A reading which fails or refuses to recognise limits, as the narrative of the mutiny has shown, results in indiscriminate, and potentially unending, massacre. The effect of such a reading of *status* and *seditio* is less immediately physical, but it threatens a collapse of meaning; if all things are sedition the reader can no longer refer to 'the beginning of the mutinies' and must have recourse to the arbitrary marker '1.16.1', an assignation as random as a telephone number.

This problem is also experienced at the level of political action; if any action aimed at delimiting disorder is no more than a prolongation of that disorder at some level, the necessity for action is undermined before it has begun. Tacitus' ironic 'unmasking' of the principate as a continuation of the civil war it claimed to calm seems then to offer no possibility of political redemption or real change. Yet the insistent reading lessons which constitute the text of *Annals* I suggest that Tacitus addresses his

---

[12] 'Civic dissent, because some people go in different directions from others, is called sedition (*dissensio civium, quod seorsum eunt alii ad alios, seditio dicitur*)' (Cic. *Rep.* 6.1).

work to some future reader whose progress through the narrative is a process which changes their reading practice. If the *Annals* is, as I am arguing, directed towards effecting some kind of change, how does that fit with the ironic collapse of all distinctions into the discourse of sedition, a collapse which potentially makes any sort of action or reading impossible?

If Tacitus is training the reader in ironic interpretation, an interpretation which subverts the ostensible manœuvres of the text it reads, unmasking its hidden and contradictory realities, where does Tacitus' reader draw the line in the practice of ironic interpretation? To take the prime example of this section, if Tacitus ironically reads the text of the principate as 'really' civil war, does Tacitus' newly-trained reader go along with this, reading ironically side by side with Tacitus, or does she turn the application of that ironic exposure onto the manœuvres of Tacitus' own text? And is that further application to be defined in terms of continuity or of contrast with Tacitus' own? Which of the two readings of Tacitus thereby produced is the 'really' Tacitean one? The final reading of this chapter will be focused on an example which gives rise to these questions and which suggests one possibility for future change.

A senatorial debate towards the end of *Annals* 1 is centred on the question of how to curb the theatrical licence which has broken out again. The disturbances in the theatre are termed *dissensio* at the point in the narrative which records mob violence against the praetorian cohort 'when they prevented disagreements (*dissensionem*) among the crowd' (77.1). When these events come to be discussed in the senate in the following sentence they are termed *seditio*, a 'translation' which we have already seen to be etymologically sound, and far less disruptive than the translation of *seditio* into *status*. The account of what happens in the senate, however, interacts in interesting ways with the definition of disorder.

> There was a senatorial debate on this sedition, and opinions were given that the praetors should have the authority to flog the actors. Haterius Agrippa, as tribune of the plebs, interposed his veto, and was rebuked in a speech by Asinius Gallus, with silence from Tiberius, who held out these *simulacra* of liberty to the senate. But the interposed veto remained valid, because the god Augustus had once advised that the actors should be immune from flogging, nor was it allowable for Tiberius to infringe on Augustus' statements. (77.2–3)

41

Before the reiteration of Augustan precedent for the theatrical disorder which is (like) a sedition, we have the voices of dissent raised in the senate. The noisy rebuke (*increpuit*) of Asinius Gallus is contrasted with the silence (*silente*) of Tiberius. One question the Tacitean reader could pose is whether senatorial dissent is like theatrical discord, and indeed one possible reading of this passage is that it exemplifies the potentiality of collapsing all differences into disorder. But Tacitus also offers us an explicit interpretation of the senators' disagreement, one which is distinctively Tacitean: these disagreements were the '*simulacra* of liberty (*simulacra libertatis*)', which were held out to the senators by the princeps. Tacitus here takes what could be read as senatorial freedom of speech and subjects it to ironic exposure as something *other than* 'actual' freedom: a *simulacrum*, a false appearance. What is the 'properly' subversive reading of this phrase?

Senatorial speech as a sign of freedom has already been a preoccupation of the last chapters of *Annals* I. When Gnaeus Piso draws attention to Tiberius' implicit influence on senatorial decisions his intervention is introduced into the narrative with the words 'there remained even then vestiges of dying liberty (*vestigia morientis libertatis*)' (74.5). Here we seem to be offered a sign of 'actual' liberty, a freedom whose reality is, paradoxically, upheld because it is said to be 'dying'. Interestingly, the sign of liberty here consists of Piso's (ironic?) words to Tiberius '"if you speak after everyone else, I am afraid that I might, without knowing, disagree with you" (*dissentiam*)'. The traces of real liberty seem to work against the *simulacrum* of liberty, since openly fearing dissent is not quite the opposite of open dissent, but rather is *other than* ... Piso's irony in respect of liberty is irony also in respect of sedition. There are multiple ironies in Piso's words, not least in Tacitus' contextualising of them, so that openly stating Tiberius' power as princeps becomes a sign of senatorial freedom. One conclusion it thereby suggests is the inherent paradox of liberty under a princeps. If the reality of freedom is both paradoxical and already ironised, it scarcely offers a stable position from which to consider what a *simulacrum* of liberty might be.

I have already examined in the introduction the concluding sentence of *Annals* I, which exemplifies the reciprocal relationship of truth and falsehood in Tacitean historical analysis.

> (Tiberius' statements) were plausible in words, in matter empty and deceitful, and the more they were covered with the mask of liberty, the more they would break out into more damaging servitude.

42

speciosa verbis, re inania aut subdola, quantoque maiore libertatis imagine tege-bantur, tanto eruptura ad infensius servitium. (81.4)

Does the 'mask' of liberty offer us a gloss on the *simulacrum* of liberty, a phrase which allows for many different translations?[13] Like *imago*, the term *simulacrum* can have the sense of 'false appearance', and in that sense we are encouraged to read the dissent between Agrippa and Gallus as the false appearance of freedom which conceals its opposite, actual servitude. But we could also draw a distinction between the two terms by pointing out that the 'mask' of liberty appears in a context where it is specifically set in correlation to the truth which it does not quite cover. Indeed, in the final sentence of the book 'mask' and 'servitude' are glossed respec-tively as 'words' and 'matter'.[14] The *simulacrum* of liberty, by contrast, stands alone; if it is a false appearance, the exact nature of the truth is not revealed.

Another way of considering the *simulacrum* of liberty is as a semblance of the real thing, but focusing not so much on its difference from real liberty (a 'mere' semblance) as on its similarity; it is a semblance because it resembles liberty. Is senatorial disagreement here a metaphor for liberty? Once more we return to the question which reverberates through this chapter: when is something *like* liberty and when *is* it liberty? What are the limits of metaphor and by whom are these limits drawn?

This can be seen to be a central point for Tiberius' senators and Tacitus' readers. One of the sceptical readings of the *Annals* often put forward is that Tiberius was, in these moments, *really* offering executive responsibility to the senate, who actually did have the freedom to state their views before the princeps. This reading then suggests that the liberty offered by the princeps is interpreted as 'mere' semblance either by Tiberius' senators or by Tacitus as the narrator. Tacitus' text here becomes the object of ironic exposure, as the false appearance of his interpretation is stripped away to uncover the truth: actual liberty.

But, as I stressed in the introduction, these various types of decoding implicitly set up 'truth' or 'reality' as the goal of reading; in this reading

---

[13] Clearly the mask of liberty here has a particular relationship with the dying liberty evinced by Piso's words. The *imago* is specifically a funeral mask; I will return to the implications of the funeral mask in the next chapter.

[14] Although there are problems with this too, in that the first half of the clause then sug-gests that the uncovered 'truth' is empty and deceitful. See introduction for a further analysis of this sentence.

practice to identify something as 'appearance' is a prelude to casting it aside as unwanted residue. Instead, we can return to the *simulacrum* and consider its significance *as simulacrum*. In the theatrical context of the specific senatorial debate under discussion here, the term *simulacrum* has the added resonance of a *performed* semblance, an 'act' in more ways than one. Introducing the dimension of performance causes us to repeat the question of metaphor more pressingly: how do we differentiate between the action of a free man, and the action of a man who acts as if he were free?

The term *simulacrum* has a further dimension, related to the theatrical context. A *simulacrum* denotes a mock battle, enacted for the entertainment of the onlookers and, in many cases, for the education of the participants. The mock battle serves as preparation and training for the real thing. By this reading the mock exercise in liberty prepares and trains the senators for the exercise of actual freedom; is this what Tiberius offers to the senate? Can we read the clash between Agrippa and Gallus as a mock battle, a rehearsal in or for liberty? Does its status as *simulacrum*, as something other than the real thing, point to its future fulfilment by or as the real thing? Must the senators perform the *simulacrum* in order to guarantee a future for liberty?

I would argue that this interpretation of the *simulacrum* as 'prospective', as holding out hope for future change, can be operative even within the most ironic readings of Tacitus. The *simulacrum* of liberty marks the absence of liberty in the present, but can gesture towards a future presence of liberty. To put it another way, we can conceive ironically of the senatorial dispute as an empty semblance of liberty, which is enacted in the full knowledge of its meaninglessness in contemporary life, but in the hope of its potential to regain meaning in a future which it could thereby transform. The enactment of the *simulacrum* by the senators, and its transmission to the future by Tacitus, allows misreading and meaninglessness to become bearable in their present because the charge of redemption has been placed on the shoulders of future readers. And that charge to the future *gives meaning* to the servitude and loss of political language experienced in the present.

This possible future is banished from Tacitus' narrative; indeed ironic style makes it difficult to speak explicitly of such hopes. Instead, the rest of the *Annals* represents the unravelling of the Roman political world under the pressures of meaning imposed by the principate. A particular threat is posed to memory and history by the interacting movements of assimilation and disjunction which I have begun to trace in this brief analysis of metaphor. The threat to history is, of course, a pressing issue for Tacitus the historian, and one to which we will now turn in an analysis of Germanicus and Agrippina.

Germanicus and the reader in the text

The desire of the text is ultimately the desire for the end, for that recognition which is the moment of the death of the reader in the text. Yet recognition cannot abolish textuality, does not annul that middle which is the place of repetitions, oscillating between blindness and recognition, between origin and ending. Repetition toward recognition constitutes the truth of the narrative text.

Peter Brooks, *Reading for the Plot*

Genealogy is one cluster within a society's ideological apparatus through which pressure is brought to bear toward realizing a future in conformity with a valued representation of the past.

John Henderson, *Figuring out Roman Nobility*

Germanicus is an important figure in Tacitus' narrative, because his position in the history of the principate raises crucial questions about how meaning is created in the interplay between past and present. It is generally accepted that the tradition about Germanicus, to which Tacitus is contributing in *Annals* 1–2, has its source in writings from the reign of Caligula, the son of Germanicus.[1] As the father, brother and grandfather of three successive Julio-Claudian emperors, Germanicus acquires historical significance retrospectively. According to which sort of history you read, he either foreshadows the greatness of his successors[2] or represents the virtues which they pervert.[3]

As an addition to this perspective on Germanicus, readers of Tacitus have remarked on the extent to which Germanicus seems out of place in the Tiberian regime. He is often read as a doomed republican in the new

---

[1] Borszák (1969) 589; Goodyear (1972) 239–40. The Caligula narrative is missing from Tacitus' *Annals*, but the process of interaction between past and present also takes place between Germanicus and the emperors Claudius and Nero.

[2] Sen. *Consol. ad Polyb.* 16.3; Suet. *Calig.* 13.1.

[3] Suet. *Calig.* 1–6; Sen. *De Const. Sap.* 18.1 and especially *De Ben.* 4.31.2.

world of the principate. This is the characteristic of Germanicus focused on particularly by Christopher Pelling.

> Just as Tacitus can regard the principate as a regrettable necessity . . . so he can regard Germanicus rather as he regards the past, particularly the republican past: nostalgically attractive, brilliant, the sort of thing it is good to write about (4.32–33); but out of keeping with the real needs of the modern world. Tiberius introduces many of the themes of the principate, both the distaste and the sense of reality. In the same way, Germanicus helps us to grasp the alternative, with his style of politics and his style of war. Brilliant, yes, but brilliantly anachronistic.[4]

Both of these aspects of Germanicus in the *Annals* present Germanicus as a symbol of the past: an entity which acquires meaning only in the present from which it is viewed and towards which it is seen to be directed at the moment of viewing. The Tacitean Germanicus demonstrates that the past cannot be seen on its own terms; on the one hand he becomes recognised as the embryonic and unfulfilled princeps only when his son becomes emperor, and on the other he represents a past which becomes 'the republican past' only when it is viewed from the present of the principate.

The meaningful interaction between past and present which we might term 'reading history' is therefore central to how Germanicus is perceived by readers in and of Tacitus' narrative. He can be seen as the lynchpin of continuity from heroic republican to glorious princeps, or he can be viewed ironically as a symbol of discontinuity between past and present. The episodes I will concentrate on in this chapter are the scenes in which Germanicus reads traces of the past in his visits to former battlefields, and in which Germanicus himself is read by contemporary viewers as an image of the past. As I will examine in the final section in this chapter, the same sort of reading is practised when characters in the narrative look at Germanicus' wife Agrippina, whose stance and gestures make of her body a historical corpus.

When Germanicus is introduced at the start of the German mutinies, the first explanation for his popularity is given as his ancestry. Germanicus is seen as the successor to his father Drusus (brother of Tiberius) in that he is a possible champion of the republic, and this is introduced as part of the reason for alleged conflict between Germanicus and Tiberius: 'for the memory of Drusus was of great weight with the

---

[4] Pelling (1993) 77–8.

Roman people, and it was believed that, if he had come to power, he would have restored freedom; hence the same favour and hope in Germanicus (*unde in Germanicum favor et spes eadem*)' (1.33.2). Similarly, when Germanicus dies and is interred in the mausoleum of Augustus, the laments of the people align his death with that of republican hopes: 'they were crying out that the republic had fallen, that nothing was left to hope (*nihil spei reliquum*)' (3.4.1). In keeping with this characterisation is Tacitus' record in passing that Germanicus rededicated the temple of Hope (*Spes*) at Rome (2.49.2); Germanicus as the embodiment of hope stands as a mediation point between the past and the future. As the embodiment of hope for a restored republic he could be seen to be a figure associated primarily with the past, a past which from the perspective of the narrator and reader is irredeemable.

But Germanicus' characterisation in particular as the embodiment of republican *hope* renders this more complex. As we have seen in the previous chapter, the German mutiny is motivated in part by hopes which also reside in Germanicus: 'with great hope (*magna spe*) that Germanicus Caesar would not be able to bear the rule of another man' (1.31.1). This hope is assimilated to the hopes of the Pannonian army: 'a change of emperor showed to them the licence of confusion and the hope of booty from civil war (*ex civili bello spem praemiorum*)' (1.16.1). Germanicus here represents the potential for the worst excesses of the republic, and resembles not so much his father Drusus as his grandfather Augustus, whose rise to power through civil war is charted in the early chapters of *Annals* 1. The resemblance to Augustus is implicitly borne out in the contrast between Germanicus and Tiberius, which is offered as an alternative explanation for Germanicus' popularity: 'for the young man had a civil nature (*civile ingenium*), and wonderful affability (*mira comitas*) different from Tiberius in speech and countenance' (1.33.2). The qualities of civility and affability are also cultivated by Augustus in his indulgence of the theatrical mob, discussed in the previous chapter:[5] 'Augustus had

---

[5] Pelling (1993) draws a distinction between Augustus' (and even Tiberius') and Germanicus' form of civility – 'this is the shrewd style of the accomplished autocrat ... not the natural manner of a Germanicus', 79 n. 44 – by pointing out that actions are often shown to be *considered* civil by the two emperors, whereas Germanicus is not represented as calculating the civility of his actions. Rather than distinguishing between 'calculating' and 'natural' behaviour I would like to stress the extent to which the reader is shown what passes for the emperors' interpretations of their own actions, while Germanicus' actions are presented as interpreted by his contemporaries, and by the reader of the narrative.

indulged them in this entertainment . . . he thought it was civil (*civile*) to mix with popular pleasures' (54.2). Since the result, as it were, of the excesses of the republic is the principate, the hopes which rest on Germanicus can be seen to span the political spectrum, from idealised freedom to the restoration of the republic under the *name* of princeps. Through his foreshadowing in the narrative of his imperial descendants, moreover, he embodies the potential tyranny[6] which represents the ultimate betrayal of political hope.

THE TEUTOBERGERWALD

There are many scenes in the first two books of the *Annals* where Germanicus appears as a figure for the reader of history (most notably when he stands before the monuments of Egyptian Thebes at 2.59, which I will examine in chapter five, or when he visits Troy). But the two scenes I will focus on in this section and the next are, first, Germanicus' visit with the German legions to the site of Varus' massacre in the Teutobergerwald (1.61) and, secondly, his visit to Actium (2.53). The first of these, a long and striking passage, demonstrates that the process of reading history is also the process of creating history, and that the relationship between the reader and the traces of the past which he shapes into history involves more than an imaginative identification with the past. Rather, the past which is shaped in this moment of reading is one which leads inevitably to that reader; the past to which the reader looks is precisely one which *looks back* at the reader. In this sense the reader is always the reader in the text.

The text of Roman history, in this instance, is embedded in the German landscape. When Germanicus and his legions first arrive at the place it is described in terms of its effect upon the onlooker: 'they advanced into sorrowful (*maestos*) places, disfigured in sight and memory (*visuque ac memoria deformis*)' (1.61.1). The interpretation of the place seems at first to be drawn from the visible traces on the landscape (disfigured in sight), what we could call an 'affective' response to the site. At the same time, memory, prior knowledge of what has happened here, contributes to the sense of the place as 'disfigured'; this would be what we call a 'cognitive' response. The Teutobergerwald's unsightliness depends on this interaction of affective and cognitive response, which

---

[6] Borszák (1970); Gillis (1977).

explicates its first description as 'sorrowful places': it is both visually gloomy and a reflection of the sorrow which the visiting Romans project onto it. The characterisation of the Teutobergerwald as 'disfigured' (*deformis*) points us towards the process of reading the battlefield which is narrated in the rest of chapter 61. This process of reading *forms* a narrative of the battle from the shapeless, unformed (*deformis*) matter of the battlefield. This reading is put forward by expert translators, soldiers who survived the massacre and who return to explain the traces of the past on the basis of their prior knowledge. The ordered recollection of the battle, however, is in turn shaped by the traces on the field; the account of the massacre given here is organised not by chronology but by space.

> They recalled (*referebant*) that here (*hic*) the legates had fallen, there (*illic*) the eagles were taken; where (*ubi*) first Varus was wounded, where (*ubi*) he found death with the unfortunate stroke of his own hand; from which tribunal (*quo*) Arminius had addressed the men, how many pillories for the captives, what graves, and how he had mocked the standards and the eagles in his arrogance. (1.61.4)

Tacitus mirrors the extent to which the historical narrative read by the visitors is organised by space when, in the middle of this chapter, he focuses on the middle of the battlefield. At this point the survivors of the massacre are not present as interpreters, but the visible remains of the past are, nevertheless, vividly interpreted: 'in the middle of the field were whitening bones, scattered or piled up as they fled or stood their ground (*medio campi albentia ossa, ut fugerant, ut restiterant, disiecta vel aggerata*)' (1.61.2). If read literally this sentence is nonsensical; the subject of the verbs of motion being 'the bones'. In order to make sense of the sentence the reader of the text must bring the bones back to life, to be read retrospectively as signs for the living men they once were. Looking back to this moment in the past requires that the visitors to the site reanimate the soldiers of Varus in precisely these actions of fleeing and resisting in order that the positions of the bones, scattered or piled up, make sense.

The relationship between the readers and the object of reading is explicated at the beginning of the episode, where the motives for visiting the site are summed up as pity (*miseratio*).

> Desire took hold of Caesar, a desire to pay the last honours to the soldiers and the general, while the whole army which was present was

50

moved to pity because of their relatives and friends, and also because of the calamities of war and the lot of humanity. (1.61.1)

In addition to a generalised imaginative identification with these examples of the human condition, the army of Germanicus perceives an affinity between itself and the army of Varus. The line of continuity drawn by pity and elaborated by the process of recollection in the subsequent account of the battle is given added charge by Tacitus' reader's own recollection of why Germanicus' army is there at all: to revenge the massacre and to recover the three standards. Indeed, the immediately preceding chapter has narrated the recovery of the first of these. In short, the significance of Germanicus' presence on the battlefield is determined by the earlier massacre; the massacre, in turn, is rendered significant by the remembrance enacted by Germanicus and the other visitors to the site. Meaning is rendered in reciprocity, or, as I have put it earlier, the reader looks back to a past as a past that looks back at him.

This episode seems to stage a fulfilling, if poignant, encounter with the past, a 'successful' reading of history, as it were. The actions of Varus' men are read off the scattered bones and their significance is seen to impress itself on Germanicus' army and on Tacitus' reader. Moreover, the presence of expert interpreters who explicate the invisible traces of the past (the tribunal, the graves) presents a reading which does not undermine the reading of the bones. What we are presented with, therefore, is very different from the contradictory readings and staged misrecognitions of, for example, the mutiny episodes.

The limits of this historical reading are pointed up, however, in the conclusion, which by echoing the opening creates a distinct structure to the whole episode.

> Therefore the Roman army which was present, in the sixth year after the massacre of the three legions, buried the bones, with no one recognising whether he covered with earth the remains of a stranger or of a relative, so everyone buried as if his friends, as if his kinsmen, with increased rage against the enemy, sorrowing and at the same time hostile.

> *igitur Romanus qui aderat exercitus sextum post cladis annum trium legionum ossa, nullo noscente alienas reliquias an suorum humo tegeret, omnes ut coniunctos, ut consanguineos aucta in hostem ira maesti simul et infensi condebant.* (1.62.1)

The repetition of 'the army which was present'[7] binds together the reactions of the army at the beginning and end of the account. The act of interment as a conclusion to the reading process also bears traces of the act of narration (*condere* means 'to inter' and 'to commit to writing'). The bones, which were reanimated in the earlier interpretation, are here settled into the end of their historical account: they fled, resisted, were read and buried. At the same time, however, the limitations of a historical understanding of the bones are pointed up by Tacitus' reminder that the precise identity of the dead men is not known. The ignorance of the soldiers in this regard at the very moment of burial is countered by their creative interpretation, reading the bones *as if* they represent the friends and relatives of the soldiers: *ut coniunctos, ut consanguineos* (1.62.1). This reminds us of how at the beginning of the episode the soldiers were moved to pity 'because of their relatives and friends' (1.61.1). Most importantly, the soldiers invent the past of the bones in order to render them significant in the present; here they are read as the bones of relatives so that the soldiers can play the role of a grieving and, crucially, vengeful community.

The narrator emphasises the invention of the past in this respect by marking the soldiers' lack of firm knowledge about the status of the bones with the words 'with no one recognising' (*nullo noscente*), an echo of the inexpert interpreters of the mutinies: 'with no one, except for those in the know, recognising (*nullo nisi consciis noscente*) what was the beginning of the massacre, what the end' (1.48.3). As I argued in the previous chapter, the characterisation of the soldier as ignorant in interpretation frequently offers a challenge to the reader to accept or reject that characterisation in the context of the surrounding narrative, that is, an interpretative challenge. At 1.62.1 the ignorance of the soldiers first of all points up their inventive reading of the bones at the moment of burial. It also suggests that meaning is a gesture achieved in the face of utter contingency. The army's first response to the site, where the emotion of pity is elicited in part from an identification with human fate in general, raises the question why a more specific recognition is necessary in the burial scene. Since the narrative represents to us soldiers who recognise the bones as worthy of burial, the narrative of an additional absence of recognition, one which does not preclude honour to the dead and acknowledgement of the past, seems gratuitous. One reason for the inclusion of

---

[7] Noted by Woodman (1979) 145.

this absence is clearly to effect a heightened sense of pathos. The non-recognition of relatives is also a central example of misreading which runs through the narrative as a whole (a particularly dramatic example being the collapsing amphitheatre at Fidenae at 4.62–3, examined in the next chapter). In this case the non-recognition of the bones questions the extent to which Germanicus' army achieves a 'correct' reading of the site, a reading of the past as it was, and demonstrates perhaps the inherent impossibility of such a reading.

The 'monument' of the battlefield itself is constructed by Germanicus and his army just as much as the subsequent tumulus which they build over the bones of Varus' legions. But the reading of Varus' army which they put forward limits the identity of the massacred legions to their actions on the battlefield and their (imagined) relationship with the later army. As I pointed out earlier, the reason for Germanicus' presence in Germany is at the outset of the narrative linked to Varus' defeat, an event which the legions are meant to obliterate: 'to wipe out the infamy of the loss of Q. Varus' army (*abolendae . . . infamiae ob amissum cum Quinctilio Varo exercitum*)' (1.3.6). The memorialising of the massacre which takes place in this episode, therefore, at first seems to run counter to this mission. Indeed, by requiring their 'infamy' abolished Varus' dead legions could be said to call into being the existence of Germanicus and his army, who then require not the obliteration, but the continued memorialising of the Varan army in order to render themselves meaningful.[8] The identification with the Varan massacre as the sort of thing that could happen to any army becomes more than a general musing on the fate of all men, when the association between Germanicus and Varus is read retrospectively as a fatal line of transmitted signification. In the reciprocal relationship between Germanicus' and Varus' armies, where each is rendered meaningful by its relationship with the other, Germanicus' desire to offer a resolution to Varus' history (*solvendi suprema*, 'paying the last honours', 'finishing the final things') involves not only burial and memorialising of the past but also action in the present, dealing with the 'unfinished business'.

One of Tiberius' interpretations of the burial (an interpretation at first implicitly discredited by the narrative) is that it burdens the soldiers with the ghosts of Varus' men: 'he believed that the soldiers would be slowed down in battle by the image of the massacred and unburied

---

[8] The fulfilment of that meaning could be seen to be the redemption of the eagles.

(*imagine caesorum insepultorumque*), and that the enemy would be more terrifying' (1.62.2).[9] This interpretation seems to be borne out in the subsequent account of the German campaign, when Caecina, the commander, is visited in a dream by the ghost of Varus: 'an ominous dream (*dira quies*) terrified the general: for he seemed to see and hear Quinctilius Varus smeared with blood emerging from a swamp as if calling him, but that he did not follow but pushed away the hand stretched towards him' (1.65.2). In this fulfilment, however, the suggestive term of Tiberius' foreboding, 'image' (*imago*),[10] is absent; the ghost is subsumed into the dream in the phrase *dira quies*.[11] Caecina's resistance to Varus represents a reluctance to repeat the disaster, while in the battle next day Arminius' identification of the Roman soldiers as Varus' legions – '"see Varus and the legions again, bound to the same fate!"' (1.65.4) – represents his desire to place the new army in the position of the old, defeated army. Arminius' reading of the soldiers as the legions returned from the dead (to be killed again) summons up the apparition feared by Tiberius, but the ghosts here appear not to the Roman soldiers, to slow them down, but to the Germans, to spur them on. Caecina's earlier resistance to the ghost of Varus, which figures as a resistance to repetition, enables the invocation of Varus' legions here to operate as a sign not of repetition but of reversal. The success of the campaign, intended to wipe out the memory of Varus, can be seen to be prefigured in the apparition smeared with blood (*sanguine oblitum*), which appears as a sign both of the previous disaster, smeared with Roman blood, and of the subsequent reversal, erased with German blood.[12]

The conclusion to the German campaign, and the end therefore of

---

[9] Goodyear (1981) 100 glosses *imago* here not as 'ghost' but as 'vivid memory'; I would, however, question the extent to which a firm line can be drawn between a mental picture and an apparition, whether experienced by an individual or represented in a text.

[10] *Imago* is a Latin term which it is particularly difficult to render in English. I have translated it in this context as 'image', but in the next section especially I have retained the Latin in the main text in order to retain the dual notion of 'image / ghost / reflection / representation / funeral mask'.

[11] In the Lucanian line which, as Goodyear has noticed, may have influenced Tacitus here the *imago* reappears: 'tomorrow's sleep will be terrible and made gloomy by the image of the day, and everywhere will show the deadly battle' *crastina dira quies et imagine maesta diurna | undique funestas acies feret* (Luc. *BC* 7.26–7). Awareness of this allusion, I would argue, makes conspicuous the absence of the *imago* at 1.65.2, the search for which could then lead back to 1.62.2.

[12] *Oblitum* from *oblino, OLD* 4, but one could also reread *oblitum* as from *obliviscor*.

Germanicus' relationship with this piece of the Roman past, is the triumph celebrated at Rome halfway through the second book of the *Annals*. The enactment of a triumph has a strong closural function in the narrative of a campaign, marking the victorious and decisive end to a sustained series of military actions.[13] The triumph releases Germanicus from his reciprocal signifying relationship with Varus, from the necessity to make his present meaningful in relation to that particular past and to make that past meaningful in relation to his present. But, as I have pointed out at the beginning of this chapter, Germanicus as a historical figure is always rendered significant in this continual movement between retrospection and what we might call anticipation.[14] As a military commander Germanicus is significant in terms of his relationship to Varus and other commanders of past armies; as a Julio-Claudian, he occupies a pivotal position in dynastic history. Here meaning is hereditary.

This hereditary significance is re-invoked at Germanicus' triumph, when his appearance, or rather his representation, is focalised through the spectators, who become readers of history in their act of interpreting what they see.

> An exceptional representation of the man himself increased the sight of the onlookers (*augebat intuentium visus eximia ipsius species*). But there was an underlying hidden fear as they considered (*reputantibus*) that the favour of the crowd had not been fortunate for his father Drusus, that his uncle Marcellus, for whom the enthusiasm of the plebs was ardent, had been snatched away in the middle of his youth, that the loves of the Roman people were brief and unlucky. (2.41.3)

The sight of Germanicus and of his children seems to generate hope in the onlookers. An exact meaning for the term *augebat . . . visus* is elusive. The commentator F. R. D. Goodyear maintains that the primary meanings of *augebat* are 'intensified' or 'delighted' (although he finds neither satisfactory).[15] In the light of similar passages which place Germanicus'

---

[13] It is worth noting in passing that Germanicus does not accept this emplotment of events and begs to be allowed to continue the campaign, but Tiberius, in decreeing the triumph, imposes his own narrative structure with the words 'enough events now, enough happenings (*satis iam eventuum, satis casuum*)' (2.26.2).

[14] I have borrowed these terms from Brooks' (1984) analysis of narrative, 23. 'If the past is to be read as present, it is a curious present that we know to be past in relation to a future we know to be already in place, already in wait for us to reach it. Perhaps we would do best to speak of the *anticipation of retrospection* as our chief tool in making sense of narrative, the master trope of its strange logic.'

[15] Goodyear (1981) 317–18.

wife Agrippina in the centre of the onlookers' gaze,[16] I will argue that *augebat visus*, which I have translated as 'increased the sight', conveys the sense that the scope of what the onlookers see is broadened when they look upon Germanicus and his children. In other words, Germanicus and his children come to represent not only themselves but other individuals in the past and the future to whom they are linked in a chain of dynastic history.

The scope of vision centred on Germanicus but embracing also the past is made explicit when those looking on Germanicus consider his ancestors. The term used is *reputare*, literally 'to think back', and the scene from the past to which these onlookers think back mirrors the scene which they inhabit at this moment. In other words, the people at Germanicus' triumph draw a line of continuity between their own enthusiasm for Germanicus and the favour felt in the past for Germanicus' ancestors. The memory of what happened to these ancestors is projected forward to the possible premature death of Germanicus himself. This projection takes the form of fear, but is founded on memory and on a belief in continuity. This continuity hinges upon the people's recognition of Germanicus as a conduit between the past, represented by their memory of Drusus and Marcellus, and the future, represented perhaps by his children, or perhaps by the underlying fear. Germanicus, it could be argued, is not the object of hope so much as of the anticipation of retrospection. That is, the onlookers at the triumph look at Germanicus as a monument, and in that gaze anticipate the moment when they will look on his memory, when his life has been completed and they will lament 'that nothing was left to hope' (3.4.1).[17] This lamentation is anticipated when the spectators associate their own support for Germanicus with the possibility of his early death.

IMAGINARY ROME

The image of Germanicus carried in his triumphal procession, which triggers the retrospection of anticipation, is called a *species*, but the overwhelming sense of Germanicus' mortality which this image conveys to the onlookers and to the reader turns the triumph into a funeral proces-

---

[16] I will examine these passages in the last section of this chapter.
[17] On the association between triumphal and funereal procession, see Flower (1996) 107–9.

sion, and suggests that this representation of Germanicus is not a *species* but an *imago*. We have encountered the term *imago* in the last chapter, when analysing Tacitus' claim that the 'mask of liberty' (*imago libertatis*) fails to cover the destructive servitude of Tiberian Rome. Here I will examine the significance of the *imago* in its more specific cultural context of the Roman funeral, from which context it operates as a particularly potent symbol of historical memory.

The *imago*, the funeral mask, is invested with a sense of mortality; one's *imago*, through which one's glorious deeds are preserved and recalled, comes into being only after the moment of death.[18] Like any text, the *imago* has significance only in relation to a spectator to which the message of the past is addressed, or, as I have argued, in relation to a spectator whose position in the present is such that they are able to make of the text a message from the past. The *imago*, moreover, is an object carried, even worn, by an impersonator in a ceremonial display of the past, an event perhaps analogous to the recitation of a historical text. Most importantly, the relationship between past and present, ancestor and descendant, which is embodied in the *imago*, can be read as one of metonymy, a relationship of contiguity and causality, association as much as similarity.[19] Here we are moving away from the predominantly metaphorical aspect of historical representation, which the last chapter explored, and towards a metonymical chain which links, for example, Germanicus and Drusus, not because they are *like* each other, but because the past of one informs the present of the other.

This can be examined further by looking at the most extensive picture of the process of 'imaginising' an individual, provided by Polybius.

> 53.1. Whenever one of the illustrious men dies, after his funeral is brought to an end he is carried by the remaining order to the rostra, as it is called, in the agora, sometimes visible because standing up, more rarely lying down ... 4. After these things, burying him and performing the customary rites they place the image (εἰκόνα) of the man who has died in the most conspicuous place in the house, surrounding it with a wooden shrine. 5. The image (εἰκών) is a mask made extremely

---

[18] See Schneider and Meyer, *RE* 9.1, 1097–1104; Daut (1975); Winkes (1979); Bettini (1991); Flower (1996). For history as the procession of *imagines* see Kraus (1994a) 16–17.

[19] The central structuralist texts on metonymy are Jakobson (1981) and Lodge (1977); see also Brooks (1984) 259–60 and, for the reciprocity of metaphor and metonymy, Gallop (1985) 114–32.

similar (ὁμοιότητα) to the man both in shape and in delineation. 6. In the public sacrifices, displaying these images they adorn them zealously, and when someone illustrious from the family dies, they bring the images to the funeral, putting them on whoever seems most similar (ὁμοιοτάτοις) in size and general outline. 10. There cannot easily be a finer spectacle for a young man to look on, one who is a lover of glory and nobility (φιλοδόξωι καὶ φιλαγάθωι); for who would not be persuaded by looking on the images of men glorified for their virtue, all in the same place as if living and breathing (οἷον εἰ ζώσας καὶ πεπνυμένας)? What spectacle would seem finer than this? 54.1. Besides, the one speaking over the man about to be buried, when he has narrated the story of this man, he begins from the most ancient of the other images present, and he speaks of the success of each and of their deeds. 2. From this eternal renewing (καινοποιουμένης ἀεί) of the fame of noble men for their virtue the renown of those who accomplished fine things is made immortal (ἀθανατίζεται), the glory of those who did good for their country is made known to many and transmitted (παραδόσιμος) to posterity. (Polyb. 6.53.1–54.2)

There are two visual and one verbal chain of relationships from ancestor to descendant here. The first (53.4–6) might be termed a 'metaphorical' chain, based on similarity; the relationship between corpse and ancestral mask is one of likeness, while the impersonator who bears the mask is also chosen on the basis of likeness. This relationship is embedded in the term for 'image', εἰκών, derived from εἴκω, 'to be like', and is emphasised in many explanations on the use of the ancestral portrait and the ancestor mask in Roman culture.[20] The second visual association evoked in Polybius' account (53.10) does not depend on resemblance so much as on memory and emulation. The young man's appreciation of the sight of the ancestral masks depends upon his being 'a lover of glory and nobility' (φιλόδοξος καὶ φιλάγαθος).[21] In other words the masks in this instance are on display as a visual sign of past deeds; the relationship between mask and event in the past is not mimetic or metaphoric, based on representation or resemblance, but metonymic/synecdochic, since the mask stands for an individual who was a part of the event in the

---

[20] So for example Gregory (1994) 87; Gombrich (1982); Flower (1996); various specific readings of Tacitus offered by Woodman and Martin depend upon this sense of the *imago* being predominant, cf. n.31 below.

[21] Similarly the descendants are said to display their ancestral masks 'zealously' or 'emulously' (φιλοτίμως).

past.[22] This chain of associations needs to be emphasised if the historicising significance of the εἰκών/*imago* is to have any force. This is underlined by Polybius' representation of the funeral speech as having an exegetical function in relation to the display of the masks, narrating the deeds which are represented metonymically by the ancestral masks (54.1–2). Both oration and display achieve a juxtaposition of past and present;[23] Polybius maintains that the narrative immortalises (ἀθανατίζεται) past glories and that the ancestral masks make it seem as if the ancestors are alive (οἶον εἰ ζῶσας) and present.[24] The meeting of past with present ensures continuity, as knowledge of the past is renewed/reinvented (καινοποιουμένης) and transmitted (παραδόσιμος) to the future. The spectacle of the funeral, therefore, embraces not only the corpse and the ancestral masks, but also the young spectator fired with emulous zeal by the glories of the past.

The *imagines* towards which a Roman orator points in both funeral and other orations, therefore, represent the glorious past of a family, the latest product of which is the speaker himself. They represent both glorious past and the possibility of its repetition in the future. Hence, to pick examples from the *Annals*, Gaius Cassius is indicted on the grounds that he maintains an *imago* of his tyrannicide ancestor in his household, interpreted as a desire for civil war: 'Cassius was accused because he cultivated an effigy of Gaius Cassius among his ancestral images, thus inscribed: "to the leader of the party"; and that in fact he had sought the beginnings of civil war and a revolt from the dynasty of the Caesars' (16.7.2). The *imago* of Cassius does not stand for a dead past but for one which is dangerously

---

[22] Sallust reinforces this point when remarking on the power of the ancestral images to fire the mind to virtue: 'indeed it is not the wax or its shape which holds such power in itself, but the memory of deeds (*memoria rerum gestarum*) which makes the flame rise in the hearts of uncommon men' (*Iug.* 4.6). Not only is the 'cognitive' privileged over the 'affective' response here, but also the moral qualities of the reader are perceived to be crucial if the *imago* is to have any effect. See also Gregory (1994) 90–1.

[23] Pliny also articulates the sense that the masks at a funeral represent the totality of the family through time (and therefore the process of family history): 'the images would be assembled at family funerals, and invariably (*semper*), when someone died, every (*totus*) person who had ever (*umquam*) been a member of that family was present' (*NH* 35.6). Flower (1996) 277: '[s]ociety, both past, present, and future, was presented as a cohesive whole embodied by the living and deceased family members. The *imagines* and their associated messages, either spoken or inscribed, handed on traditions, whether preserved or invented, by rehearsing them.'

[24] The display of the masks standing around (παραστῆσαι) is similar to the display of the corpse itself standing up (ἑστώς) at the rostra.

contiguous with the present.[25] Gesturing towards an ancestral image is also employed for pathos, to draw attention to the reversals of fortune. So Aemilia Lepida, when indicted for false ascription of paternity, arouses the pity of an audience at Pompey's theatre by calling on her ancestors: 'having entered the theatre with some noble women, calling on her ancestors with tearful lament, and on Pompey himself, whose monuments and images could be seen standing there' (3.23.1). Here, in addition to the images, the very theatre becomes the *imago* of Pompey, juxtaposing a glorious ancestor with a descendant in distress; this wider context frames the audience's recollection of the contrasts in Lepida's own life, her nobility and subsequent 'degradation'. This effect is in part achieved by the display of Lepida herself[26] as an image which evokes memory, a phenomenon to which I will return in the next section.

The highly rhetorical use of the *imago* is also in evidence in M. Hortensius Hortalus' appeal for financial support from Tiberius (2.37–8). Here the speaker seeks a repetition of Augustus' earlier support for the propagation of the Hortensian family. Hortalus begins his appeal by directing his gaze towards an *imago* of his grandfather, the orator Hortensius, as the symbol of the illustrious past of the family, a past which could be revived in the four children of Hortalus, also placed within view, before the threshold of the Curia.[27] This particular example illustrates very well the metonymic structure inherent in the *imago*. First of all the *imago* stands for Hortensius himself, then it stands in meaningful relationship to Hortalus and finally to the children of Hortalus; as an attribute of their past, the *imago* is an attribute of their person, of them-

---

[25] Gregory (1994) 91–2. The anxiety surrounding the images and memory of the tyrannicides is central to the most famous Tacitean sentence, 'but Cassius and Brutus shone forth because of this very fact, that their effigies were not to be seen' (*sed praefulgebant Cassius atque Brutus, eo ipso quod effigies eorum non visebantur*) (3.76.2). At the trial of the historian Cremutius Cordus at 4.34–5 Cordus draws a parallel between the visible *imago* and historical memory: '"Are they not dead this past seventy years, and in the same way as they are known by their images (which not even their conqueror destroyed) so do they not retain a part of their memory through writers?"' (4.35.2). The previous absence of precisely these *imagines*, as 3.76.2 shows, does not silence written memory as perpetuated by dissident historians. But cf. Martin and Woodman (1989) 183–4.

[26] For a close reading of this entire passage see Woodman and Martin (1996) 219.

[27] Hortalus also gazes at an *imago* of Augustus, whose grant of money led to his setting up a family; clearly this *imago* stands in meaningful relationship to Tiberius, who represents the possibility of a repeated grant, a possibility which he chooses not to fulfil.

selves. Indeed, the prominent display of the children makes of them another form of *imago*: a visual image which represents not only the individual family member but the whole family and its history.[28] The gaze which focuses on the *imago* is not simply directed towards the past; Hortalus is 'looking on the image of his ancestor (*imaginem intuens*)' with an eye to the future well-being of his children. Similarly the *imago* of the ancestor can be seen to stand for the descendant, *and vice versa*. Hence, the descendant himself can take the place of an *imago* and direct the gaze of the spectator back towards his ancestors and forward to his progeny, a process of viewing which we have already seen in operation at Germanicus' triumph, where the onlookers (also called *intuentes*) look on an image of Germanicus and see his father Drusus and uncle Marcellus, creating an underlying fear, while their hopes are augmented not only by the spectacle of Germanicus but also by the sight of his children.[29] As I have already remarked, they stand for their father's memory, and, as the next link in the metonymic chain of dynastic history, they figure as *imagines*, being significant insofar as they stand for the past. Later in the narrative the eldest son, Nero, attracts the gaze and elicits a joyful response from the senators precisely because he appears almost as a manifestation of Germanicus.

> Nero gave thanks for this to the senators and to his grandfather, creating joyful emotions in his listeners, who with the memory of Germanicus still fresh thought that they saw and heard him again.
>
> *egit Nero grates ea causa patribus atque avo, laetas inter audentium adfectiones, qui recenti memoria Germanici illum aspici, illum audiri rebantur.* (4.15.3)[30]

Nero here is almost an impersonator of his father (carrying his *imago*) but the conflation of the two is underpinned in the text not by resemblance but by memory, the prior knowledge of the senators about the

---

[28] Here we can see the close assocation between metonymy and synecdoche, discussed in Lodge (1977) 75–7. Woodman and Martin refer more nebulously to 'the remarkable Roman capacity for seeing one individual in terms of another': (1996) 85 (on Germanicus and his father).

[29] This congruence of forward and backward views recurs in the repeated 'iconic' representations of Agrippina, which will be examined in the next section. What is worth noting again in this context is how the viewing enacted within the narrative draws attention to the same process enacted *by* the narrative from a later perspective.

[30] The memory of Germanicus which elicits a favourable response towards a descendant recurs at the appearance of the next Nero at 11.12.1, discussed in chapter seven.

association between the two: a cognitive rather than affective response.[31] Their relationship here is, therefore, not so much metaphoric (based on resemblance) as metonymic (based on contiguity), and dependent upon readers who bring historical knowledge to the moment of interpretation. When Germanicus embarks upon his tour of the eastern provinces (beginning at a site which recalls Augustus' imitation of Alexander, Nicopolis), the first pause in journey and narrative is at Actium, a visit which parallels in microcosm some of the elements of the visit to the Teutobergerwald.

> He went to the coast famous for the Actian victory and the spoils consecrated by Augustus and the camp of Antony with a recollection of his ancestors. For, as I have mentioned, his great-uncle was Augustus, his grandfather was Antony, and in that place was a great image of sorrows and joys.

> *sinus Actiaca victoria inclutos et sacratas ab Augusto manubias castraque Antonii cum recordatione maiorum suorum adiit. namque ei, ut memoravi, avunculus Augustus, avus Antonius erant, magnaque illic imago tristium laetorumque.* (2.53.2)

In contrast to the visit to the German battlefield, here there are no guides, nor are discrete features of the site unfolded in a spatially ordered narrative which mirrors a guided tour. In the place of 'first . . . then . . . in the middle . . . together with . . . here . . . there . . . where' (*prima . . . dein . . . medio . . . simul . . . hic . . . illic . . . ubi*) are the simple co-ordinating conjunctions *et . . . que*. But the extent of prior knowledge about Actium is much

---

[31] Impersonation dependent upon resemblance is discussed in the next chapter. Martin and Woodman on this passage once more point out that 'the Romans had a remarkable capacity to see one individual in terms of another' ((1989) 140), but seem to maintain that resemblance between Nero and Germanicus is what underpins the senators' response here. I would argue that the evocation of Germanicus as a vivid image represents a cognitive rather than an affective response, in that resemblance between Germanicus and Nero is not mentioned and therefore is subordinate to memory. Woodman and Martin also argue that Agrippina the elder's claim to be the *imago* of Augustus (4.52.2) hinges on 'family likeness' (217), which seems an even weaker argument. Agrippina presents herself as an *imago* in contrast to the 'mute effigies' before which Tiberius offers sacrifice. The notion of a metonymic relationship is here privileged over the merely mimetic; the statues represent Augustus in terms of likeness, but Agrippina represents a part of Augustus, 'descended from the heavenly blood'. The notion of speaking ('mute effigies' in contrast to Agrippina's indirect speech) may also be of significance here; on women's speech, see chapter six.

greater than that of the Teutobergerwald, while the visible signs of a sea-battle are inevitably restricted to monuments onshore; hence the place is 'famous' (*inclutus*), indicating not only its fame but the predominantly aural nature of its reputation,[32] heard of before seen. Indeed, the minimal signs of the past are here overwhelmed by prior knowledge. Germanicus attends the camp 'with recollection' (*cum recordatione*), which places his memory almost on a spatial plane alongside the camp and the dedicated ships. Tacitus' interjection 'as I have mentioned' (*ut memoravi*) first sends the reader back to the chapter on Germanicus' ancestry (2.43), and secondly draws attention to the narrator's implication in the memorialising process. The significance of Actium, it seems, is entirely dependent upon this preponderance of memory brought to the site by Germanicus and his narrator. An *imago* rather than a monument is present at the site, but this *imago* is not tied to a specific physical presence.

The emotions evoked at the site encompass the range of sorrow and joy to be expected in a spectator whose ancestors fought on both sides of the battle.[33] Here we have the alternative to the figure of the soldier in Germany, who buries bones 'as if his kinsmen' despite his fundamental ignorance as to whether they are foreign or familial. Germanicus' full awareness of his family ties at Actium does not enable him to make the distinction between one side or the other any more than can the soldier in Germany, despite his identification with only one side. Moreover, the soldier assimilates all remains into the category 'kinsmen' in order to maintain an uncontradictory emotional response to the place and event (angry and sorrowful) while Germanicus, who *knows* that all traces here are of his relatives, remains caught between the extremes of sorrow and joy. But the final phrase of the episode bears further examination. The extent to which Actium is figured *as* Actium because of the memories of its visitor comes out in its ambiguity: 'and in that place was a great image of sorrows and joys' (*magnaque illic imago tristium laetorumque*). Reversing the tenor of the earlier 'with recollection', which at first seems brought to the site by Germanicus, and then appears almost to coexist with the other visible traces of the past, the *imago* at first seems to be the site of Actium itself so long as Germanicus, the descendant of the protagonists, is looking on, but then by implication it appears to be what Germanicus

---

[32] From the Greek *kluo*, 'to hear'.

[33] As I have argued above, Germanicus' ancestry spans the political spectrum, sometimes at odds with the hope that resides in him; the range of responses available to him here highlights this tension.

himself has brought to Actium, another form of memory, perhaps embodied in himself as *imago*. Is the *imago*, then, a visible or an invisible trace of the past? Whether the 'image of sorrows and joys' is embedded in place or person, an important feature of the representation here is how Germanicus responds to the images he views, a crucial element in the portrayal of a reader. As Leach remarks of Aeneas before the temple of Juno at *Aen.* 1.459, 'Virgil interposes the hero's subjective response between us and the object he describes.'[34] The subjective response of the reader in the text is, from the narrative point of view, perhaps the most important part of the reading episode. But in Germanicus' other readings his response seems muted, even absent. In the visit to the Teutobergerwald the emotions of pity, sorrow and anger are ascribed to the whole army, while Germanicus himself is described at the start of the episode as fired with desire (*cupido*) to pay the visit, but has no individual emotional response upon viewing the remains. Similarly, when he traverses Greece the motivating force is said to be 'out of a desire (*cupidine*) of recognising ancient places celebrated by fame' (2.54.1). Apart from these two instances of desire and the sorrows and joys at Actium there are no instances of Germanicus responding with emotion to the sites and monuments of the past, an absence which is all the more striking when brought into contrast with the displays of emotion exhibited elsewhere by Germanicus.[35] Indeed, if we read the *imago* at Actium as Germanicus himself, then the emotional response is assumed to come from elsewhere, from an implied spectator or from the reader of the narrative. The intrusion of the narrator in the first person earlier in this sentence increases our distance from Germanicus as the spectator of Actium, allowing us, perhaps, to see him in this landscape as the descendant who carries on the memory of the past.

But the absence of an emotional identification with the past on Germanicus' part at other places in the narrative threatens to overwhelm the response to Actium and empty it of meaning, rendering it a 'semblance' or 'shadow' of emotion: another range of the meanings of *imago*. Actium as a historically significant site should elicit the joy and sorrow of Antony's and Octavian's descendant, but these emotions in the text are

---

[34] Leach (1988) 312.
[35] Attempted suicide (1.35.4; 2.24.3); weeping (1.40.3; 1.49.2); anger (2.57.3; 2.70.1); fear (2.70.1). On Germanicus as an emotional young man, see Rutland (1987) 155, 158, and Goodyear (1972) 261.

dependent on the *imago*, and how we read the *imago* therefore becomes crucial. The metaphorical range of meanings offered to the reader enables or disables the metonymic power of the *imago* to organise history; the more prior knowledge about *imagines* the reader brings to the text the more unstable a term it becomes for determining Actium or its visitors. Is the *imago* that of Germanicus or of Actium; is it Actium when Germanicus is present; does it signify an absence? Do we conflate it with the visible traces of the past or with the memory brought to the site by the various readers? Is it a term for the transmission of meaning or for its failure? In the absence of an interpreter/guide at narrative or story level the reader of the Tacitean text is arguably left stumbling over traces which elude recognition. The *imago* becomes an empty semblance, a mere representation, when no impersonator takes it on and no onlooker recognises its meaning.

The problematics centred in the *imago* of Actium have important resonances for the end of Germanicus, his crystallisation into memory, the moment when he becomes significant in relation to a later reader. The oracle of Clarian Apollo at Colophon, who sings composed verse despite basic illiteracy, foreshadows Germanicus' death, 'through ambiguities/circumlocutions (*per ambages*), as is the custom of oracles' (2.54.4). In the midst of these episodes about the practice of reading, this prophet, 'ignorant of letters' (*ignarus litterarum*), strikes an odd figure. Illiteracy, inability to read, is here linked to knowledge of secrets invisible to the eye of mere mortals;[36] moreover, the illiterate prophet, with his knowledge of the future, becomes a figure of a narrator, telling of events which will have been, a tale addressed not so much to the unknowing character as to the knowing reader. At the same time the knowledge of the prophet challenges the expertise not just of the reader in the text but of the reader *of* the text. Germanicus, presumably, does not decode the ambiguities of the oracle, but that does not leave the reader who possesses prior knowledge of Germanicus' death with any superior insight into the ambiguities of the prophecy, which is presented to us already decoded as what we already know, the early death of Germanicus. In this case, the ambiguities of the oracle become clear, readable, to Germanicus when he reads his own name inscribed upon curse tablets at Antioch (2.69.3). That act of reading also constitutes Germanicus' recognition of

---

[36] See also the illiterate freedman, privy to Tiberian secrets, at 6.21.1, examined in the next chapter.

his own impending death; in this respect, as Peter Brooks put it in the quotation with which I started this chapter, 'recognition . . . is the moment of the death of the reader in the text'. The enigma (*ambages*) which is solved in the resolution of Germanicus' life is enacted by his wanderings, through which (*per ambages*) he reaches his premature death. If we return to the most ambiguous moment in those wanderings, the *imago* at Actium, we could conclude that the moment of recognition at this site is deferred to the point of Germanicus' death, when he becomes replaced by an *imago*, that the moment of recognition at Actium is not afforded to Germanicus but to another onlooker, in an anticipation of retrospection back from the moment in the future when Germanicus' life has become part of history.

But the moment when Germanicus has become an *imago* is not the end of Tacitus' narrative, and, as I pointed out at the beginning of this chapter, Germanicus' narrative significance is determined by subsequent emperors (whose significance in turn depends upon Germanicus). The moment of recognition, when Germanicus' life and travels find their end to be the *imago* set up for others to follow, inaugurates a further series of repetitions which constitutes the ongoing Julio-Claudian narrative. This is figured by the continuing slippage of the *imago*, whose precarious meaning is reinvented and undermined again in the process of the ongoing reading of the past. This is performed through the nexus of funeral imagery starting at Germanicus' cremation in Antioch. The funeral, a strong closural ceremony at which the family *imago* plays a prominent role, is here marked by conspicuous absence: 'Germanicus' funeral, without images or procession, was notable for the praises and the memory of his virtues (*funus, sine imaginibus et pompa, per laudes ac memoriam virtutum eius celebre fuit*)' (2.73.1). Here the visible display which is absent (images and procession) is in contrast to the vivid memories, invisible signs of the past, brought to the event by onlookers, the praises and memory which distinguish the funeral.[37] When Germanicus' remains are finally interred at Rome, the absence of a funeral is again marked, as Tacitus records the contrast in the minds of the people between Germanicus' funeral and that of his father Drusus. As at the triumph at 2.41, the onlookers become figures of historical readers,

---

[37] In Junia's funeral the visible display is present but outshone by the absences rendered significant by memory. Woodman (Woodman and Martin (1996) 498) argues that Tacitus' reference to *effigies eorum non visebantur* 'compels us to infer that Cassius and Brutus were somehow "really" present. This was the mark of true glory . . .'

offering an interpretation of the present which hinges upon a past which makes the present interpretable. Whereas at the triumph the comparison with Drusus triggered a fear of repetition, acknowledging the similarity between the two, at the funeral Drusus is evoked in order to point up a contrast with his son.

> There were those who missed the procession of a public funeral and compared it with the honours and splendours which Augustus had performed for Drusus, the father of Germanicus . . . the images of the Claudians and Julians had surrounded the bier . . . where were these ancient practices, the effigy of the dead man set in front of the couch, the songs carefully composed to memorialise his virtue and the praise-giving and the tears or at least the semblance of grief?

> *fuere qui publici funeris pompam requirerent compararentque quae in Drusum, patrem Germanici, honora et magnifica Augustus fecisset . . . circumfusas lecto Claudiorum Iuliorumque imagines . . . ubi illa veterum instituta, propositam toro effigiem, meditata ad memoriam virtutis carmina et laudationes et lacrimas vel doloris imitamenta?* (3.5.1)

The final questions, in particular, underscore the onlookers' reading of Germanicus' funeral as a procession of absences. Woodman and Martin in their reading of the passage conclude that the onlookers' complaints are malicious and in part groundless, and that Tacitus implies as much in his narration, in particular by the strong parallels with Drusus' funeral in his earlier narrative of Germanicus' return to Rome.[38] But the selective reading of the past presented by the onlookers demonstrates the extent to which a reader, in order to characterise the present in terms of lack, must endow the past with plenitude. The questions which the onlookers frame at the end of the passage have already been answered by the same speakers: where are the trappings? They are in the past. The questions also receive an answer from the narrative itself, since many of the trappings have featured in Germanicus' funeral at Antioch; the 'songs carefully composed to memorialise his virtue and the praise-giving' sought at Rome are present in the 'praises and the memory of his virtues', and the effigy of the dead man is replaced by the display of the corpse itself before cremation. The main absence at the Roman funeral not accounted for at Antioch is that of the *imagines*, an absence which renders Germanicus' funeral discontinuous with the past, representing a failure of

---

[38] Woodman and Martin (1996) 98–9; *contra* Flower (1996) 247–52.

67

transmission, a gap which the onlookers have to work to bridge with their complaints and questions.[39]

This gap is highlighted further by a later comparison, not made by onlookers but required of the reader. When Tiberius' son Drusus dies at the beginning of book 4 his funeral enacts historical continuity from Trojan origins in precisely the way that Germanicus' funeral does not.

> His funeral was especially illustrious for its procession of images, since the origin of the Julian family, Aeneas, and all the Alban kings and Romulus the founder of the city, followed by the Sabine nobility, Attus Clausus and the other effigies of the Claudians could be seen in a long row.

> *funus imaginum pompa maxime inlustre fuit, cum origo Iuliae gentis Aeneas omnesque Albanorum reges et conditor urbis Romulus, post Sabina nobilitas, Attus Clausus ceteraeque Claudiorum effigies longo ordine spectarentur.* (4.9.2)

The wording at the start of this passage strongly echoes that of 2.73.1; here we are supplied with the plenitude of *imagines* whose absence was remarked at both funeral ceremonies for Germanicus. Indeed, we are explicitly told at the outset that further honours to Drusus' memory represent an addition to those voted to Germanicus: 'the same things were decreed to the memory of Drusus as had been for Germanicus, with many more added'.[40] The addition, associated with the long procession of *imagines*, only serves to highlight the moment of historical disjunction experienced at Germanicus' funeral, and articulated there in terms of comparison with the elder Drusus' funeral. From 4.9.2, then, the reader is invited to look back at 3.5 and at 2.73.1, in a retrospective glance similar to that of the onlookers at the funerals themselves. The younger Drusus (son of Tiberius) then stands in meaningful relationship to the elder Drusus, a relationship figured both by the plenitude of *imagines* at both funerals and by their shared name, which stands as a verbal *imago*, a meeting-place of past and present.

In the middle remains the absent *imago* of Germanicus, the figure on which the significance of the Julio-Claudian dynasty depends. Tacitus goes on to construct a narrative of the descendants of Germanicus which

---

[39] The onlookers' verbal summoning-up of Drusus and Augustus at 3.5 supplies the *imagines* which are visually absent.

[40] On honorific parallels between Germanicus and the younger Drusus see Levick (1966).

draws upon the themes inherent in this first representation. But his portrayal of Germanicus here demonstrates that the process of reading the past ultimately hinges on an image whose significance is continually reinvented by the present and whose absolute value is elusive.

THE ICONIC WOMAN

We have already seen how the display of the *imago* which represents the ancestral dead is analogous to the display of the body of the descendant, dead or alive. Aemilia Lepida in the theatre of Pompey, for example, not only gestures towards the monuments and images of her illustrious ancestor (3.23.1) but also, in directing the gaze of the audience towards herself, stands forth as an embodiment of her family past. Germanicus too, in his triumph, becomes a spectacle evoking the shades of his father and uncle (2.41.3). As I argued in the first section, the triumph scene contains a nexus of retrospective and prospective views, enacted both by the reader of the text and the onlookers in the text. Indeed, the sight of the onlookers in this episode and their response to the scene in part triggers the reader's response and invites comparison between the two perspectives. Such 'iconic' moments[41] in the narrative, where a visual display and a first-level response to the display is offered to the reader for her response in turn, are frequently centred on the body of the well-born imperial woman, who stands both as *imago* of her ancestry and, through her childbearing potential, as a figure of the future. Agrippina the elder in the early books of the *Annals* is the pre-eminent example of this figure; as an *imago* of her grandfather Augustus, through her fecundity on which the narrative frequently focuses, and through the verbal echo of her name, repeated in the Neronian books.[42]

The first display of Agrippina in the narrative is during the account of

---

[41] Iconic narrative (as termed by Jakobson) in its structure mirrors the structure of the story told. Genette (1980) 107, 115 discusses this in the context of singulative, repeating and iterative narrative. I am using the term in a slightly different sense to denote narrative which presents a visual image and (for the most part) a response within the narrative to that visual image. Since the examples I am looking at are 'freeze-frame' images of living characters I am reluctant to use the term 'ecphrasis'; the relationship of these examples to the *imago* (εἰκών) in part suggested the term 'iconic'. Clearly what also takes place in these episodes is variable focalization, on which see Genette (1980) 185–98. On the possible influence of Roman friezes on Tacitus' narrative, see Tanner (1991) 2706–12.

[42] On the textual and historical effects of this doubling, see chapter six.

the German mutiny. Her departure from the turbulent camp presents an image to the soldiers reminiscent of scenes at the capture of cities, thereby impressing upon them the role of enemies of Rome and instigating a return to order.[43] The scene is presented to us in intensely pathetic terms.

A womanly and wretched procession was advancing, the wife of the leader a fugitive, carrying her tiny little son in her bosom, the wives of friends weeping all around, who with her were being dragged from the camp; nor were those who remained any less miserable. This was the appearance not of a flourishing Caesar, not in his own camp, but as if in a conquered city; the groaning and wailing even attracted the soldiers' attention.

incedebat muliebre et miserabile agmen, profuga ducis uxor, parvulum sinu filium gerens, lamentantes circum amicorum coniuges, quae simul trahebantur; nec minus tristes qui manebant. non florentis Caesaris neque suis in castris, sed velut in urbe victa facies; gemitus ac planctus etiam militum aures oraque advert-ere. (1.40.4–41.1)

The response of the soldiers is divided between consideration of Agrippina and of her infant son Caligula.

Hence there was shame and pity and the memory of her father Agrippa, of her grandfather Augustus; there was her father-in-law Drusus, there was herself, of distinguished fecundity, of outstanding chastity; moreover there was her infant, born in the camp, brought up in the legionaries' tents, whom they called by the soldierly name of Caligula.

pudor inde et miseratio et patris Agrippae, August<i> avi memoria; socer Drusus, ipsa insigni fecunditate, praeclara pudicitia; iam infans in castris genitus, in contubernio legionum eductus, quem militari vocabulo Caligulam appellabant. (1.41.2)

---

[43] Paul (1982) lists the standard elements of the 'captured city' (*urbs capta*): killing of men; destruction of city by fire, carrying-off of women and children; plunder of temples, murder of children, separation of child from parent; rape; wailing of women and children. See also Ziolkowski (1993). The fate of women and children is clearly at the forefront of this example; *trahebantur* in particular, which Goodyear explains as having a moral rather than a physical force, is consistent with the threat of physical violence which is (partly) the cause of the woman's lament in the *urbs capta topos*. Cassandra, to pick the most prominent example in Latin literature, is dragged (*trahebatur*) in *Aen.* 2.403.

The primary emotions of shame and pity are amplified and come to depend upon memory, specifically ancestral memory; it is not merely female distress that causes these emotions but the implied contrast between the treatment accorded to Agrippina and that due to her as daughter and granddaughter of the legions' former commanders. Between consideration of Agrippina and of Caligula occurs an initially confusing juxtaposition: 'there was her father-in-law Drusus, there was herself, of distinguished fecundity, of outstanding chastity'.[44] Goodyear cites and dismisses Wolf's supposition that 'T. wants to suggest that the presence of Drusus, their old commander, is as much a concrete reality to the mutineers as Agrippina and Caligula whom they can actually see'.[45] But the presence of Drusus in the nominative, juxtaposed with *ipsa* (*Agrippina*) suggests that here too we have a spectator's gaze which looks at the descendant and sees the ancestor.[46] As I have already argued, this assimilation can be based on contiguity (underpinned by memory) more than actual resemblance. The juxtaposition of Drusus and Agrippina here also marks the transition point from retrospective to prospective gaze – her father-in-law Drusus (past), herself (present), of distinguished fecundity (future) – a transition point centred in the pregnant body of Agrippina herself. From this point the reader's view diverges from that of the mutineers, who look on Caligula as a present figure in both senses (*iam infans* denoting both 'here' and 'now') while the narrative's reader looks back to Caligula's infancy with the awareness of what he will have been (*iam* as 'then' rather than 'now').

Indeed, ironic foreknowledge is elicited from the reader in the preceding description of the fugitive family, quoted above. In this respect the portrayal of Agrippina is strikingly similar to Velleius Paterculus' account of Livia in flight with the infant Tiberius, where the narrator's and reader's perspective is more explicitly figured in the text.

> Livia, the daughter of the most noble and brave man Drusus Claudianus, the most conspicuous of Roman women for her birth,

---

[44] This representation comprises the three elements of female display in imperial propaganda, as summarised by Wood (1988) 409: 'demonstration of bloodlines . . . the hope for the birth of heirs . . . embodiments of various virtues'.

[45] Goodyear (1972) 286, citing in (momentary) support of Wolf Germanicus' apostrophising of Drusus' *imago* at 1.43.3.

[46] We have already seen how Polybius characterises the effect of ancestral *imagines* as being *as if* the ancestors were alive and present (Polyb. 6.53.10). See also Flower (1996) 91 and *passim*.

honesty and beauty, whom afterwards we saw as the wife of Augustus
. . . then fleeing from the armies of her soon-to-be husband Caesar, carrying in her bosom Tiberius Caesar, less than two years old, avenger of
the Roman empire and the future son of that same Caesar . . . .

*Livia, nobilissimi et fortissimi viri Drusi Claudiani filia, genere probitate forma
Romanarum eminentissima, quam postea coniugem Augusti vidimus . . . tum
fugiens mox futuri sui Caesaris arma, minus bimum hunc Tiberium Caesarem,
vindicem Romani imperii futurumque eiusdem Caesaris filium, gestans
sinu . . .* (Vell. 2.75.3)

Velleius' reader is first offered an image from the more immediate past
('afterwards', *postea*) which is then contrasted with an earlier image, heralded by 'then' (*tum*). But this last image is presented to the reader with
multiple temporal perspectives, so that Livia's enemy, Caesar, is overlaid
with Livia's future husband, Caesar, and the infant she carries is both 'less
than two years old' and 'the avenger of the Roman empire'. The image of
the fugitive woman carrying her infant son in her bosom (*gestans sinu*) is
what links Velleius' passage to Tacitus' in this instance; while the images
in both passages are allusive, evoking past and future to spectators and
readers, the relationship between the two images is also allusive. Just as
the mutineer, primed with foreknowledge of Agrippina's ancestry, looks
at her and sees her father-in-law, so the reader learned in Latin historiography is encouraged to look at Agrippina and Caligula and see Livia and
Tiberius. The Velleius quotation draws on the ironies of Livia's former
and subsequent situation by characterising individuals from the perspectives both of the story and of the narrative, as well as by introducing the
story with a reflection on the vicissitudes of fortune.[47]

The future reversals of Agrippina's and Caligula's fortunes are not made
explicit in Tacitus' narrative, except through a contrast of appearance and
reality which implicitly calls on the reader's foreknowledge. Agrippina
here gives the appearance of a woman going into captivity, but in the
reader's eyes she perhaps dangerously plays on the dividing line between
being *like* a woman going into captivity, and *being* a woman going into
captivity.[48] This is borne out by the parallel image later in the narrative of
a 'real' captive woman, the wife of the German leader Arminius.[49]

---

[47] 'Who could sufficiently wonder at the changes of fortune, at the doubtful chances of
human affairs? Who would not either hope or fear for things different from the
present and contrary to what is expected?' (Vell. 2.75.2).
[48] On the limits of metaphor, see preceding chapter.
[49] In other texts she is called Thusnelda, but remains nameless in the *Annals*. On the parallels between Arminius and Germanicus see Pelling (1993) 79–81 and Baxter (1972).

The wife of Arminius, also the daughter of Segestes, with a spirit more
her husband's than her father's, neither overcome with tears nor suppli-
ant in speech, with her hands pressed together in her bosom, looking
on her pregnant womb.

*uxor Arminii eademque filia Segestis, mariti magis quam parentis animo, neque
<e>victa in lacrimas neque voce supplex, compressis intra sinum manibus
gravidum uterum intuens.* (1.57.4)[50]

The parallels between Agrippina and the wife of Arminius (*gravidam
coniugem . . . uterum eius . . . sinu* (1.40.2–4) *sinum . . . gravidum uterum*
(1.57.4)) sharpen the focus of the text on the womb, while the latter
image offers a form of correction to the former, as the German woman
demonstrates how to endure captivity with dignity. The image of
Arminius' wife, together with that of Agrippina, is evoked in subsequent
iconic episodes in the narrative, examined below.

Agrippina herself resists the role forced upon her by her husband in
this tableau; her resistance is voiced in terms of an appeal to her ancestry,
and is overcome by an appeal to her fecundity.

To his wife spurning departure, when she bore witness (*se testaretur*)
that she was descended from the god Augustus and was not unworthy
(*degenerem*) in the face of danger, he finally, embracing her womb and
their common son with much weeping, urged her to go away. (1.40.3)

In a rhetorical move similar to the appeals to *imagines* examined in the
preceding section, Agrippina offers, as evidence of her ancestry and
nobility (*degener* spans both senses), herself: *se testaretur*.[51] Germanicus'
response is an embrace which encloses Agrippina, Caligula and the
unborn child in a gesture which fuses the infant and pregnant woman
into one image, so that in the subsequent scene Agrippina is 'carrying
her tiny little son in her bosom' (1.40.4) and the mutineers' gaze moves
from the woman (*ipsa*) to her womb (*fecunditate*) to her child (*infans*).
While Germanicus' journeys through books 1 and 2 are directed towards
his enshrinement in an empty *imago*, his embrace here associates

---

[50] The focalization in this passage is somewhat different to the Agrippina tableau. We are
afforded internal focalization with *mariti magis quam parentis animo*, whereas
Agrippina's inner emotions are presented in the text by their outward signs. Arminius'
wife also possesses a gaze of her own – *uterum intuens* – which is not the case with
Agrippina.

[51] Agrippina's awareness of the extent to which she embodies her ancestry is also
brought out in her famous challenge to Tiberius in the course of her persecution,
where she claims primacy over the statues of Augustus as a 'true *imago*' (4.52.2).

Agrippina inextricably with her uterus, which she carries to Antioch and back to Rome as an image not of hope but of doom.

Agrippina is repeatedly recognised in the text as a figure of fecundity; her first mention in the text is as the mother of Germanicus' many children (1.33.1), and in the extended comparison of Germanicus and Drusus (son of Tiberius) she is said to surpass Drusus' wife Livia 'in fecundity and reputation (*fecunditate ac fama*)' (2.43.6). Moreover, as we have seen, her distinguished fecundity is a pivotal feature of the captured-city tableau during the mutiny. The next iconic representation of Agrippina occurs after Germanicus' death, when Agrippina embarks on her journey back to Rome.

> But Agrippina, although worn out with weeping and physically ill, not bearing anything which might delay her revenge, embarked on the ship with the ashes of Germanicus and with her children, while everyone pitied her, that a woman most eminent in nobility, just lately with the most excellent marriage, accustomed to be seen in the midst of respect and gratitude, was now carrying the funeral remains in her bosom, doubtful of her revenge, worried for herself and for her unfortunate fecundity which offered so many hostages to fortune.

> *at Agrippina, quamquam defessa luctu et corpore aegro, omnium tamen quae ultionem morarentur intolerans, ascendit classem cum cineribus Germanici et liberis, miserantibus cunctis, quod femina nobilitate princeps, pulcherrimo modo matrimonio inter venerantes gratantesque aspici solita, tunc ferales reliquias sinu ferret, incerta ultionis, anxia sui et infelici fecunditate fortunae totiens obnoxia.*
> (2.75.1)

As Goodyear remarks, the weight of the 'long and carefully planned sentence' falls on the ablative absolute and dependent clauses, in other words, on the response of the spectators to the sight of Agrippina. Goodyear tellingly adds '(i)n such structures the main clause functions for T. as a pivot, not a climax'.[52] The pivotal clause here achieves a juxtaposition similar to that seen at 1.41.2 (*socer Drusus, ipsa insigni fecunditate . . . iam infans*) as Agrippina's embarkation is accompanied by the past, the ashes of Germanicus, and by the future, the children. The juxtaposition, with Agrippina herself between past and future, is more striking when focalized through the spectators, who envisage her as an earlier, happier object of attention ('just lately . . . to be seen') and project her

---

[52] Goodyear (1981) 421.

fears for the future from the present view of her ('now . . . doubtful . . . worried'). A number of perspectives are included within this passage, then: the perspective of those who looked on her in happier days, to whom no foreboding is ascribed; the perspective of those who pity her now, who look back to the earlier view in order to heighten the pathos of the present scene; and the view forward of Agrippina to her uncertain future, a view projected by the present onlookers from the present signs of uncertainty and anxiety, and validated by the reader with her aware-ness of the certainty of Agrippina's future misfortunes. The reversal of Agrippina's fortunes is strikingly portrayed by the replacement of her young son in the earlier scene (1.40.4) with the ashes of her husband (2.75.1).[53] As a gloss on the replacement her 'distinguished fecundity (insignis fecunditate)' (1.41.2) has become 'unfortunate fecundity (infelici fecunditate)' (2.75.1). Again these textual echoes serve for the narrative's reader as an equivalent of the visual echoes which evoke the memory of the spectators in the narrative.

The final iconic presentation of Agrippina directly mirrors her embarkation at Antioch: the disembarkation at Brundisium in the pres-ence of mourning crowds (3.1).[54] The association between the two episodes is underlined by similar references to Agrippina's emotional state: 'worn out with weeping (luctu) . . . not bearing (intolerans) anything which might delay her revenge' (2.75.1); 'wild with weeping (luctu) and not knowing how to bear it (nescia tolerandi)' (3.1.1).[55] As in the embarka-tion scene, the picture of Agrippina with her children and her husband's ashes is presented to the reader juxtaposed with the response of the onlookers at the scene. At Antioch, however, the spectators offer a complex reading of Agrippina, incorporating memories of her former state and projecting her possible future. The picture of Agrippina at Brundisium, though echoing the image focalized through the Antioch

---

[53] The 'remains' (reliquias) here can be reread as not yet devoid of hope, analogous to Virgil's revival of the defeated Trojans (reliquias Danaum (Aen. 1.30)) to found a great empire. The last male descendant of Germanicus is represented in the same terms as the Roman people's great hope: 'that remaining male offspring; and for his mother Agrippina . . .' (illa reliqua suboles virilis; et matri Agrippinae . . .)' (11.12.1), discussed in chapter seven. On the meanings of reliquus in the earlier chapters of Annals 1, see O'Gorman (1995b) 104–8.

[54] The vividness of this scene, and the legendary chastity of Agrippina, made this a popular subject for eighteenth-century painters; see, for example, von Erffa and Staley (1986) pl. 38; Macmillan (1986) pls. 17, 25, 43. I am grateful to Michael Liversidge for drawing my attention to these pictures.   [55] Woodman and Martin (1996) 81.

spectators, is presented in narrative voice, while the response of the onlookers is restricted to a universal wordless cry.

> After having disembarked from the ship with her two children, holding the funeral urn, she cast down her eyes and from everyone there was the same groan.

> *postquam duobus cum liberis, feralem urnam tenens, egressa navi defixit oculos, idem omnium gemitus.* (3.1.4)

The narrative then turns the reader's gaze onto the spectators themselves for a moment of interpretative evaluation to which I will return. The picture presented to the spectators comprises elements from the two images of Agrippina at Antioch: the narrator's 'she embarked on the ship with the ashes of Germanicus and with her children'; and the onlookers' 'she was carrying the funeral remains in her bosom' (2.75.1). This merging of views in the Brundisium scene suggests to the reader a spectator's view without Tacitus presenting it as such, leaving the spectator to function as a symbol of loss of meaning in the face of grief. The parallel of many features draws attention to the variation in detail from 'she was carrying the funeral remains in her bosom' (*ferales reliquias sinu ferret*) to 'she was holding the funeral urn' (*feralem urnam tenens*). The triptych of Agrippina images presented to us over the first three books moves us from consideration of her pregnant womb and its product, the tiny child in her bosom (1.40.4), to its replacement by the funeral urn which she carries off the boat at Brundisium.[56] This development serves as a visual reminder of the change from distinguished to unfortunate fecundity and as a foreshadowing of the violent deaths of her children.[57]

In a collection of passages which draws attention to the interpretative act of looking, the wordless response of the crowd at Brundisium is strikingly in contrast to the indirect speech of those at Antioch or the German camp. It is also different from the laments to be found later in Tacitus' narrative, all of which present the people's grief in some sort of 'logical' context.[58] For example, the cry 'that the republic had fallen, that nothing was left to hope' (3.4.1) depends upon an imaginative link

---

[56] On the uterus as an urn see Hanson (1990) 137.

[57] Nero and Drusus are put to death by Tiberius; Caligula is assassinated; Agrippina is put to death by her son Nero; Drusilla succumbs to illness in the reign of Caligula; Julia is put to death by Claudius.

[58] For a textbook structuralist and ahistorical reading of the popular reaction to Germanicus' death, see Versnel (1980).

between Germanicus and the state (or Germanicus and the hope of a restored republic) while the complaints about Germanicus' funeral at 3.5 are based on a comparison with his father's funeral, and therefore represent a historicising account of the event on display. The groan at Brundisium, on the other hand, represents an absence of interpretation or even an abdication of the role of interpreter, an absence which is all the more marked given that the picture presented to the onlooker calls out for interpretation, from the reader's point of view, by its evocative relationship with the earlier pictures of Agrippina in the narrative. The gap between the reader of the narrative and the reader in the text momentarily widens, but only momentarily. As Tacitus swings the reader round to face the crowd at Brundisium he once more challenges his reader's ability to read, as the grief which renders the crowd wordless, unreading, also renders them unreadable: 'nor could you distinguish (*neque discerneres*) kin from strangers, the laments of men from those of women' (3.1.4).[59]

Just as the absence of *imagines* at Germanicus' cremation in Antioch and interment at Rome represents a moment of discontinuity in the dynastic history, so too the absence of an interpretative response to the scene at Brundisium threatens to empty the significance of Agrippina's womb, which has become a site of the past (the funeral urn) as well as of the future (the tiny son). Agrippina later dramatically claims to be the true *imago* of her ancestor, but the *imago* is, as we have seen, constructed by the spectator, whose interpretation renders it meaningful, precisely what does not occur at Brundisium. As I argued in the first section, the action of looking at the *imago* operates as a reading of the past, looking back at an event from which the future is viewed as what will have been: looking at the *imago* which looks back at its onlooker. Agrippina at Brundisium does not return the gaze of the crowd ('she cast down her eyes' (3.1.4)[60]), which may be what renders her, in their eyes, momentarily meaningless.

---

[59] Compare the challenge to the expert interpreter in the account of the mutinies, discussed in the preceding chapter (1.32.3).

[60] On the recurrence of this glance downwards in the iconography of Agrippina, cf. Wood (1988) 411. Gilmartin (1975) 110 regards this as a 'purely visual' effect.

Reading Tiberius at face value

In the preceding chapters I have concentrated on readers of political and dynastic history in the narrative of the *Annals*, those who draw out continuity or discontinuity between political structures and persons in the past and present. The readers examined in this chapter exercise or try to avoid exercising their interpretative skills on the emperor Tiberius, who in turn subjects his contemporaries to a hostile scrutiny. Tiberius is at the centre of Tacitean misreading and obscurity, so much so that he has often been taken as an oblique self-portrait of the historian. What is represented as the prime obstacle to reading Tiberius, what we could therefore term the predominant element of Tiberius' representation, is his repression and dissimulation of thoughts and emotions. This feature is so pervasive in Tiberius' representation that it conjures up a fantasy of the 'real' Tiberius, a fantasy for Tacitus' readers which threatens to be a nightmare for the people of Tiberian Rome. What I will be arguing in this chapter is that Tiberius represents the Tacitean narrative, in that the difficulties of reading the princeps are a dramatisation of the difficulties of reading the *Annals*.

These difficulties, as I outlined in the introduction, have to do with reading a surface which continually calls attention to itself *as* surface, thereby predicating hidden depths and exciting the desire to plumb those depths, uncovering hidden truth. Hence any reading of the surface, however coherent and plausible, is disrupted by the uncertainty of how that reading measures up to the hidden truth. In the case of the emperor Tiberius, the surface repressions and perversions of inner thoughts are punctuated by the eruption of what is hidden beneath; these eruptions, far from constituting moments of certainty for the reader, only increase the sense of fear and lack of control. This is primarily because the hidden truth of Tiberius is a terrifying cruelty. This is recognised by the people of Rome from a very early stage in the narrative, when they are considering the possible successors to the ageing Augustus.

Tiberius Nero was mature in years, had been tested by war, but with the ancient arrogance bred into the Claudian family, and many signs of cruelty, although they were repressed, broke out.

Tiberium Neronem maturum annis, spectatum bello, sed vetere atque insita Claudiae familiae superbia, multaque indicia saevitiae, quamquam premantur, erumpere. (1.4.3)

This preliminary assessment of Tiberius is borne out by the narrative of the next six books. The conclusion to book 6, the obituary of Tiberius, considers his life as a development from repression to increased outbreaks of cruelty.

There were distinct stages also to his behaviour: outstanding in lifestyle and reputation while he was either a private citizen or in office under Augustus; hidden and deceitful with feigned virtues so long as Germanicus and Drusus were alive; similarly mingled with good and bad while his mother lived; unspeakable in his cruelty but with lust concealed while he favoured and feared Sejanus: finally he burst forth in crimes and misdemeanours after having put aside shame and fear he made use only of his own nature.

morum quoque tempora illi diversa: egregium vita famaque quoad privatus vel in imperiis sub Augusto fuit; occultum ac subdolum fingendis virtutibus donec Germanicus ac Drusus superfuere; idem inter bona malaque mixtus incolumi matre; intestabilis saevitia sed obtectis libidinibus dum Seianum dilexit timuitve: postremo in scelera simul ac dedecora prorupit postquam remoto pudore et metu suo tantum ingenio utebatur. (6.51.3)

The obituary traces a gradual revelation of hidden cruelty and lust over the period of Tiberius' life, as each individual who represents a moderating influence on him is removed by death. With hindsight, the obituary suggests, we can read what was there all along, although it was at first concealed; retrospection is a privileged position of reading. But the early assessment of Tiberius near the beginning of the *Annals*, while Augustus is still alive and Tiberius is supposedly still 'outstanding in lifestyle and reputation', makes the same point from a position of anticipation as the obituary makes in retrospect: in advance of any reading exercise cruelty is set up as the hidden truth which will inevitably be uncovered.

Hence the obituary at the end of the Tiberian books validates the judgement made by the Roman people at the beginning as a correct interpretation of their next ruler. But the congruence between anticipation and retrospection here raises the question of why reading Tiberius is continually staged in the narrative as a problematic and uncertain process. If the key to Tiberius is presented to his subjects and to Tacitus' readers at the outset, why does reading Tiberius at face value continue to *represent* a difficulty?

One reason, as I have suggested above, is that the awareness of a hidden truth disrupts the certainty of reading a surface. In addition, the nature of the hidden truth in this case, the 'unspeakable' (*intestabilis*) cruelty of the ruler, makes revelation a terrifying experience; the only certainty the reader of Tiberius attains is the certainty of doom. Finally, the eruption of Tiberius' inner truth is continually represented as an arbitrary phenomenon, not as a result of a particularly effective interpretation enacted by any Roman. The reader's lack of control over when the repressive surface breaks to reveal the hidden truth creates a sense of the profound uselessness of readerly expertise.[1]

Hence, Tiberius represents a paradoxical text, one that is continually asserted to be unreadable, but which has always already yielded up its secrets. The people's response to the terrifying secret is to replicate the ruler's own repression and perversion of signs by themselves 'looking elsewhere'. It could be said that the strategy of unreadability which Tacitus represents Tiberius as pursuing is just as much a creation of the Roman readers, and of Tacitus himself; the various images of suppression constitute an attempt to *represent* suppression. In addition, Tiberius' dissimulation is represented as a reading strategy; his removal of the ability of other Romans to understand, and thereby to manipulate the signs of the ruler suggests that Tiberius himself not only monopolises the power of interpretation but creates a position where the privileged reader exercises interpretation while remaining effectively invisible to any rival interpreter. This reading position can be seen to be usurped explicitly by Sejanus in book 4, and implicitly by Tacitus throughout the narrative.

In the first section of this chapter I will look at some moments where Tiberius and the senators try to read each other, and at how our attempts to read these passages draw us into the position where we become, in Klingner's words, 'the reader of Caesar'.[2] In the second section I turn to Tiberius' reading of two specific characters, Sejanus and Agrippina. We have already seen in the preceding chapter how Agrippina operates as a

---

[1] An example of Tiberius' revelations which are terrifying to the senate is the episode where he has the account of his grandson Drusus' dying words (including curses against the emperor) read out in public (6.24).

[2] Klingner (1955) 193, quoted in full in chapter one.

historical text, offered as a representation of family history to readers in and of the *Annals*. In book 4 of the narrative Tacitus represents her in continual contrast to Sejanus, and juxtaposes the emperor's readings, or misreadings, of both. Again, the reader of the *Annals* is drawn by the contrast into a position of complacency about her superior insight into the events, a complacency which once more is disrupted by the difficulties and ambiguities of the narrative. In the final section two further readers are introduced: the astrologer Thrasyllus and the historian Cremutius Cordus. Each one uses his particular skill to produce a narrative interpretation of the past and the future; each narrative must be read by the emperor, whose response determines the survival of the skilled interpreter. The implications of these two episodes are underscored by their juxtaposition in the *Annals* with digressions in which Tacitus addresses the question of reading the past and the future. A further challenge is presented to Tacitus' reader who must interpret these juxtaposed digressions and episodes, and consider the many relations between them.

MISREADING

The recurrent qualities of Tiberian rule are hesitation and delay, withdrawal and absence, disguised or suppressed emotion and ambiguity, punctuated by immoderate anger, heartfelt outbursts and terrifying revelation. In the political environment primarily concerned with debate before the emperor and in the senate, the absent presence of Tiberius is profoundly disconcerting. The narrative of Tacitus points up this perversion of normal political interaction by focusing almost obsessively on Tiberius' emotionless face. The rhetoric of Roman public (and indeed private) life makes physical appearance a crucial factor in self-representation and persuasion; the Roman orator by facial expression, bearing and gesture conveyed to his audience a non-verbal message both specific (in relation to his speech) and general (in relation to his personal authority).[3] The key to an orator's influence over his audience's emotion, according to Cicero, is the working together in harmony of speech content, tone of

---

[3] For an examination of the cultural specificity of gesture, and particularly of its role in the rhetorical system of ancient Rome, see Graf (1991); Gleason (1995). Gombrich (1982) 61–77 examines ritualized gesture as a representational element in later art, while Brilliant (1963) 49–78 offers an analysis of gesture in Julio-Claudian sculpture and coinage. On non-verbal communication in ancient literature see Newbold (1990) on Tacitus and Ammianus, and Lateiner (1987) on Herodotus and (1995) on Homer.

voice, face and movement.[4] Linked to this rhetorical theory is the science of physiognomy, concerned with the idea that permanent character or transitory emotion is manifested on the outward form of the body. In this science, the character of a man is interpreted by the signs visible on the face and body (*indicia* or *signa* in Latin; σημεῖα in Greek). Within the hierarchy of these signs the face and the eyes are most important. In her work on the ancient physiognomists, E. C. Evans has remarked on the physical descriptions of characters in historical writings, which tend to occur as a character is about to address an assembly of some sort.[5] Examples of this in the *Annals* concentrate on attitude, gaze and gestures: Hortalus before the senate ('Hortalus, now casting his eyes on the image of Hortensius situated among the orators, now on that of Augustus, began in this manner' (2.37.2)) and Drusus Caesar at a military assembly ('Drusus was standing asking for silence with a gesture of the hand' (1.25.2)). Because these descriptions appear at points in the narrative where the character described appears to other people, the image of the gesturing character is focalised through the onlookers. Hence a central issue in such scenes is how their body, face and gesture are read by the other characters.

The physical descriptions of Tiberius in his dealings with the senate pick up on the subject of reading face and gesture only in order to record its suppression and displacement. So, for example, when Tiberius refuses to present himself to public view as Germanicus' body is brought back to Rome, Tacitus represents Tiberius' actions as concealment of his face.

> Tiberius and Augusta kept out of public view, thinking it beneath their majesty if they were to lament openly, or in case, with the eyes of everyone examining their faces (*vultum eorum scrutantibus*), they might be understood (*intelleg<er>entur*) to be faking. (3.3.1)[6]

Tacitus ends the chapter by saying 'Tiberius and Augusta did not go out of their house (*domo non excedebant*)' (3.3.1). Concealing emotion is achieved not by an expressionless but by an absent face, one which

---

[4] 'For delivery is as it were the speech of the body (*quasi sermo corporis*), with which the mind should be harmonious ... After the voice, the face is most effective; but it is governed by the eyes, and in all those things which are a part of delivery is a certain force given by nature; so that by delivery the ignorant, the common people and even barbarians are greatly moved' (Cic. *De Orat.* 3.223).   [5] Evans (1935) 56.

[6] Woodman and Martin (1996) 90 remark '[i]t is ironical that T. here affects to believe that Tib., the master of pretence, dared not appear in public for fear of revealing his hypocrisy'.

remains behind closed doors. But the withdrawal from potentially hostile interpretation is itself an interpretable action. By suggesting that Tiberius is unable to deceive when placed under scrutiny, and therefore is forced to withdraw from public view, Tacitus in effect holds up the emperor's face before the reader as an explanation for his actions. This explanation, and the imagined scrutiny by those who might really understand what they see, hovers between Tacitus' reader and the hidden emperor.

The image of the closed door as a mask which hides Tiberius' emotions from the scrutiny of the Romans later becomes transferred back onto the face of the emperor. Even when present at the trial of Cn. Piso later in book 3, Tiberius represents a terrifying absence of emotion.

> He was terrified by nothing so much as that he saw Tiberius without pity, without anger, holding firm and shut close, lest he be broken into by any emotion.
>
> *nullo magis exterritus est quam quod Tiberium sine miseratione, sine ira, obstinatum clausumque vidit, ne quo adfectu perrumperetur.* (3.15.2)

The emperor himself is the closed door, shut against the appeals of his Roman subjects (lest any emotion break *in* on him) and likewise shut against any manifestation of his inner thought (lest any emotion break *out* of him).[7] The terror of this for Piso is that it indicates Tiberius' dissociation from Piso's acts against Germanicus, but the closed face of the emperor also represents a more general terror in that it indicates Tiberius' withdrawal from the sort of communication on which hinges normal Roman social interaction. The abandonment of this mode of social communication momentarily makes of Tiberius an unreadable and unreading entity for the Roman senator. But the closed face, like withdrawal behind closed doors, is not uninterpretable; the inscrutability and uncommunicativeness of the emperor become indicators of his tyrannical nature.

Emphasis on the face of Tiberius quickly shifts to a consideration of the imagery of the closed door. The image both obscures and represents the face of the emperor. The act of looking at the emperor head-on is thus easily deflected for all readers of Caesar. I have already pointed out that the science of physiognomy makes the human body a text whose meaning is the human mind, and does so by making physical

---

[7] See Woodman and Martin (1996) 166–7; they persuasively read this passage as referring primarily to Tiberius closing his ears to appeals.

characteristics 'signs' (*signa* or *indicia*) of character or emotion. The signs of Tiberius' cruelty (the keynote of his character in the *Annals*, as we have seen) are manifested not as *indicia* upon his face but as trials for treason in the senate, the *indicia maiestatis*. The case of Scribonius Libo Drusus in book 2 is a good example of the displacement of Tiberius' emotion from his face to the mechanism of prosecution.

> Caesar, not spurning the accusation / a trial (*indicium*) declined a meeting (*congressus abnuit*) with Firmius Catus. In the meantime he honoured Libo with a praetorship, invited him to dinner, not alienated in his expression, not disturbed in his speech (*non vultu alienatus, non verbis commotior*) (thus he buried his anger (*iram condiderat*)). (2.28.2)

Tiberius' secret actions, his encouragement to the prosecutor Firmius Catus and complicity with the ruin planned for Libo, are at odds with his manifest actions, his conviviality with Libo and avoidance of Catus. The contrast is highlighted by the echoes in the two manifest actions *congressus abnuit . . . convictibus adhibet*, where the repeated *con-* prefix of meeting is first denied with the separative *ab-* prefix and then encouraged by the *ad-* prefix of summoning. Tiberius' face and words are held up as signs of deception; his face does not reflect his estrangement from Libo. But even as Tiberius' face here deceives Libo, and seemingly fails to deceive the more knowledgeable reader, Tacitus' phrase *non vultu alienatus* undermines our certainties. The reader has been given the insight that Libo lacks, but that insight renders the phrase more ambiguous. In one sense Tiberius *is vultu alienatus* in that his facial expression is at odds with his intention. Moreover his intention is signalled by the trial, the *indicium* which is not manifested on his face; in that respect Tiberius is estranged not from Libo but from his own expressions of inner thought. The phrase *non vultu alienatus*, in other words, shifts in its referents when placed under scrutiny.

The treason trials which manifest Tiberius' cruelty are a pervasive feature of *Annals* 1–6, and represent another *charged* arena of conflicting interpretations by readers in and of the text. Trials for the crime of *maiestas minuta*, the 'lowering/diminution of the standing/dignity of the *populus Romanus* and by extension its representatives',[8] scrutinise the significance of individuals' acts, to determine whether they are meaningful symbolic gestures against the state, or meaningless in relation to the

---

[8] Goodyear (1981) 141 n. 1.

public affairs of Rome. In other words, an accusation of *maiestas* renders potent the 'metaphoricity' of gestures. The trials themselves also stand in the narrative as symbols of tyranny, the imposition of public interpretation upon (often) private acts. This process and its evolution is traced by Tacitus when Tiberius introduces the trials.

> He had brought back the law of *maiestas*. It had the same name (*nomen idem*) among the ancients, but came into trials in other ways (*alia in iudicium*): if anyone diminished the army by betrayal or the plebs by seditions, or generally diminished the majesty of the Roman people by any corrupt deed: actions were accused, words were unpunished (*facta arguebantur, dicta impune erant*). (1.72.2)

The original application of *maiestas* entails an interpretation of actions, not words; in contrast the trial itself has become a word, 'the same name' (*nomen idem*), with a very different referent in action, 'into trials in other ways' (*alia in iudicium*).[9] The referent of the contemporary *maiestas* is the interpretation of words, and Tiberius' precedent is, not surprisingly, Augustus: 'Augustus first conducted a judicial inquiry (*cognitionem*) into slanderous writings under the cloak (*specie*) of this law' (1.72.3). The judicial inquiry (*cognitio*) for the purpose of defining an individual as innocent or guilty is conflated with the investigation for the purpose of knowledge, understanding or recognition (*cognitio*). Augustus' and Tiberius' inquiries into the meanings of words used about *them* become conflated with Tacitus' and the reader's inquiry into the meaning of the words used about the principate.

The trials as they appear in the *Annals* seem an exercise in injustice at the levels of both action and narrative. It seems a sign of tyranny that a Roman knight is brought to trial and threatened with exile for selling a statue of Augustus (1.73.2). It also seems arbitrary and unfair (and has been remarked as such)[10] that the trials in books 1 to 6 are explicitly mobilised by Tacitus as signs of Tiberius' tyranny even as he narrates the princeps' protests at the charges, and the eventual acquittal of the accused. In other words Tacitus enacts the tyranny of wilful (mis)interpretation in his narrative of a procedure which he sees as standing for precisely that aspect of political tyranny. The *maiestas* trial, therefore, is

---

[9] This is a good example of Tacitus using a single term and its shift in meaning over time to chart the political changes of the principate and to articulate his protest. We see here the 'in other ways' (*alia*) of ironic contrast, examined in the introduction.

[10] Walker (1968) 20–2.

most a symbol of tyranny when as a symbol it is disjunctive; within the trial, when the metaphoricity of the gestures alleged do not seem self-evident; within the narrative, when an acquittal is secured and the cruelty of the princeps is *therefore* drawn as a conclusion.

The trials, then, effect a displacement of Tiberius' character from his face and words to the senate, but also stage a series of hostile (mis)read-ings of individual actions. Finally, the trials themselves stand as blatantly falsified signs of cruelty when most of them end with acquittal. Suppression and displacement of signs are allied with simulation; signs are either deliberately misleading or aggressively misread.

Curiously, the deception and dissimulation of the emperor is supposed to be a strategy for uncovering the hidden thoughts of others (much as the ambiguities of Tacitus' narrative require the reader to 'come out' in favour of one interpretation). This supposition is made early in the *Annals*, when Tiberius does not immediately or openly assume the role of Augustus' successor.

> Afterwards it was recognised that his hesitation was put on in order to scrutinise the wishes even of the chief men; for twisting their words and expressions into crime he stored them away.
>
> *postea cognitum est ad introspiciendas etiam procerum voluntates inductam dubitationem; nam verba vultus in crimen detorquens recondebat.* (1.7.7)

Tiberius *cloaks* himself in hesitation (the clothing imagery of *inductam* is highly significant) in order to put the senators under scrutiny (*intro-spiciendas*). Their inner thoughts (*voluntates*) are displayed upon their faces (*vultus*)[11] and in their words. Interestingly, however, this display of thought is seen as dependent upon Tiberius' metaphorical self-conceal-ment; the hesitation marks an absence, a gap which is filled by the sena-tors' words and expressions. But the hesitation/absence cloaks the presence of the scrutiniser, who gathers the words and expressions into his hiding-place (*recondebat*). The deviation in this reading process is that, before storing up the signs of the senators' thoughts, Tiberius twists them around (*detorquens*), thereby violently changing the meanings of the sena-tors' expressions from *voluntates* to *crimen*. The term *detorquens* suggests aggressive misreading, while the early term *introspiciendas* suggests a per-

---

[11] The late Latin etymologies of *vultus* are of relevance here: 'the face, which is named from the will (*a voluntate nominatur*), is a mirror of the soul' (Cassiod. *De Anim.* 3.78H); 'the face is so-called because through it the will of the spirit is displayed (*animi voluntas ostenditur*)' (Isid. *Orig.* 11.1.34).

ceptive close reading: does one term invalidate the other? The sentence presents further difficulties for Tacitus' reader since the concluding phrase 'twisting etc.' is introduced as an explanation and elaboration of the preceding phrase, as the weak conjunction *nam*, 'for', indicates. Tiberius' wilful misinterpretation of words is given to us as proof of his scrutiny from a concealed position. The gap between the first claim and its supposed substantiation, as in the case of the treason trials, first indicates that Tiberius is as much the object as the subject of aggressive misreading, but secondly acts as a gap which the reader of Tacitus must fill with her own interpretative response to its perceived inadequacy.

The failure to explain arises out of the tension between the conjunction *nam* and the incompatibility of two words which it conjoins, *introspiciendas* and *detorquens*. This failure drives the reader back to the opening words of the sentence, which make a strong claim about the firm knowledge on which the matter of the sentence is based: 'afterwards it was recognised (*postea cognitum est*)'. Although the sentence seems to characterise Tiberius as the privileged reader against the senators' will, the subordination of the first half of the sentence (in indirect speech) to this retrospective knowledge positions Tiberius as the object of interpretation by a reader who remains hidden. In that respect the sentence replicates the very strategy of reading from a hiding-place which it goes on to describe in the case of Tiberius. Similarly, it leaves another gap for Tacitus' reader to fill, in this instance by not supplying an agent for *cognitum est*: by which reader was the fact subsequently recognised? One provisional answer is 'by senators'; not only the senators of the Tiberian regime but also senators in general, including the senatorial historian Tacitus. This interpretation subordinates Tiberius' position as privileged reader to the retrospective (and equally aggressive) readings of the senate, who retain their hegemonic control of the historical record. Another provisional answer is 'by Tacitus' reader', for whom the deceptions and concealments of the Tiberian regime are revealed in the full play of imagery. But the disjunction I have already noted between the two halves of the sentence work to undermine the privileged, retrospective knowledge of this reader. The explanatory power of the concluding phrase, heralded by *nam*, is nullified not only by this disjunction but also by the hidden and deceitful actions which it describes. This works to problematise Tiberius' actions first of all as proof: how can his twisting and storing-up of words be evidence for any certain knowledge? Also, and more importantly, the destabilising of Tacitus' reader's knowledge puts her in

87

the same position as the senator who fills the gap and the hidden reader who scrutinises; it blurs the boundaries between active wilful reader and passive hapless object of reading. Tacitus' reader, drawn in by substantival clause and subordinating conjunction, becomes once more implicated in the power struggle of princeps and senator.

This brief sentence conveys an overwhelming sense of the unattainability of certain knowledge through a process of reading. Under scrutiny the understanding which it seems to convey recedes, but that elusion itself offers a sort of understanding of Tiberian Rome as a dangerous play of surfaces. Soon after this account of Tiberius' hesitation comes a well-known passage which highlights the dangerous position of the senator as reader of the princeps. As in the passage we have just examined, Tiberius' dissimulation is assumed (in both senses of the word) to cover the appropriation of Augustus' place at the head of empire.

> Tiberius, even in the kind of matters which he would not conceal, either by nature or custom, always used hesistant and obscure words: but at this time, with him trying to hide his meaning deeply, they were rather more entangled in uncertainty and ambiguity. And the senators, for whom the one fear was if they might seem to understand, burst out in complaints, tears and prayers.

> *Tiberioque etiam in rebus quas non occuleret, seu natura sive adsuetudine, sus-*
> *pensa semper et obscura verba: tunc vero nitenti, ut sensus suos penitus abderet,*
> *in incertum et ambiguum magis implicabantur. at patres, quibus unus metus si*
> *intellegere viderentur, in questus lacrimas vota effundi.* (1.11.2–3)

The opening sentence of this passage effects a tight alignment between the reader of Tiberius and the reader of Tacitus, as the account of Tiberius' mode of speaking formally replicates the qualities it describes. So Tiberius' 'hesitant words (*suspensa verba*)', words left hanging and unfulfilled, are presented in a sentence which delays the subject (*verba*) by interposing adverbial phrases and an adjectival clause. This implicit parallel becomes more important as the reaction of the senate to his speech is described, inviting the reader of Tacitus to consider her position in relation to these senatorial readers.

Curiously, what we seem to have here is an episode about correct reading. Tiberius' intention is to conceal the meaning of his words (*ut sensus abderet*); the senators' fear of giving the appearance of understanding represents an understanding of Tiberius' intention. What is ironic about this is that misunderstanding Tiberius is a response which indicates true understanding of Tiberius. The final sentence, which portrays the senators both reading the emperor and offering themselves to him to be read in turn, also implies our own reading of the senators, their inner thoughts (fear) and overt acts (complaints, tears, prayers). We are required, once more, to ascertain a precise relationship between the two halves of the sentence, thought and deed. In particular, the flurry of complaints, tears and prayers seems to operate as a cloak to understanding, as a sign of misunderstanding. The reader of Tacitus then supposes a disjunction between the inner fear and these outward signs. But misunderstanding, as I have already pointed out, operates in this instance as a sign of understanding, so the reader also supposes a conjunction between the object of fear (seeming to understand) and the outward signs. Tacitus' reader, caught in the interplay of conjunction and disjunction in this sentences, replicates the dilemma of the senators, who represent their understanding by their very attempts to avoid the appearance of understanding.

In this particular case, when Tiberius attempts to hide his meaning, the words he uses are 'entangled in uncertainty and ambiguity (*in incertum et ambiguum implicabantur*)'. The same sort of entanglement can be seen to be the predicament of Tiberius' senators and of Tacitus' readers, whose interpretations might be said to replace the hesitant and obscure words in the net of ambiguity.

'DECEIVING THE READER'[12]

When we try to read Tiberius at face value we look at the treason trials, at Tacitus' imagery, at the senators, at ourselves: anywhere but at the princeps. The dangers of reading and misreading are further explored in the episodes of book 4 which focus on Sejanus and Agrippina, on Tiberius' readings of them and on our readings of all three.

Sejanus dominates book 4 of the *Annals* after his striking introduction in the very first chapter of that book. One feature of this multi-layered introduction is the characterisation of Sejanus as an especially privileged reader of the princeps.

> Soon he had bound Tiberius by various arts, so much so that he rendered the emperor who was obscure to everyone else unguarded and uncovered to this one man, not so much because of his skill (since he

---

[12] Masters (1994).

89

was overcome by those same arts) as because of the anger of the gods against the Roman state, whose ruin was the same when Sejanus flourished as when he fell.

mox Tiberium variis artibus devinxit, adeo ut obscurum adversum alios sibi uni incautum intectumque efficeret, non tam sollertia (quippe isdem artibus victus est) quam deum ira in rem Romanam, cuius pari exitio viguit ceciditque. (4.1.2)[13]

The arts of Sejanus seem to be interpretative skills which render him unique in Rome. As such Sejanus appears to stand as a figure for the narrator, who similarly uncovers the hidden thoughts of his characters. Like Tacitus, and indeed Tiberius, Sejanus occupies the position of privileged insight by his self-concealment, as the character sketch goes on to elaborate.

> Concealing himself, an accuser of others ... in public, affected modesty, within, lust to aim for the heights of power.

> *sui obtegens, in alios criminator ... palam compositus pudor, intus summa apiscendi libido.* (4.1.3)

This introduction of Sejanus implies that his unique interpretative skills are acquired by adopting a similar strategy to that of Tiberius, such as we have already seen in the last section from a close reading of parts of book 1. Indeed the parallel in reading practice between Sejanus and Tiberius seems to be encouraged by the use of the same term in the same episode of book 1 to describe the emperor's approach to power. Tiberius is seem by some to have 'crept' (*inrepsisse*) into power through his adoption, while Tacitus describes Sejanus 'creeping gradually' (*paulatim inrepere*) into military favour at the start of book 4. But Sejanus' skills or arts by which he holds the emperor captive are also represented as precisely the arts which cause his downfall. Sejanus thus stands as an exemplary warning of the dangers as well as the rewards of this type of reading.

Although the opening chapter of book 4 constitutes the formal introduction of Sejanus, he has appeared briefly in book 1, accompanying Tiberius' son Drusus to Pannonia. There he is characterised not as *criminator*, 'accuser', but as *ostentator*, 'demonstrator', in a phrase which Goodyear calls 'bold and pregnant ... and also a little obscure'.[14]

---

[13] The variety of preposition + accusative (*adversum alios*) followed by dative (*sibi uni*) (see Martin and Woodman (1989) 82) reflects the advantageous position held by Sejanus in contrast with other contemporaries.   [14] Goodyear (1972) 220.

Along with Drusus came the praetorian prefect Aelius Sejanus, who had been appointed as a colleague to his father Strabo, with great influence over Tiberius, a guide to the young man and a demonstrator of dangers and rewards to the rest (*ceteris periculorum praemiorumque ostentator*). (1.24.2)

As Goodyear puts it, '(w)ho exactly are *ceteri*?'; since Sejanus plays no active role in the rest of the events of book 1, this brief characterisation seems to point forward to the introduction of book 4. Arguably the *ceteri*, the audience to whom Sejanus displays himself as an example, are the other readers of Tiberius within the narrative as well as the readers of Tacitus' text. But since the strategies which Sejanus adopts are seen to be Tiberius' own strategies, the emperor himself could be the target audience; Sejanus could demonstrate the dangers of self-concealment to Tiberius. Indeed, it is possible to say that what Tacitus says about Sejanus, that he was overcome by his own arts, is just as true when applied to the dissimulating emperor, who dies smothered under a heap of clothes.[15]

The irony of Sejanus' exemplary role to the emperor and senators is that he occupies this role by being unreadable through his deceptions and concealments. As such he represents a problematic example for Tacitus' reader too, since her sense of privileged insight into the characters of the *Annals* invites her to consider her own possible parallels with Sejanus.

The counterbalance to Sejanus in *Annals* 4 appears to be Agrippina, who is first mentioned in this book as the main object of the emperor's suspicion on account of her promotion of her sons' interests. She is described as 'badly concealing her hopes (*spem male tegens*)' (4.12.3); this characterisation sets her in direct contrast to Sejanus who, as we have already seen, is 'concealing himself' (*sui obtegens*). This contrast continues throughout book 4, not only in the continued characterisation of Sejanus as dissimulating and Agrippina as unable to conceal her thoughts, but also in the parallel episodes where first Sejanus and then Agrippina request imperial permission to marry and are refused. The contrast culminates in the juxtaposed dinner-party episodes where Tiberius subjects each character in turn to a close scrutiny. I will examine these episodes in detail in the rest of this section.

This schematic opposition of Sejanus and Agrippina lures the reader into one mode of interpretation, but we could also consider Sejanus'

---

[15] See above on *inductam*.

characterisation to be a warning about the dangers of such readings. Sejanus is not just a concealer of himself; he is also an accuser of others. This characterisation sums up the dynamic of book 4, where Tiberius fails to see Sejanus' deceptions because his attention is directed by Sejanus to the open behaviour of Agrippina, the supposedly straightforward object of reading. We could consider how the ambiguous Tacitean text, presenting us with the systematic opposition of Sejanus and Agrippina, distracts the reader in the same way that the ingenuous Agrippina distracts the emperor. In both cases a straightforward object of reading is presented to a reader by a dissimulating text, which works to undermine the reader while his attention is thus diverted. The contrast between Agrippina and Sejanus, therefore, should make Tacitus' reader feel very uncertain.

Uncertainty of reading is the dominant theme of the dinner-party episodes, for in each case Tiberius reads the face of his companion and arrives at conclusions which the narrative demonstrates to be false. The first of these is the dinner party with Agrippina, where Tiberius' mis-reading is set up in advance by the deception of Sejanus.

> But when Agrippina was sorrowing and unprepared, Sejanus struck her a deeper blow (*altius perculit*), when he sent people to her who under the guise (*speciem*) of friendship warned her that poison was being prepared for her, that she must avoid dining with her father-in-law. And she, not knowing how to simulate (*simulationum nescia*),[16] when she sat beside him at dinner, did not bend in expression or speech (*non vultu aut sermone flecti*) and touched no food, until Tiberius noticed, or perhaps because he had heard about it; and in order to probe her more keenly (*quo acrius experiretur*), praising some apples which were placed near him he passed them to his daughter-in-law with his own hand. Agrippina's suspicion was increased by this and she passed on the apples, untouched by her mouth (*intacta ore*), to the slaves. Yet no open remark (*vox coram*) ensued from Tiberius, but turning to his mother he said it was no wonder if he decided on more severe measures against a woman by whom he was alleged (*insimularetur*) to be a poisoner. (4.54)

Agrippina's face is at the centre of scrutiny; her anxiety can be read in her immobility of expression (*vultus*) and in her refusal to allow the apple to touch her mouth (*os*). Her face is supposed to afford access to her inner

---

[16] Compare Agrippina at 3.1.1 'not knowing how to bear it' (*nescia tolerandi*).

thoughts; the apple which is offered in order to probe her deeply appears almost as a metaphor for close reading. Despite Agrippina's openness, her display of anxiety, and her inability to deceive, her expressive face remains opaque to the emperor. His close-reading apple fails to penetrate her and he remains as much a prey to Sejanus' deception as she does. The failure of Tiberius' reading is pointed up by his use of the term *insimulare* when he accuses Agrippina of making allegations. His accusation thus echoes *against* the narrative's claim that Agrippina is *simulationum nescia*, 'not knowing how to deceive', suggesting a contrast between Tiberius' reading of Agrippina and the narrator's. This contrast is pointed up when the reader recalls that the deceitful Sejanus has been shown by the narrative to have actually made the allegation that Tiberius is a poisoner; in effect this episode explicates the earlier characterisation of Sejanus as *sui obtegens, in alios criminator* (4.1.3).

Not only does Tiberius misread Agrippina, but she too seems to misread him; because Sejanus has deceived her into fearing poison she misunderstands Tiberius' offer of the apple. But here the narrative does not directly contradict Agrippina's reading. Tiberius is said to have offered the apple 'in order to probe her more keenly', where 'keenly' or 'rather bitterly' jars with his praise of the apple (presumably for its sweetness), suggesting that, verbally, at least, Tiberius' apple does bear traces of poison. Allowing such traces to become prominent in the text, however, makes Tacitus' reader subject to Sejanus' deception, which, we can see, informs the whole chapter. Tiberius misreads not Agrippina, but Sejanus' deception; Agrippina likewise misreads not Tiberius but Sejanus' deception. The deception could be seen to interpose itself between the two individuals, and perhaps between Tacitus' reader and the episode. Because Sejanus in a sense scripts this encounter, moreover, it is possible to read an asymmetry between this dinner party and the next, where Tiberius scrutinises Sejanus.

> And by chance (*forte*) during these days a doubtful danger (*anceps periculum*) which happened to Caesar increased the groundless rumours and offered to him a substantial reason why he should rather trust (*fideret*) in the friendship and loyalty of Sejanus. They were dining in a villa called Spelunca between the Amunclane sea and the Fundanian mountains, in a natural cave. When the rocks at the mouth (*os*) suddenly fell in, some of his attendants were crushed: hence universal fear and flight of those gathered at the dinner. Sejanus, hanging over Caesar with knee and face and hands (*genu vultuque et manibus super Caesarem*

suspensus) placed himself in the way of the falling stones and was found in that attitude (*habitu*) by the soldiers who came to the rescue. He became greater because of this and although he advised what was ruinous he was listened to with trust (*fide*) as a man who did not care for himself. (4.59.1–2)

As with the preceding episode about Agrippina, the object of scrutiny is the human body. Here the posture or attitude of the body (*habitus*) is interpreted; Sejanus' interposition of his body between the emperor and the danger is read as a sign of trustworthiness and loyalty. The passage begins and ends with the same term to denote Tiberius' trust (*fideret, fide*) and suggests that the episode is a straightforward matter for reading. This is, however, undermined by the opening characterisation of the event with the phrase *anceps periculum*, a doubtful or double danger. The commentators Martin and Woodman point out that the danger is *anceps* 'because it could have gone either way . . . also in the sense that it was capable of two interpretations'.[17] The doubleness of the interpretation can emerge if we first concentrate not on Sejanus' posture but on his face. He is said to be 'hanging over Caesar with knee and face and hands'; most readers have wondered why Sejanus' face is included in the description of his posture. It works against the realism of the text and the syntactical sense of the sentence; in attempting to restore both sense and realism commentators assign to the face of Sejanus an expression. Martin and Woodman, for example, acknowledging the difficulty of this sentence, suggest that *vultu . . . suspensus* might be translated as 'with anxiety written all over his face'.[18] Nipperdey, according to Furneaux, assigns 'an expression of anxiety and devotion'.[19] These interpretations serve to emphasise the absence of expression on Sejanus' face in the narrative itself; in that absence of expression Sejanus is *suspensus* in another sense too, like the obscure and hesitant words (*suspensa verba*) of Tiberius early in book 1, as I discussed in the first section. Just as the words left hanging by the emperor require senatorial responses to fill in the gaps, so the expressionless and almost meaningless face of Sejanus here requires an interpretative supplement by the commentators and other readers of Tacitus.

But if Sejanus' face appears meaningless to Tacitus' reader, how can she judge Tiberius' interpretation of Sejanus to be false? If we return to a

---

[17] Martin and Woodman (1989) 227; *anceps* in the narrative, therefore, replicates its role in the story. [18] Martin and Woodman (1989) 228. [19] Furneaux (1884) 512.

consideration of Sejanus' posture, we see that he is said to place himself in the way of the falling rocks, an act interpreted as loyalty. But if we start by suspecting Sejanus (as Tacitus strongly suggests we should) then we could consider reading his posture differently. Sejanus' interposition of himself between the emperor and the falling rocks could then be read as another distraction of the imperial reader from the 'proper' object of reading. Tiberius finds himself face to face with Sejanus, who appears unproblematically loyal, instead of facing the doubtful danger. The supposedly straightforward object of reading, the *vultus*, distracts Tiberius from the ruinous deception which threatens to undermine him, symbolised by the collapsing mouth (*os*) of the cave. This danger represents in microcosm the dangers of Tiberius' Rome. In particular, the threat of being crushed under falling rocks could be read as an omen, warning Tiberius of the dangers of dissimulation through a premonition of his eventual smothering. Sejanus' act of protection in the cave represents a distraction from these unwelcome truths.

The reading episodes centred on Sejanus and Agrippina seem to exercise a dissection of the processes of deceit, but the ultimate strategy of Sejanus, who distracts Tiberius by diverting his attention to a seemingly straightforward object of reading, can also be seen to be a strategy of the Tacitean text, which points us towards the simple contrast of Sejanus and Agrippina and distracts us from the multiple deceptions of its own narrative. The dangers of dissimulation are heralded by the incident in the cave, and can be said to be dangers for the reader of the text as well as readers within the text. This is explicated by the climactic disaster of book 4, the collapse of the amphitheatre at Fidenae, which is the final episode to be examined in this section.

The collapse of the amphitheatre carries through the destruction which is only threatened by the collapse of the cave, and is therefore not 'doubtful' (*anceps*) in the sense of being a danger which could have gone either way. It is a doubtful danger, however, in that it can be interpreted in different ways, and indeed can be read as an episode about doubtful interpretations. This can be explicated if we first look at the immediate effect of the collapse.

> Those people were to be pitied whom life had not abandoned while part of their body had been torn off; they could / tried to recognise (*noscebant*) their spouses and children by sight (*visu*) during the day, by their screams and groans during the night. (4.62.3)

As Martin and Woodman point out, *noscebant* here can mean either 'kept on recognising' or 'tried to recognise'.[20] This has considerable implications for the meaning of the sentence; the maimed victims are tortured either by the constant recognition of their suffering family, or by their inability to recognise them. The inability of Tacitus' reader to recognise which of these meanings might be more pitiable only replicates the uncertainty at a narrative level. Later in the episode the maiming of the victims contributes to their unrecognisability.

> As the debris began to be moved aside, they rushed together, to embrace and kiss the dead; and often there was a battle (*certamen*), if the face was disfigured but the general outline and age were similar (*si confusior facies, sed par forma aut aetas*), so that it caused an error of recognition (*errorem adgnoscentibus*). (4.63.1)

The 'error of recognition (*error adgnoscentibus*)' can be seen as an oblique comment on the continuing ambiguity of *noscebant* in the preceding chapter. The disfigurement which causes misrecognition returns the effects of dissimulation (suppression of signs from the imperial face and subsequent collapse) onto the faces of his subjects. The confusion with relation to face or appearance (*facies*) then spreads to the city, where the distinction between past and present is blurred.

> Throughout those days the city, although sorrowful in appearance, was like the practices of the ancients, who after great battles would sustain the wounded with donations and care.
>
> *fuitque urbs per illos dies, quamquam maesta facie, veterum instituti<s> similis, qui magna post proelia saucios largitione et cura sustentabant.* (4.63.2)

The support (*sustentabant*) provided by the city, in place of the architectural support lacking in the amphitheatre,[21] gives an appearance of antiquity to the place.[22] This echoes Tacitus' introduction to the disaster: 'an

---

[20] Martin and Woodman (1989) 235.

[21] The extent to which the narrative mirrors the amphitheatre perhaps picks up on the occasional use of architectural metaphors to describe literary composition, the most relevant being Cic. *De Orat.* 2.63, discussed at length in Woodman (1988) 78–85. See also Cicero's account of trustworthy narrative in oratory: 'narrative is . . . as it were a seat and foundation for setting up belief (*fundamentum constituendae fidei*)' (Cic. *Part.* 31).

[22] Martin and Woodman (1989) 237 comment on the slight ellipse here, since the 'logical' similarity between past and present is in the actions of the citizens, not in the city itself.

unforeseen evil matched (*aequavit*) the massacre of mighty wars' (4.62.1). The collapse of the amphitheatre causes a comparison of the present with the past: the disaster is equal to (*aequavit*) a great battle, while Rome's response is similar (*similis*) to ancestral practice during war. But the very similarity of appearance between past and present suggests that our reading of the episode is comparable to the relatives' reading of the mangled bodies. The equality or similarity (*aequavit, par*) which suggests the comparison enables readers to make sense of what they read, but threatens also an error of recognition (*error adgnoscentibus*) and a contest of interpretations (*certamen*).

The sense of futility and perversion in the reading episodes examined so far is so pervasive that Tacitus' reader is not so much challenged as actively discouraged. Is misreading the end of all readings? How can a potential be transmitted to the future through the collapsing structure of this narrative? Tacitus asks these questions in his most famous digression on the uses of his history in book 4, which is juxtaposed with the trial of the historian Cremutius Cordus. Central to these episodes is the question of how the historian addresses himself to the future. What is implicit in this question is the extent to which the historian creates a future to which his work is addressed; the limits of the historian's control over meaning in the present are seen to be not transcended but replicated in the future. In book 6 Tacitus directly addresses the possibility of reading the future from the position of the present in a digression which is juxta-posed with his account of the successful predictions of the astrologer Thrasyllus. This pair of digressions with their associated exemplary episodes invites us to consider the issues of reading within the temporal framework of past, present and future.

First let us consider the structure of the two digressions. In both cases the argument is tripartite, but that tripartite structure does not explicate the argument so much as mislead the reader. So, for example, the digres-sion on reading the future sets out three different types of belief in fate, which is a prerequisite to the question of whether the future can be read. Each of these beliefs is applied to the question of why evil befalls good men. Therefore the first (Epicurean) doctrine, that everything happens by chance and is no concern of the gods, concludes, 'and so very fre-quently sad things happen to good men and joy to those who are worse'

(6.22.1). The second doctrine (Stoic), stating that the course of life, once chosen, proceeds according to natural laws, draws a distinction between the appearance of adversity and the true good, the firmness of character shown in dealing with fortune.

> It is not evil or good, as the common people think: many who seem to be afflicted with adversity are in fact happy, but very many, although surrounded by wealth, are the most wretched of men, if the former bear their heavy lot with constancy and the latter use their prosperity without thought. (6.22.2)

In this case it is the misinterpretation by the common people of the signs manifested by a man which leads to confusion and uncertainty about the entire course and determination of life. The final system of belief put forward by Tacitus is the 'popular' belief: 'but for most of humanity the belief cannot be banished that what is coming to each man is destined from his birth' (6.22.3). The tripartite structure here leads the reader, after reading the first two sections, to make certain suppositions (or 'predictions') about the third part of the argument. Hence the reader might expect the narrative to elaborate on this popular belief, which would explain that evil befalls good men because their fate is written in the stars. But the third part of the exposition swerves, and turns instead to the falsity of many supposed acts of foretelling: 'some things fall out differently from what is said because of the deceptions of those who speak of what they do not know (*ignara*)' (6.22.3). The belief of many in predestination is protected from unpredicted events by their belief in the ignorance of false prophets; this claim, rather than paralleling the arguments of the two preceding doctrines, inverts the latter (Stoicism), which accounts for apparent inconsistencies by ascribing misinterpretation to the people. But against this third instance Tacitus throws the weight of history: 'thus is worn away the credibility of an art (*fidem artis*) to which clear testimony (*clara documenta*) has been given by both antiquity and our own times (*et antiqua aetas et nostra*)' (6.22.3). The tripartite structure of the argument, therefore, does not mirror the relationships between the parts of the argument thus structured; the reader is faced with the question of whether to follow the argument or the structure.

Similarly, in the digression on history, Tacitus links the usefulness of historical narrative to three eternally recurring modes of government. He goes on to specify the type of knowledge necessary under each regime, knowledge which the historical narrative is presumed to supply.

Therefore when the plebs were strong or when the senators had power, as in previous times, the nature of the common people had to be understood (*noscenda vulgi natura*) and the means by which they could be moderately treated, and the men who had thoroughly learnt (*perdidicerant*) the character of the senate and the aristrocracy were believed to be skilled in their era (*callidi temporum*) and wise men. (4.33.2)

In other words, scrutiny and recognition of the inner nature of one's rulers (whether they be the people or the senate) is deemed wise. It would follow, then, that Tacitus' convoluted sentence might end with advice to those living under autocracy to scrutinise the nature of the emperor. It is clear that the Julio-Claudian regime is referred to here by the verbal echoes with the beginning of the first book,[23] but specific reference to scrutiny of the ruler is passed over.[24]

> It will be useful to investigate and hand down these things, since few men can wisely distinguish good from bad, useful from harmful, and more are taught by the events of others.
>
> *haec conquiri tradique in rem fuerit, quia pauci prudentia honesta ab deterioribus, utilia ab noxiis discernunt, plures aliorum eventis docentur.* (4.33.2)

Scrutiny and recognition of the past is offered (in the place of examining the present emperor) the result of which is the ability to discriminate between good and bad, rather than the specifically power-related results of the other types of knowledge under other systems of government: 'the means by which they could be moderately treated' (4.33.2).[25] Again, the

---

[23] 'Thus with the state turned around (*sic converso statu*)' (4.33.2), 'therefore with the state of the country overturned (*igitur verso civitatis statu*)' (1.4.1); 'nor with any health of affairs except if one man were to command (*neque alia rerum <salute> quam si unus imperitet*)' (4.33.2), 'no account can be agreed other than if it is given by one man (*non aliter ratio constet quam si uni reddatur*)' (1.6.3), 'there was no other remedy for the discordant nation than that it be ruled by one man (*non aliud discordantis patriae remedium fuisse quam <ut> ab uno regeretur*)' (1.9.4).

[24] Lana (1989), in his examination of *introspicere* as a term of historical enquiry, interprets this passage as a statement about degrees of understanding required under different types of government (*noscere* for democracy, *perdiscere* for oligarchy and *introspicere* for autocracy), which, while useful, does not take into account the elision of past and present time in the narrative (31). The swerve in the third leg of Tacitus' argument, also, passes him by.

[25] Syme (1958) 374 sees the shift in subject of scrutiny from the holder of power to the individuals living under his rule as authorial resistence to the principate: '[i]t was an historian's duty to insert a full measure of senatorial transactions, however unexhilarating or even repellent, if his *Annales* were not to degenerate into a dynastic chronicle and end as a sequence of imperial biographies'.

first two parts of the argument invite readers to predict the third, which however defies their predictions.

The structure within each digression, therefore, undermines the reader's faith in the formal properties of argumentation. Each argument concludes in a way which fails to satisfy the reader. The substance of the final argument, since it fails to connect with the structure within its own digression, could be seen to require further connections to render it conclusive. One way of reading these digressive arguments is to put them in significant relation to each other. In the digression on history, for example, the final argument is diverted from historical scrutiny of the imperial ruler to a consideration of how to distinguish good men from bad; this is precisely the distinction which informs the first part of the digression on fate. Similarly the last argument about reading the future suggests that history shores up the credibility of prophecy. In each digression the different questions of reading past and future are seen to be implicated to such an extent that any attempt to focus upon one quickly slides to the other. At first this may seem to point to the mutual interdependence of these types of reading: history validates prophecy; belief in a stable and predictable future gives history its meaning beyond present readership.

Juxtaposed with these digressions on reading are the episodes in which readers of past and future have their interpretative skills examined by the emperor. The first of these, the trial of Cremutius Cordus for treason, emphasises the extent to which history, a narrative of past events, is received as oblique political comment on present events. Cremutius is on trial because his history praises the tyrannicides Brutus and Cassius. We have already seen in the first section of this chapter how the treason trial operates not only as a displaced sign of Tiberius' cruelty but also as a site of wilful misreading, through the misplaced significance assigned to the actions of the accused and through the misleading use of the trials in Tacitus' narrative to suggest continual condemnation. Under such circumstances the reader expects hostile scrutiny to be turned upon Cremutius' history, but instead the narrative focuses on Cremutius himself, who interposes an interpretation of the trial. He begins his defence having already determined to end his life (*relinquendae vitae certus*) and has therefore foreclosed on the trial's outcome. His speech constitutes a history of the place of history in politics, concluding with a defiant claim for the future of his history, guaranteed by his own fate.

If condemnation falls upon me, there will be no lack of men to remember (*meminerint*) Cassius and Brutus – and me. (4.35.3)

Cremutius thereby imposes his own interpretation on the judgement of the court even before it has taken place. Tacitus' narrative promotes this claim by making a further comment about the preservation of Cremutius' history. Although the senatorial decree requires the burning of all copies, some are concealed and later published. Tacitus interprets this as an instance of the universal truth that no tyrant can suppress historical memory.

> Hence one is more inclined to ridicule the stupidity of men who believe that by their power in the present they can extinguish memory (*memoriam*) even for subsequent ages. (4.35.5)

These proud assertions by Cremutius and Tacitus of the immortality of historical memory are undercut by the preceding digression on the utility of history. We have already examined the central tripartite argument of that digression, but should now consider the surrounding statements about the meaning and relevance of the past in the present and future. The digression is generally agreed to be rather pessimistic; the opening chapter, in praise of close reading, is structured around Tacitus' claim that his subject matter is inferior when judged against the glorious deeds of antiquity. The paragraph is framed by statements which echo each other.

> I am not ignorant of the fact that much of what I have related and will relate seems (*videri*) perhaps minor and trivial (*levia*) . . . However it is not without its uses to scrutinise (*introspicere*) those things which seem trivial at first glance (*primo aspectu levia*), from which often the movement of great affairs arises. (4.32.1–2)

This claim is elaborated by the tripartite argument we have already examined, which concludes with a diversion of scrutiny from the nature of the ruler to the morals of his subjects. Tacitus then reverts to the disadvantages of his own particular historical period, in particular its monotony (*rerum similitudine*) and its capacity to be (mis)read as oblique comment upon the present reader.

> The descendants of many who suffered punishment or infamy in Tiberius' reign are still living. And even when the families themselves have died out, you find people who believe they are being accused

through another's misdeeds on account of a resemblance of character (*ob similitudinem morum*). Even glory and virtue have enemies, as alleging the opposite from too much proximity (*ut nimis ex propinquo diversa arguens*). (4.33.4)

Tacitus ends his digression with a statement which denies ultimate control of meaning to the historian; his history's meaning is determined by future readers regardless of his intentions. This works against Cremutius' attempted retention of control over his history by arguing that the accusers' interpretation is simply not appropriate. Tacitus' claim that even the praise of virtue will be assumed to have direct contemporary relevance forecloses on Cremutius' claim that praise of the tyrannicides has *only* to do with the past.[26] We have already seen how Cremutius' interpretation of the charge pre-empts the process of the trial; Tacitus' digression can be seen to pre-empt and to undermine Cremutius' claims, and his own. Tacitus' conclusion to the trial, where he claims that tyrannical suppression of literature only secures glory for the artist (*gloriam peperere*) is ironically undercut by his claim in the digression that glory, perpetuated in historical memory, is subject to hostile reinterpretation by future readers.

Tacitus begins his digression in praise of close reading; scrutiny (*introspicere*) will uncover the meaning of apparently trivial matters. By the end of the digression he appears to deplore the excess of close reading (*nimis ex propinquo*),[27] when readers refuse to accept the surface meaning of events and wilfully interpret his text as a commentary on their own lives. These readers have replaced the emperor Tiberius as arbitrary and hostile interpreter of signs. We saw in the first section how Tiberius scrutinised the senators' inner thoughts (*introspiciendas voluntates*) and twisted the meanings of their words. In his digression of book 4 Tacitus represents this reading practice as one turned upon his own writing. This could be seen to be a result of Tacitus' warning earlier in the digression that the subjects of an emperor should look to history to distinguish good acts from bad. In effect, he places his historical narrative between the reader's scrutiny and the face of the emperor. Tacitus' text becomes, like Sejanus in the collapsing cave, both the object and the agent of misreading. Its role in the future

---

[26] "'Are they not dead these past seventy years?'" (4.35.2).

[27] This is read as temporal proximity by Furneaux (1884) 483, Koestermann (1965) 117, Martin and Woodman (1989) 176, since Tacitus has just claimed that no one takes offence at ancient history. My examination of this passage is aimed at exploring what effect is achieved by reading this in terms of spatial proximity.

is, perhaps, to become the victim of the reading strategy it has exhorted its readers to adopt. But that possible future could also be seen to be evoked as a warning to Tacitus' readers of the implications of this strategy. A text which is read 'as (if) alleging the opposite from too close a proximity' exercises the reader's interpretative skills, as does the ambiguity of the phrase itself when it is placed under pressure. This ambiguity arises in part from the floating nature of the adverb *nimis*, so that we are presented with the options 'as if (excessively) alleging (too much of) the opposite from (too close a) proximity'. Most translations put *nimis* with *ex propinquo* on grounds of word order; proximity between the words invites us to read them together. It thereby suggests that too close a proximity overrules other determinants of interpretation, such as, for example, definition, so that opposites that are too close together (or perhaps too closely contrasting) are read as the same.

This leads us to the final exemplary reader of this chapter, the astrologer Thrasyllus. One of the marks of Tiberius' reign is his repeated attempts to control access to interpreters of the future.[28] This is presented not as a feature of the imperial regime but as a characteristic of Tiberius himself; the episode involving Thrasyllus is supposed to have taken place when Tiberius was a private citizen living on Rhodes. Reading the future is an interpretation of what is obscure and hidden, and is therefore a very appropriate concern of Tiberius, who goes about testing the skill of astrologers in a characteristically secretive way.

> Whenever he consulted anyone on such a matter, he used an elevated part of the house and the loyalty of one freedman. This man, ignorant of letters (*litterarum ignarus*), physically strong, would go along a pathless and precipitous route (*per avia ac derupta*) (for the house projected over the rocks) in front of the astrologer whose art Tiberius had decided to probe (*experiri*), and on the way back, if the suspicion of meaninglessness and deception had fallen on him, the freedman would toss him into the sea below, lest there be any sign of the secret (*ne index arcani existeret*). (6.21.1)

This inquiry into astrological skills mirrors the senatorial inquiry or treason trial with which Tiberius will subsequently test his subjects. But Tiberius' probing of the astrologer's art is also reminiscent of his attempted penetration (*experiretur*) of the mind of Agrippina by offering her an apple, as examined in the preceding section. In his reading of a

[28] Such as the expulsion of soothsayers from Italy (2.32.3).

reading Tiberius makes of the astrologer himself a sign (*index* as a variant on *indicium*) which must be erased. The secret for which the astrologer stands remains a secret in the text: is it the substance of consultation? The fact of the consultation? The route to the villa? The successful astrologer, Thrasyllus, escapes the fate of his predecessors by reading, not Tiberius' horoscope, but his own, thereby bearing out the implication of the narrative that the astrologer himself is a sign which bears interpretation.

> Having measured the positions and distances of the stars first he was at a loss, then he trembled, and the more he scrutinised (*introspiceret*) the more he trembled with wonder and fear, and finally he cried out that he was at a critical point, doubtful for him and almost final (*ambiguum sibi ac prope ultimum discrimen instare*). (6.21.2)

We could read Thrasyllus in contrast to Cremutius; what the astrologer reads is an 'ambiguous (*ambiguum*) critical point' which saves his life. What Cremutius is given to read at the start of the trial is that forbidden subject, the face of the emperor: 'Caesar with fierce expression (*truci vultu*) heard the defence, which Cremutius, determined (*certus*) to end his life, began thus' (4.34.1) Cremutius' certainty about his own death resonates with the openly hostile expression of Tiberius, suggesting that there is a relationship between the two, that Cremutius' determination arises from certainty about what he sees. If we read this in relation to Thrasyllus, we find a precarious path mapped out between the uncertain reading that saves and the certain reading that condemns.

The critical point (*discrimen*) on which Thrasyllus sees himself stand (*in-stare*) corresponds to the edge of the cliff, as well as to the astrologer's dependence upon the ambiguous Tiberius for safety. The path to the house, therefore, operates as a metaphor for reading, and demonstrates the dangers of *seeming* to misread.[29] Earlier in the narrative the readings of astrologers have been presented as simultaneously uncovering the truth and misreading it, when it is predicted that Tiberius will never return to Rome, a prediction which is read as foretelling his imminent

---

[29] It is worth pointing out that Thrasyllus' correct reading of the situation could just as well have ended his life, given Tiberius' reaction to attempted unmasking of his dissimulation at other points in the narrative. The ultimate judgement (*ultimum discrimen*) of the astrologer's reading depends upon the emperor. The fear of the senators, on the other hand, is of seeming to understand, as we have seen in the first section above (1.11.3).

death.[30] The 'incredible' survival of Tiberius for a further eleven years, as Tacitus remarks, uncovers the thin dividing line between true and false interpretations.

> Later the narrow dividing line between art and falsehood was uncovered, and how truth is covered by obscurity.

> *mox patuit breve confinium artis et falsi, veraque quam obscuris tegerentur.*
> (4.58.3)

The 'narrow dividing line' (*breve confinium*) which the astrologers tread here is analogous to the 'final critical point' (*ultimum discrimen*) on which Thrasyllus stands when he offers his reading to Tiberius for approval, the narrow path along the cliffs. The sentence itself, with its balancing of oppositions 'art' and 'falsehood', 'truth' and 'obscurity', offers the reader of the narrative a narrow dividing line in the pause between *falsi* and *veraque*, suggesting that a further opposition – or assimilation – can be constructed between art and obscurity; this could be called reading opposites from too close a proximity.

---

[30] Again, the narrative colludes with the misreading by reporting Tiberius' departure as *excessisse Roma* (4.58.2). For *excedere* as dying, particularly in the context of Augustus' death in book 1, see chapter two and O'Gorman (1995b).

Obliteration and the literate emperor

The erasures, blanks and disguises that are the stock-in-trade of the political censor are features too of the very writing upon which he exercises his
vigilance.

Malcolm Bowie, *Freud, Proust and Lacan: Theory as Fiction*

The obliteration of Claudius' style we must accept with what resignation
we can muster, nor perhaps is the loss serious.

Kenneth Wellesley, 'Can you trust Tacitus?'

The collapsing amphitheatre at Fidenae symbolises the threat that
Tiberian dissimulation poses to the future, a threat countered (and replicated) in the partial assimilation of past and present which makes history
possible. Despite Tacitus' claim that historical memory is resistant to
tyrannical repression, the struggle for control of the past in anticipation
of an imagined future remains dominated by imperial power of permit-
ted meanings. This struggle for control can be situated in Tacitus' text:
the conflict between the senatorial tradition of history and the imperial
politics it narrates. The dynastic history which we have already seen
emerging in the figures of Germanicus and Agrippina threatens to overwhelm this tradition. Tacitus emphasises the construction of dynastic
history in his narrative of the later Julio-Claudian emperors, Claudius
and Nero. In particular the figure of Claudius, the historian turned
emperor, can be read within the dynamic of a dynastic history which he
first seeks to construct and by which he is later circumscribed, when narrative control is taken over by his second imperial wife, the younger
Agrippina. This chapter will be concentrated on book 11 of the *Annals*,
before Agrippina has come to dominate the narrative.

The transmission of power to sons or adopted sons (Augustus to
Tiberius to Caligula) is disrupted by Claudius, the first Julio-Claudian
emperor who does not come from the Julian family. Dynastic history
works to naturalise hereditary power (we will see the empresses' role in

this history in the next chapter) while senatorial history protests by focusing on the casualties of such transmission, the discarded rivals, the violence and the lies. Claudius' assumption of power poses a challenge to history-writing from either dynastic or senatorial perspectives. Claudius himself constructs his legitimacy by continual imitation of Augustus. Tacitus records this and points it up ironically by citing Augustan precedent for the gradual manœuvring of Nero into the succession, which has fatal consequences for Claudius and his children. An additional irony to Claudius' construction of an Augustan ancestry for his principate lies in the repudiation by Tacitus of any narrative explanation for Augustus' own assumption of power, as we have seen in chapter one. The detached status of Augustan *imperium* (which counters Augustus' own inscription of it as a restoration of the republic) undermines Claudius' use of Augustan precedent to write himself into a historical continuity.

I have already mentioned in several contexts a key feature of irony which implicates the reader in the dynamics of Tacitean prose: the gaps not only in the structure of the narrative but also between ostensible and hidden meanings which seem to require supplementation by the reader, who then bears responsibility for the meaning of the text. Perceived disjunction is more glaring at the start of *Annals* 11 as we have it, which begins in mid-sentence after the loss of four and a half books. Hence it is apposite that what I want to examine in this chapter is the loss and suppression of history as an important theme of *Annals* 11, and Tacitus' self-representation as the historian who preserves traces of obliteration.

THE ABC OF HISTORY-WRITING

Claudius' self-definition as princeps is centred on his appropriation of the past through various symbolic acts which also serve to situate Claudian Rome in time and space. So, for example, his assumption of the office of censor points up his concern with the maintenance of Roman tradition, and his closing of the *lustrum* marks out a segment of Roman civic time.[1] Similarly Claudius' celebration of the secular games defines a symbolic era for Rome, and situates this reign at a significant juncture in time. Other defining acts include the extension of the pomerium, the boundary of the city, and the extension of senatorial rights to Gallia Comata. Both of these boundary extensions serve to redefine Rome and

---

[1] On the importance of the ceremonial of *lustratio* see Suolahti (1963) 45–6.

Roman-ness in spatial terms, and could be said to reflect the extension of the empire itself, earlier achieved by Claudius' campaigning in Britain.[2] All of these spatial and temporal redefinitions of Rome have implications for the (self-)representation of the emperor. They are all, moreover, acts which recall Claudius' imperial predecessors, particularly Augustus. Through this imitation Claudius lays claim to links with the 'true' Caesars, allowing him legitimacy as their successor. At the same time Claudius' redefinitions challenge their precedents; his celebration of the secular games 64 years after Augustus has celebrated them implicitly sets up a rival reckoning of the centuries which have passed since Rome's foundation. Similarly, his redrawing of boundaries (through both the pomerium and the franchise) overwrites the boundaries of his predecessors.

These overwritten traces can be resurrected by a reader who wishes ironically to disclose what disrupts continuity from emperor to emperor. So, for example, when Tacitus introduces the account of the secular games he positions them within three chronologies: senatorial, foundational and Augustan.

> During the same consulship the secular games were exhibited, in the eight hundredth year after the founding of Rome, the sixty-fourth year since Augustus had celebrated them. (11.11.1)

The familiar pairing of consular and foundation dates is augmented and at the same time disrupted by the third temporal marker, Augustus' celebration of the secular games in 17 BC.[3] While the temporal space between the foundation and Claudius' declaration of the *saeculum* is at odds with the idea of an era lasting one hundred and ten years, the reminder of temporal irregularity between not only the Augustan games and the Claudian but also the Augustan games and the foundation, serves to characterise tradition in terms of disharmony. Interestingly, this juxtaposition of chronologies can be said to invalidate the Augustan as much

---

[2] The conquest of Britain is adduced by Claudius himself, in the extant speech at Lyons, as a reason for extending senatorial rights to Gaul. See, for example, Claudius' speech: 'now if I were to narrate the wars from which our ancestors began, and up to which we have proceeded, I am afraid that I might seem excessively insolent in seeking to boast of the glory of the empire which I have extended across the Ocean' (col. 1, lines 37–9). The inscription of his triumphal arch is supplemented to read: ' …and he has been the first to bring under the [power of the Roman people] the [barbarian] nations [across the ocean]' (*CIL* 6.920). Tacitus' account of the campaign is lost.

[3] See Feeney (1998) 28–31 on the secular games.

as the Claudian creation of symbolic time. But by undermining the Augustan precedent for the secular games in this way Tacitus also undermines Claudius' claims to continuity with the Augustan principate.

Claudius' restoration of the Roman past in these symbolic redefinitions, therefore, brings to the fore the tension within the act of memorialising, which entails a partial or total erasure of the past. The history written by the emperor in order to legitimate his position effects the obliteration of histories which undermine his assumption of power.

Yet this feature of the Claudian narrative does not convey an overwhelming sense of the emperor's control over history and memory; on the contrary, Claudius is portrayed as unaware of events occurring around him and as passive before the manipulations of his wives and freedmen. In that respect he is more like the anti-historian, embodying none of the qualities of insight, scepticism and vigilance for the truth. Hence it could be argued that Claudius' shaky control over history is turned against him; his attempts to write himself into a narrative about continuity of power make him susceptible to a narrative about the inevitability of losing power. An example of this is in the use of the Augustan precedent. As we have already seen, Claudius stages symbolic acts in imitation of Augustus, thereby legitimating his position as Caesar. When his new wife, Agrippina, aims to introduce her son into the Claudian family (and eventually to oust the heir, Britannicus) the argument used to persuade Claudius to adopt his wife's son is Augustan precedent: Augustus' adoption of his stepsons Drusus and Tiberius while his own grandsons were still alive (12.25.1). The adoption of Nero is therefore predetermined by the historical narrative that Claudius has already constructed about himself, but that narrative then circumscribes Claudius, imposing on him the necessity for actions which will bring about his downfall.[4]

Hence Claudius could be read as a warning to the reader of history, the one who interprets narratives of the past as oblique commentary on the present. Although this process of reading may be seen to *confer* meaning on the past, its counterpart is the collapse of a distinction between present and past, which undermines precisely this conferral of meaning. This can be examined through one chapter in *Annals* 11, the digression on the history of the alphabet.

Claudius' invention of three new letters appears to be a rather quirky

---

[4] Hence the emergence of Nero *as* Nero (and not Domitius) is structured around the idea of repetition, as I will argue further in chapters six and seven.

minor event in his reign, demonstrating, if anything, the eccentric nature of the emperor's learning. Tacitus introduces this event at the end of the chapter which began with Claudius assuming the office of censor.

> And he added new forms of letters and made their use common (*ac novas litterarum formas addidit vulgavitque*), having learnt that the Greek alphabet was not all begun and completed at one time. (11.13.2)

What Claudius has learnt about the history of the alphabet could be seen to be the substance of most of the ensuing digression, so that it seems at first as if the narrative voice has been temporarily taken over by the emperor. This suggestion is upheld by the early part of the digression itself, where the first inventors of the alphabet assume narrative authority in telling the history of their invention.

> The Egyptians first gave shape to the meanings of the mind through the shapes of animals . . . and they cited themselves as inventors of letters. (11.14.1)

Tacitus' narrative validates that authority by handing over the rest of the sentence to Egyptian indirect speech, and by evoking material evidence for the Egyptian claim, the survival of their inscriptions. These two deferrals to Egyptian authority, allowing them to speak indirectly in the text and pointing to the extant inscriptions, might be seen to be paralleled in Tacitus' treatment of Claudius in this episode, both the partial surrender of the digression to his narrative voice and the reference, at the end of the digression, to surviving inscriptions which bear the Claudian letters. The predominant sense seems to be of Claudius' control over the signs he has invented. The meaning of this invention is linked with civilisation, laws and memory.[5] The existence of the letters attests to Claudius' status in his history as a civiliser; they also stand metonymically for the history itself.

Both the Egyptian and the Claudian letters appear in inscriptions which are seen in the narrator's present as indelible traces of past

---

[5] Various precedents for alphabetical invention are mentioned in the digression. Cadmus, Cecrops, Demaratus and Evander are linked to the rule of cities, and in three of those cases to the foundation of cities, while Linus is often accredited with the invention of music; Palamedes with that of draughts and astrology; Simonides with the system of mnemonics. Foundation, laws, monogamy, walls, together with the skills just mentioned, all have to do with marking out, shaping and representing the world in its different aspects, whether natural (astrology), social/political (walls, laws, monogamy), or symbolic (mnemonics).

memory. This is highlighted by the shift from imperfect/perfect tense to present in both parts of the account.

> The Egyptians first gave shape (*effingebant*) to the meanings of the mind through the shapes of animals – these most ancient monuments to human memory are discerned (*cernuntur*) engraved on rocks. (11.14.1)

> Following this example Claudius added (*adiecit*) three letters which ... can be seen even now (*adspiciuntur etiam nunc*) on public bronze on which statutes are publicised, fixed throughout the squares and the temples. (11.14.3)

The letters constitute a monument to human memory on the durable materials of stone and bronze. The shift of tenses conveys the role of the letters in forging a significant link from past to present. Yet the letters can also be seen to stand for the elusive nature of meaning as much as its stability and endurance over time. The first point to note is that the meaning of Claudian letters sketched above, as signifiers of civilisation, tradition and historical continuity, is other than the ostensible meaning of the letters in inscriptions: the specific content of the inscriptions is not given. Indeed, for Tacitus' reader the matter is complicated by the absence even of the appearance of the letters from the text. While we are told that Egyptian letters take the shape of animals, there is no explicit mention of the form or sound of the Claudian letters. The durable inscriptions in bronze are thus presented in the text stripped of their appearance and content, with only their 'real' meaning conveyed.

If we read the final clause of the digression in this way we highlight the absence of the letters from the text. If the presence and durability of the letters stands for continuity in history, the possibility of their absence invokes a disjunction between past and present. Indeed, the entire sentence at the end of the digression explicitly renders the letters simultaneously present and absent.

> Following this example Claudius added three letters which, in use so long as he was in power, afterwards obliterated, can be seen even now (*quae <in> usu imperante eo, post obliteratae, adspiciuntur etiam nunc*) on public bronze. (11.14.3)

The juxtaposition of *obliteratae, adspiciuntur* effects the successive erasure and survival of the letters, and creates a problematic moment of disjunction between past and present for the reader to negotiate. One way to bridge this gap is to distinguish between the physical presence of the letters on old inscriptions and their obliteration from contemporary memory. This makes of the letters a more emphatic sign of the past, and is picked up by the phrase 'in use so long as he was in power', but makes of it 'in use *only* so long as he was in power'. The letters are a sign of impermanence rather than perpetuity. But this attempted negotiation of the rupture between past and present is only partial. If the letters are obliterated from contemporary usage and yet are still seen on old inscriptions, what are they seen *as*? In other words, their meaninglessness in contemporary life undermines their capacity to attest to a meaning in/of the past; the rupture between past and present persists. In that sense the letters come to stand for the potential meaninglessness of the past, and their continued presence, fixed on bronze, can be read as the intransigence of past traces in the face of present attempts to comprehend them. From this perspective Claudius loses control over a history of continuous power. His own writings, the letters in use *only* during his reign, stand as a monument to his mortality.[6]

When the letters fall out of contemporary memory they lose their power to signify a memory of the past. (This has implications for the claim that Egyptian letters constitute monuments to human memory.) Tacitus' use of the term *obliteratae* to denote forgetting suggests that what are forgotten constitute something other than letters, that their status as letters is lost along with their place in memory. When the reader recognises them *as* letters, she thereby remembers their former status as letters; they become not *obliteratae* ('erased') but *litterae quae adspiciuntur* ('letters which are seen'). But how can the reader remember the letter once the link with the past is broken by loss of memory? By way of answer we are given the example of the Egyptian letters, whose ability to attest to a past still meaningful in the present is asserted at the beginning of the digression. Not only are these monuments to human memory still to be seen, but also, as I have remarked, the narrative of Egyptian history continues in the digression, thereby attesting to its survival over time. The mention of surviving inscriptions in this digression reminds us of the similar

---

[6] '"To have remembered" is from "memory" (*meminisse a memoria*) . . . "to remind" (*monere*) is from the same source, because he who reminds does so just as memory would; so monuments (*monimenta*), which are on graves and next to roads for this reason, so that they can remind travellers that those whom they memorialise were mortal just as the travellers are. From this source other things which are written and enacted for the purpose of memory are called monuments (*cetera quae scripta ac facta memoriae causa monimenta dicta*)' (Varro, *Ling. Lat.* 6.49).

Egyptian inscriptions which are read by Germanicus at Thebes in *Annals* 2. In this earlier episode Tacitus' reader is presented with a moment of reading which recognises the plenitude and continued significance of ancient history.

> Then he went to see the mighty traces (*magna vestigia*) of ancient Thebes. And there were Egyptian letters remaining on the piles of buildings (*manebant structis molibus litterae Aegyptiae*), detailing its earlier wealth; one of the elder priests, commanded to interpret (*interpretari*) his native speech, recounted (*referebat*) that here once had dwelt seven hundred thousand men of military age, and with that army king Rhamses had ruled Libya, Ethiopia, Medes and Persians, Bactria and Scythia and had taken control of the lands which the Syrians, the Armenians and the nearby Cappadocians inhabit, in an empire extended from the Bithynian sea on one side to the Lycian sea on the other. And the tributes imposed on the nations were read out (*legebantur*), the weight of silver and gold, the number of arms and horses and the temple gifts of ivory and incense, the amount of corn and supplies which each country owed, no less magnificent than what is now commanded by the force of the Parthians or the power of Rome (*haud minus magnifica quam nunc vi Parthorum aut potentia Romana iubentur*). (2.60.3)

Here the content of the inscription is detailed, as well as its significance in relation to contemporary empires. Despite the antiquity and partial survival of Thebes, these traces of the past are formed into a full and coherent narrative which is both meaningful and illuminating to the present. Although the eventual fall of Rhamses' empire constitutes a warning to the Roman reader of the same fate in store for Rome, nevertheless the very construction of such a relationship presupposes a cyclical narrative of successive empires. The past makes sense not only *in* the present, but *of* the present. The key figure in this creation of historical significance is the priest who interprets the letters. Without his presence the inscription would be meaningless to Germanicus and the episode would convey instead a severe rupture with the past. The dependence of historical continuity upon the priest is thus centred not only on his role as a reader of history (*legebantur*) and a historian (*referebat*) but also on his activity of interpreting, acting as a negotiator between two mutually incomprehensible sign systems.

The figure of the priest as interpreter also stands as a sign of historical tradition by evoking the memory of similar figures in earlier historical narratives, particularly the Egyptian narrative of Herodotus.[7] The priest translating the hieroglyphics becomes analogous to Tacitus, translating Greek historiography. The translation of Rhamses' inscription is so complete that the final comparison with Rome and Parthia acquires the status of part of the inscription itself. The comment develops syntactically out of the translated inscription and, since it is not clear whether it is made at the level of story or of narrative (does the priest or Germanicus make this comment, or Tacitus?), it transcends the immediate time of reading. Translation or interpretation seems to bridge the disjunction between past and present. Germanicus at Thebes becomes a reader of history despite his ignorance of Egyptian letters. The priest who makes these letters meaningful to him (visible *as* letters) can be read as a parallel to Tacitus, who in the same way 'translates' the Claudian letters into a history of his reign. The rupture between past and present, evoked by the juxtaposition of *obliteratae, adspiciuntur* is bridged by Tacitean interpretation, which holds up the meaning of the letters as something distinct and separate from their form and content. Indeed, Tacitus' translation is held up in place of the letters, thereby effecting their obliteration from the text.

As the meaning of the past oscillates between presence and absence, the historian produces a narrative which might be seen to negotiate the oscillating movement. But what Tacitus produces as a 'translation' is a narrative which commemorates the erasure of meaning as much as its perpetuation. The narrative itself is a history of the rupture between past and present, a rupture which problematises the very notion of history. This rupture works against Claudius' representation of himself within a line of continuous tradition. In the alphabetical digression traces of the past are obliterated when they fail to be apprehended by present memory. The obliteration of Claudius' letters is an effect of the end of his reign. Implicit in this process is the power of Claudius' successors to obliterate his memory by allowing his letters to fall from everyday use. The commemoration of the emperor by perpetuating his invention thereby lapses. Tacitus' digression suggests that the obliteration is a natural result of the passing of time, or perhaps the judgement of posterity on the practicality of the new letters. But the concern with oblitera-

---

[7] Her. 2.100–6. Strabo's account of Thebes is also evoked in Tacitus' narrative, particularly in the introductory 'mighty traces of ancient Thebes (*veterum Thebarum magna vestigia*)', which echoes Strabo's phrase 'traces of its magnitude (ἴχνη τοῦ μεγέθους αὐτῆς) still exist' (Strab. *Geog.* 17.1.46).

tion recurs in later episodes of *Annals* 11, with the emphasis on the active suppression of signs of the present, wiping them from the historical record.

DAMNATIO MEMORIAE AND MEMORY LOSS

Claudius' invention of letters occurs at the beginning of his censorship; his role as censor is, therefore, intrinsically bound up with his role as alphabetical author. As censor Claudius must adopt a sign system which will determine the position of each Roman within or without the senate, a determination of meaning which has overt influence over political power. The mark (*nota*) set against one's name by the censor can result in disqualification or degradation, loss of good name (*ignominia*).[8] Symbolically the mark of the censorial sign system erases and replaces the name (*nomen*) by which one has been recognised. The erasure of one sign by another is thus made more explicitly in the case of censorship than in the case of the alphabet, but it should be stressed that censorship is not the *opposite* of writing; it is the same process viewed from a different position. When Claudius embarks upon his censorship he is in the position of controller of signs, and it is for this reason first that his invention of the alphabet is placed in the censorial context in Tacitus' text. Yet this position of control, which we have already seen undermined in the alphabetical digression, is ironically juxtaposed with his lack of knowledge about the state of his marriage and the threat to his reign.

> But Claudius, unaware (*ignarus*) of the state of his marriage and taking up the duties of the censor ... (11.13.1)

What is particularly ironic is that Claudius appears to be unable to discern his wife's infidelity so long as he is censor: 'he closed the lustrum, and this was the end to his lack of knowledge (*finis inscitiae*) about his own household' (11.25.5). These paired juxtapositions of the office of censor with the adultery of the censor's wife point up the extent to which Claudius is distracted from a very real threat to his power by his actions in the public domain. As censor Claudius situates himself within a tradition where he arbitrates over Roman morality; in the history that he attempts to construct about his reign Messalina's actions evade that arbitration by their apparent unintelligibility to Claudius.

---

[8] See Suolahti (1963) 47–52, 357.

The extent to which Messalina's actions are rendered unreadable within certain types of history is emphasised by Tacitus' interjection in the narrative of her marriage to Silius.

> I am not unaware (*haud sum ignarus*) that this may seem the stuff of myth (*fabulosum*) . . . but I am passing on what was in no way put together for the sake of wonder (*miraculi causa*), rather what was heard and written by my elders (*senioribus*). (11.27)

Messalina's actions almost turn the sober historical text into a narrative of wonders (*miracula*) verging on the mythical (*fabulosum*). Tacitus' claim, moreover, that he is aware of this difficulty (*haud ignarus*) points up the contrast between his history and that of Claudius, who is unaware even of the existence of Messalina's adultery.[9] When his censorship comes to an end, it is not so much that Claudius becomes aware as that he is forced to notice what is going on.

> He closed the lustrum, and this was the end to his lack of knowledge (*finis inscitiae*) about his own household: not long afterwards he was driven (*adactus*) to recognise (*noscere*) and to punish his wife's crimes. (11.25.5)

The rest of book 11 is taken up with the account of how Claudius is driven to act against Messalina, and elaborates on the extent to which Claudius is driven or forced (*adactus*) to recognise his wife's crimes. His recognition is entirely orchestrated by the imperial freedmen, who determine what he should see and hear, and how he should respond. Central to their orchestration, therefore, is the silencing and visible suppression of Messalina.

> But the critical point turned (*discrimen verti*) on this, whether he would hear her defence, and that his ears would remain shut (*clausae aures*) even to her confession. (11.28.2)[10]

Claudius, therefore, is placed in an exceptionally passive role in this part of the narrative, while Messalina and Narcissus, the leader of the freedmen, struggle to control what the emperor sees and hears. In particular

---

[9] For Claudius as *ignarus* see 11.2.2 and 11.13.1. His *inscitia* is mentioned at 11.25.5. See also the report which breaks up Messalina's party: 'that everything was known (*gnara*) to Claudius' (11.32.1). On the Tacitean use of *gnarus* and *ignarus* in the passive sense, see Goodyear (1972) 132.

[10] 'All to make sure that Claudius, just once in his life, would live up to his name': Henderson (1989) 170.

focus is directed on, or distracted from, the body of Messalina as a significant text. Messalina's attempts to display herself to her husband ('she resolved to go to meet and be seen (*aspici*) by her husband' (11.32.2)) can be read as an effort to reinstate her history of her role as his wife and the mother of his children. The display of Messalina evokes a parallel with the elder Agrippina, who, as we have seen in chapter three, becomes a site upon which both retrospective and anticipatory narratives converge. Messalina attempts to evoke the same sense of her body as a locus of the future when she appears before the emperor and declares herself as the mother of his children. Narcissus directs attention away from this version of history by interposing his narrative of her adulterous crimes.

> And now Messalina was in sight and was shouting that Caesar should hear the mother of Octavia and Britannicus, while her accuser drowned her out, recounting the story of Silius and the wedding ceremony; at the same time he passed on the documents signifying her lusts, by which he intended to avert the gaze of Caesar.

> *et iam erat in adspectu Messalina clamitabatque audiret Octaviae et Britannici matrem, cum obstrepere accusator, Silium et nuptias referens; simul codicillos libidinum indices tradidit, quis visus Caesaris averteret.* (11.34.2)

Messalina's self-display here fails to elicit the kind of response which the onlookers made when viewing Agrippina. Instead Narcissus' version of the past, presented as spoken and written narratives, drowns out and marginalises Messalina's claims.[11] His suppression of Messalina from and as history is compounded when she and her memory are destroyed.

As I remarked earlier, Claudius is extraordinarily passive in the midst of this power struggle. His few comments on the situation are first characterised as 'diverse' (*diversas voces*), alternating between an acknowledgement of his wife's adultery and a return to the memory of his marriage.

> Sometimes he was inveighing against the crimes of his wife, at another time returning to the memory of his spouse and the infancy of his children (*memoriam coniugii et infantiam liberorum revolveretur*). (11.34.1)

Hence in Claudius' speech at this point he gives voice to both narratives, turning back (*revolveretur*) to Messalina's history from Narcissus' and

---

[11] The extent to which this constitutes a battle of rival histories comes out in Narcissus' fear that Messalina's narrative will prevail as night approaches, when the domestic scene will evoke the memory of the past in Claudius: 'the approaching night and the memory of the wife's bedroom (*cubiculi memoria*) was a source of fear' (11.37.2).

failing to come down unequivocally on either side. This remains the case for the duration of the affair; Claudius speaks a few words in the praetorian camp after bursting out in threats at Silius' house. But his final word on the matter is his designation of Messalina as 'the poor woman (*miserae*)' as he sets her trial for the next day. Tacitus interjects in the middle of Claudius' speech here to highlight precisely this term.

> He ordered them to go and announce to the poor woman (for they say he used this very word) that she should come to plead her case on the next day. (11.37.2)

Tacitus' interjection makes this one word simultaneously more immediate and more distant; it is the very word used by Claudius, so that he seems to speak directly in the text; at the same time it is obscured by the voices of Tacitus' sources, asserting that Claudius used this very word. This problematic emphasis highlights the extent to which this word signals to Narcissus the return to dominance of Messalina's narrative, and therefore constitutes the critical point upon which his efforts turn. From Claudius' threats at Silius' house to the word *miserae* here, the pattern of diverse speech with which Claudius began can be traced. After Narcissus' destruction of Messalina Claudius falls silent on the subject; he does not even enquire into how she met her death. This final passivity on Claudius' part colludes in the erasure of Messalina's history from imperial memory.

The sight of a person evokes memory; Narcissus' obliteration of Messalina wipes out her memory in the mind of her husband. His mental resources have been entirely externalised, like his invented letters, which are obliterated in the minds of people, but remain fixed to inscriptions, attesting to their own erasure. But Messalina when alive did not merely stand for herself. Her claim to be seen by her husband is in the role of mother of his children: 'she was shouting that Caesar should hear the mother of Octavia and Britannicus' (11.34.2). The memory of the conjugal bedroom, feared by the freedmen, is inextricably associated with the consequences of their union, the propagation of the imperial family. This association is made explicit in Claudius' words at 11.34.1, 'returning to the memory of his spouse *and* the infancy of his children'.[12] At the same time as the sight of Messalina can evoke memory of her children,

---

[12] Furneaux (1884) 48 points out how semantically *infantiam* is dependent upon *memoriam* for sense.

once she is dead the sight of her children may still evoke the memory of their mother.[13] We have already seen how Germanicus' son Nero appears as an *imago* of his father, an appearance in which memory plays a significant part: 'creating joyful emotions in his listeners, who with the memory of Germanicus still fresh thought that they saw (*aspici*) and heard him again' (4.15.3). Memory not only 'resurrects' the dead Germanicus,[14] but evokes emotion (*adfectiones*) in the onlookers. This is precisely what Claudius' own children fail to do at the end of book 11.

> Indeed in the following days he gave no signs of hatred or joy, anger or sadness, not of any human emotion (*humani adfectus*), not when he saw (*adspiceret*) the rejoicing accusers, not when he saw his grieving children. (11.38.3)[15]

In this oblivious gaze Claudius' own children are deprived of the power to evoke the memory of their other parent, and are thereby deprived of their legitimacy in the context of the family *imago*. The most potent signs for Messalina, herself and her children, are removed and unrecognised. Claudius' state of oblivion now prompts the senate to wipe the city as a whole clear of the signs of Messalina.

> His oblivion was helped by the decree that her name and her statues should be removed from public and private places.
>
> *iuvit oblivionem eius censendo nomen et effigies privatis ac publicis locis demovendas.* (11.38.3)

The senate's decree (*censendo*) recalls the censorship which, as we have seen, distracted Claudius for so long from awareness of his wife's activities. The removal of her name and statues is the equivalent of the censorial *ignominia*, loss of (good) name, but also of *damnatio memoriae*, a condemnation, but also a loss (*damnum*) of memory. The removal of signs of Messalina is thrown into relief by the assignation of honours to her vanquisher, Narcissus: 'quaestor's insignia (*insignia*) were decreed to Narcissus' (11.38.4). These insignia mean little to the dominant freedman in the house of Caesar, but the juxtaposition of insignia for Narcissus and

---

[13] This ties in with the portrayal of the elder Agrippina, examined in chapter three. Agrippina too forces herself before the imperial gaze with a strong statement of how she is to be seen: 'she was the true image, descended from the heavenly blood' (4.52.2).

[14] See Martin and Woodman (1989) 140.

[15] Note the parallels with the senate watching Nero in book 4 (*adfectiones* with *adfectus*, *aspici* with *adspiceret*).

the abolition of signs of Messalina in the senatorial decrees and in the narrative highlights the nature of the struggle between the two. It also resonates with Claudius' oblivion, characterised as the absence of signs. Narcissus, with his insignia, wins the contest over historical memory.

The most vocal protest against the erasure of Messalina's history is the actor Mnester, one of her adulterers facing execution. Mnester can be seen to symbolise a debased version of Mnemosyne, a figure who stands for memory.[16]

> Mnester alone caused delay, having torn his clothes and shouting that Caesar should see the marks of the lash and remember his own speeches, in which he had put him under the dominion of Messalina's commands.
>
> *solus Mnester cunctationem attulit, dilaniata veste clamitans, adspiceret verberum notas, reminisceretur vocis, qua se obnoxium iussis Messalinae dedisset.* (11.36.1)

Mnester's reliance on sight and sound, by shouting (*clamitans*) and inviting examination of his body (*adspiceret verberum notas*), echoes Messalina's actions at 11.34.2: 'Messalina was in sight (*in adspectu*) and was shouting (*clamitabat*)'.[17] His evocation of memory is made explicit by his request that Caesar should remember (*reminisceretur*). Mnester's attempt to reinstate a version of the past which will enable him to survive in the present is overruled by Narcissus, whose response to his objections is simply *nihil referre*, 'it makes no difference'. The obliteration of Mnester, Narcissus maintains, is not a serious loss. The use of *nihil referre* in indirect speech also allows us to read *referre* not as the impersonal verb 'it matters' or 'it makes a difference' but as the verb 'to record' or 'to relate', used of narrative and of history. When Mnester's version of the past is dismissed and

---

[16] The Greek μνηστήρ can be translated as the Latin *memor*, 'remembering' or 'in memory of'. The dual meaning of its root μνάομαι, 'to remember' and 'to seduce' is interesting in this context, where Messalina's ultimate power lies in memory and desire.

[17] Display of the body and its marks in order to excite pity occurs during the mutinies of *Ann.* 1: 'some displayed reproachfully (*exprobrantes*) the marks of the lash (*verberum notas*), others their grey hair, most their worn clothes and naked bodies' (1.18.1); 'they all bared their bodies and displayed reproachfully (*exprobrant*) the scars from wounds, the marks of the lash (*verberum notas*)' (1.35.1). Marks of a lash are used metaphorically to denote mental scars at 6.6.2: 'if the minds of tyrants were disclosed, gashes and blows could be seen (*aspici*), since just as the body is torn by lashes (*ut corpora verberibus*), so the mind by cruelty, lust and evil thoughts' (6.6.2). On culture of displaying scars, see Leigh (1997) 221–33.

he is destroyed, it makes nothing of his historical narrative: 'he recounts nothing', *nihil referre*. Tacitus' inclusion of the Mnester episode seems to be making a particular point about the suppression of memory inherent in Narcissus' promotion of his own narrative.

Despite his attempts to obliterate the emperor's wife, signs of Messalina remain. The decree of the senate which consigns her to oblivion is by its very process drawn into the position of memorialising her. The children by their existence stand in her memory, although Claudius himself does not recognise it.[18] These 'empty' signs which are still to be seen, standing for what is both absent and forgotten,[19] are made visible at the level of the narrative; Tacitus shows us both the sign and its non-meaning, and in so doing reveals its meaning. So the memory of Messalina is preserved in the narrative, as is the memory of her obliteration.

In the account of the struggle between Narcissus and Messalina over control of imperial memory the reader is less often implicated in syntactical ambiguities than at other points in the *Annals*. Rather than a play of hidden and undefinable meanings she is presented with an open contest; the reader's committed interaction with the challenge of the text is not required here as it is elsewhere. Hence Tacitus' reader is rendered as passive as the emperor Claudius in the face of the two competing narratives. When Claudius asks no further questions about Messalina, and thereby colludes in her obliteration, he is implicitly contrasted with the sceptical historian who recovers the lost traces of suppressed meaning. But in the course of *Annals* 11 Tacitus has made his reader more like Claudius than like himself, and has thereby demonstrated to us how easy it is to occupy such a position of assent to an oppressive history.

---

[18] Agrippina the younger later removes from command the praetorians Lusius Geta and Rufrius Crispinus 'who, she believed, remembered (*memores*) Messalina *and* were bound to her children' (12.42.1).

[19] Again the parallel with Claudius' letters is clear. Note especially the recurrence of *adspicere* in these cases: 'the letters even now are to be seen (*adspiciuntur*)' (11.14.3); 'when he saw (*adspiceret*) his grieving children' (11.38.3). See also 4.15.3, 11.32.2, 11.34.2 and 11.36.1.

The empress's plot

Women have their uses for historians.

Ronald Syme, *The Augustan Aristocracy*

Might not one of the goals of what we so ambiguously call 'women's studies' be to call into question the oppressive effects of an epistemology based on the principle of a clear and nonambiguous distinction of subject and object of knowledge?

Jane Gallop, *Reading Lacan*

We have already seen, in chapters three and five, how certain imperial women display themselves or are displayed as sites of recollection and anticipation, as monuments or embodied texts of dynastic history. In this chapter I will examine the woman's voice as a source of historical narrative, in particular the voices of the 'successful' empresses, Livia Augusta the mother of Tiberius, and the younger Agrippina, mother of Nero. As women who marry emperors and manœuvre their sons into the succession, these empresses' plots can be read as strong narratives which both subvert and replace the prevailing trends of imperial history. The empress redirects the emplotment of her husband's reign, constructing a new teleology which points inevitably to her own son. The empress's 'plot', then, involves the manipulation and shaping of events, with the aim of presenting her son as the logical conclusion to her husband's reign. Consequently these female narratives have an especially charged relationship with Tacitus' own history, which blends with or diverges from their version of events. It is possible for a reader of the *Annals* to see these narratives as sources available for the historian's 'use' (compare Syme's ironic statement in the epigraph to this chapter), but it is also possible to adopt a reading strategy which privileges the female voice in Tacitus' narrative. This might be seen first from a brief return to Agrippina the elder.

The archetypal iconic woman at the start of the *Annals*, Agrippina the elder might be seen as silent and passive before the onlookers who subject her to historical interpretation. Yet Agrippina comes across in the narrative as an active and vocal character. She attempts to resist being sent from her husband's camp in book 1, protesting that 'she was descended from the god Augustus and was not unworthy in the face of danger' (1.40.3). This is echoed by her notorious reminder to Tiberius of her ancestry when she complains about the persecution of her friends.

> The divine spirit (of Augustus) was not present in the mute statues: she was the true image, descended from the heavenly blood. (4.52.2)

The contrast which Agrippina makes between herself and the mute statues could be read as a reference to her earlier appearances as a visual reminder of the past. Agrippina as the iconic woman replaces the statues, but reminds the onlooker that she is not by nature silent or to be silenced. This exchange between Agrippina and Tiberius is immediately followed in the next chapter of book 4 by an account of Agrippina requesting permission to remarry. Tacitus ends the account by citing his source for this event.

> I found this, which is not passed on by the writers of annals, in the diaries of Agrippina's daughter, who as the mother of the emperor Nero memorialised for posterity her life and the destruction of her relatives.

> *id ego, a scriptoribus annalium non traditum, repperi in commentariis Agrippinae filiae, quae Neronis principis mater vitam suam et casus suorum posteris memoravit.* (4.53.2)

The female source here records an event which has been omitted from annalistic history, thereby preserving the memory of individuals suppressed by the ruling power. In many ways this bears comparison with Tiberius' own commemoration of erasure, which we have traced through book 11, but what is also interesting here is the juxtaposition of the younger Agrippina's narrative voice with her mother's vociferous protests against the regime's persecution of her friends. Both women raise the voice of dissent against the emperor. What is also interesting is the question of who gives voice to whom. Agrippina the elder speaks in indirect speech, which could be said to subordinate her voice to that of the narrator. But when Tacitus cites the younger Agrippina as a source it becomes arguable that it is *she* who perpetuates her mother's voice in the historical record.

OLD WIVES' TALES

A comparable perpetuation of dissident history, one which pervades
Tacitean narrative, is the history of the so-called Stoic opposition to the
emperors. The sources for this history, according to the younger Pliny,
were preserved by the womenfolk of that circle: Arria the elder, Arria
the younger, and Fannia. These women kept alive the tradition of their
husbands' opposition to the emperors; Fannia, for example, supplied
commentarii to the writer Herennius Senecio for his life of Helvidius
Priscus the elder. The women also provided the family underpinning to
the circle, which has an almost matrilinear aspect. The elder Arria, her
daughter the younger Arria, and her granddaughter Fannia together
provide the direct line around which cluster their senatorial husbands:
respectively Caecina Paetus, Thrasea Paetus and the elder Helvidius
Priscus. The women themselves won honour and fame for their courage
and fidelity to their husbands in adversity. The elder Arria famously
stabbed herself and offered the action as an example to her husband,
with the words 'it doesn't hurt, Paetus (*Paete non dolet*)'.[1] Arria the
younger was dissuaded by her husband, before his own suicide, from following her mother's example, and was subsequently exiled twice.[2]
Fannia accompanied her husband twice into exile and after his death
was banished again in connection with the above-mentioned writings
of Herennius Senecio.[3] More than providing family structure to the
group of senators, their wives actively inspire them, acting as examples
both for their spouses and their children. Exchanges between both
Arrias and their husbands show their awareness of a tradition of
women's behaviour in the family,[4] while Fannia in her old age kept that
tradition alive. Most interesting in this context is the younger Pliny's
account of Fannia's tales about her grandmother. In this letter Pliny
records the deeds of Arria the elder which are less well-known than her
famous words to her husband, but which demonstrate a consistency in
her usual behaviour with the action which brought her fame. He intro-

---

[1] Pliny, *Ep.* 3.16 (examined below); Dio 60.16.5–6.
[2] Thrasea's words to his wife: *Arriamque temptantem mariti suprema et exemplum Arriae
matris sequi monet retinere vitam filiaeque communi subsidium unicum non adimere* (*Ann.*
16.34.2). Exile: Pliny, *Ep.* 3.11; 7.19.
[3] Pliny, *Ep.* 7.19 (examined below); Tacitus mentions Senecio's death in *Agr.* 45.1, and his
work in *Agr.* 2.1. Cf. Ogilvie and Richmond (1967) 133, and Syme (1958) 177 for the
possibility that Tacitus may have used this work as a source for the lost portion of the
Histories.   [4] Pliny, *Ep.* 3.16.

duces the account with a promise of the greatness and wonder of these less well-known actions.

> She recalled many things about her grandmother, not lesser matters (*non minora*), but more obscure; which I think will be as wonderful (*mirabilia*) for you reading them as they were for me listening. (*Ep.* 3.16.2)

The wonder of these tales makes them worthy to be recorded by Pliny for his reader, while he also emphasises the oral nature of the stories which he records. Pliny concludes the letter by reiterating his point about the greatness and yet the obscurity of some deeds.

> Do these not seem to you greater (*maiora*) than that 'it doesn't hurt, Paetus', to which she arrived by means of these other acts? While great fame (*ingens fama*) broadcasts this act, these others are unknown. Hence it is concluded, as I said at the beginning, that some things are more famous, others are greater. (*Ep.* 3.16.13)[5]

Arria's other demonstrations of courage and fidelity, according to Pliny, are bereft of the great fame through which her words to her husband are known. But Pliny's inscription of these other acts brings them out of their obscurity, an obscurity which seems to be connected with their preservation solely in oral tradition.[6]

In a much later letter, when Fannia falls dangerously ill, Pliny recalls her exile in connection with Senecio's memoir on her late husband, which suggests in connection with her tales to Pliny that Fannia was both preserving and promulgating the fame (*fama*) of her circle to various literary Romans. Pliny mentions her *commentarii* in his account of the exchange between Fannia and her accuser: 'had she given the notebooks (*commentarii*) to someone to write them up: "I did"' (*Ep.* 7.19). There is no indication whether these are the *commentarii* of

---

[5] In letter 6.24 Pliny recounts another brave suicide committed by an unknown woman, and contrasts the obscurity of her act with the fame of Arria's. Note also that Tacitus, when citing Agrippina, claims that the events found in her *commentarii* are absent from the historiographical tradition.

[6] Pliny elsewhere contrasts Fannia as an *exemplum* with the 'written women' of exemplary literature: 'she will exist, to be sure, whom we can afterwards display to our wives; she will exist, whom men also can take as an example of courage, a woman at whom we wonder, seeing and hearing her, just as we wonder at others who are read' (*Ep.* 7.19). This also seems to refer to Fannia's preservation in oral history after her death, but Pliny overlooks the role of his own writing in the preservation of the Fannia legend.

Helvidius Priscus the elder or of Fannia herself, although as we have seen from Tacitus' citation of Agrippina there is at least one precedent for a woman writing a work referred to as *commentarii*. Whoever is the original author of them, however, Fannia is indubitably the preserver both of these written materials and of Senecio's memoir, as Pliny goes on to state.

> She preserved those same books, although they were effaced (*quamquam abolitos*) by senatorial decree from necessity and the fear of the times, and she kept them and brought into exile with her the cause of her exile (*tulit in exsilium exsilii causam*). (*Ep.* 7.19)[7]

The text which causes Fannia's exile thereby strengthens her position as a true daughter and granddaughter to the Arrias; she simultaneously memorialises her husband, by preserving the text, and herself, by admitting to implication in its production and paying the glorious price; in this context Fannia's one-word admission to the prosecutor, quoted above, writes her into the history of opposition. Moreover, we can see from the foregoing citations of *my* sources for the story of Fannia and the two Arrias that Fannia herself has perpetuated this history through Pliny, who dominates the relevant footnotes.

One crucial difference between Fannia and Agrippina the younger as writers of *commentarii* lies in the fact that Agrippina is not just a source for Tacitus' writing but one object of his sceptical inquiry. Her diaries may memorialise the victims of Tiberian oppression,[8] but she herself perpetuates imperial oppression through the reigns of her husband and son. The writings of the empress cannot merely be classed as a dissident voice, but risk being merged into the *fama* of the ruling ideology. But the relationship between Tacitus and the younger Agrippina is slightly more complex, in that it becomes entangled in the relationship between the younger Agrippina and Livia Augusta. It is clear that Tacitus' portrayal of Agrippina recalls that of her great-grandmother. This is aided both by Claudius' imitation of Augustus, played up in the text (as examined at the

---

[7] Similarly the daughter of Cremutius Cordus is instrumental in the preservation of her father's works, destroyed under Tiberius (Dio 57.24.4). Tacitus himself uses the preservation of Cordus' work to symbolise the indestructibility of historical *memoria* (*Ann.* 4.35.5).

[8] An alternative supposition is made by Wood (1988) 424 who suggests that the commentaries were written during Agrippina's exile, which would make them more analogous to Fannia's politically dissident writings. Even if this were the case, Agrippina's subsequent rise to power would dramatically change the reception of her work.

beginning of the last chapter), and by Tacitus' use of Tiberius' pre-adoptive name, Nero, at the crucial moment of his accession.[9] Other juxtapositions strengthen the parallel; the marriage of Agrippina (to Domitius Ahenobarbus) at the end of book 4 is immediately followed by the death of Livia at the opening of book 5. Most explicitly, Agrippina is said to rival Livia at Claudius' funeral at the end of book 12.

> Divine honours were decreed to Claudius and the rite of the funeral was celebrated exactly as for the god Augustus, with Agrippina emulating the magnificence of her great-grandmother Livia. (12.69.3)

The implications of this parallel for the structure of the *Annals* is evident; Tiberius Caesar Augustus and Nero Claudius Caesar form the beginning and the end of the narrative; naming both in one word tightens the organisation of the work, making almost a ring-composition out of the progression of emperors and text. If we pay particular attention to the parallels between Tiberius and Nero, therefore, we tend to see Agrippina as a function of that parallel, made use of by Tacitus to further his narrative ends. But Agrippina's similarity to Livia can also be examined independently of the Tiberius–Nero alignment. The dubious circumstances of Claudius' death are often considered to be the shaping force upon the allegations about the demise of Augustus.[10] Agrippina the younger provides the model for Tacitus to flesh out Livia Augusta; if all 'good' emperors are the same, so too are all bad empresses. Furthermore, Goodyear has commented that Agrippina's *commentarii* could be conjectured as the source for Livia's alleged hostility towards Germanicus and the elder Agrippina,[11] a hostility which is given prominence in Tacitus' text. Agrippina, as both subject and object of writing, seems implicated in the creation of her predecessor. If Goodyear's conjecture has any force, there would be considerable irony in Tacitus adopting Agrippina's

---

[9] Cf. Charlesworth (1923) and Martin (1955). Tiberius Caesar before his adoption by Augustus was Tiberius Claudius Nero. Tacitus' pointed use in the opening chapters of his work of one of Tiberius' pre-adoptive names might be compared with Britannicus' salutation of Nero as 'Domitius' at 12.41.3, interpreted as 'the beginning of discord' by Agrippina. Cf. Goodyear (1972) 250: 'T. regards the adoption as a political façade, and will neither recognize it as a reality himself nor present others as so recognizing it, except in circumstances when the façade had to be preserved.'

[10] As argued by Charlesworth (1923).

[11] Goodyear (1981) 327: 'a very biased source . . . conceivably the younger Agrippina's memoirs'.

damning portrait of Livia *and* drawing strong parallels between the two women.[12]

Tacitus' use of Agrippina, then, both confirms and wilfully redirects her emplotment of events. I used the term 'plot' in the title of this chapter to convey the combination of narrative and dynastic manœuvring in the actions of the two empresses. This can perhaps best be seen from a close reading of Tacitus' account of the emergence of Tiberius as Augustus' heir.

> As Agrippa departed from life, and Lucius Caesar going out to the Spanish armies and Gaius returning from Armenia weak with a wound were removed by destined premature death or by the treachery of their stepmother Livia, and with Drusus long dead, only Nero was left of the stepsons, and everything inclined to him.

> *ut Agrippa vita concessit, L. Caesarem euntem ad Hispanienses exercitus, Gaium remeantem Armenia et vulnere invalidum mors fato propera vel novercae Liviae dolus abstulit Drusoque pridem exstincto Nero solus e privignis erat, illuc cuncta vergere.* (1.3.3)

As each potential heir comes to an end, the direction of Augustus' own end shifts, until Tiberius emerges as the only possible end (*Nero solus*) towards which all parts of the narrative, and of the sentence, tend (*illuc cuncta vergere*).[13] The role of his mother is here only hinted at as a possibility in the removal of Augustus' grandchildren.[14] The hint becomes open allegation in the second part of the sentence, and this shift parallels the contrast between the previous plotting of Livia and the subsequent open consolidation of Tiberius' position by Augustus.

> As son, as colleague in empire, as partner in tribunician power, he was taken up and displayed through all the armies, not as previously by the obscure arts of his mother, but by open encouragement.

---

[12] Subsequent readers, who have figured Tacitus as another Tiberius, could be seen to make the same moves as Tacitus here makes with Agrippina, aligning the historian with her/his unsympathetic creation.

[13] I have examined this passage in detail from the point of view of narrative beginnings and of the contrast between Tiberius here and Augustus at 1.2.1 in O'Gorman (1995b).

[14] As remarked by Goodyear (1972) 111: '(a) typically insidious use of alternative explanations ... T. does not decide between them, but often, by giving the more sinister explanation the later or more emphatic position or by elaborating it more fully or by the use of emotive language, succeeds in conveying the impression that this alternative is the more probable.' See also Develin (1983).

filius, collega imperii, consors tribuniciae potestatis adsumitur omnesque per exercitus ostentatur, non obscuris, ut antea, matris artibus, sed palam hortatu. (1.3.3)

The publicising of Tiberius as heir is not only subsequent to but also a consequence of his mother's plots, which are termed arts: her treachery and wickedness as well as her narrative arts (which are of Tiberian or perhaps Tacitean obscurity). Tacitus is required to accept Livia's and Agrippina's plots to the extent that he must record the emergence of each emperor. But the Tacitean narrative subverts the smooth running of the official story by its emphasis on the casualties of that story: the discarded rival heirs (and, later, spouses) whose presence disrupts the continuity emplotted by the empress from emperor-husband to emperor-son.

The complex textual and narrative relationships between Livia, Tacitus and the younger Agrippina are best examined in the crucial transition of power from Augustus to Tiberius at *Annals* 1.5.

> While the people discussed these and such matters, Augustus' health became worse, and some suspected wickedness on his wife's part. For a rumour had gone around that a few months previously Augustus, with only chosen people in the know and with one companion, Fabius Maximus, had sailed to Planasia to visit Agrippa Postumus; that there were many tears and the signs of affection and thus the hope that the young man would be returned to his grandfather's household: that Maximus made this known to his wife Marcia, and she to Livia. That this was known to Caesar; that when Maximus died not long after, doubtful whether by suicide, the laments of Marcia were heard at his funeral inveighing against herself, that she was the cause of her husband's death. However the matter stood, Tiberius having just entered Illyricum was summoned by urgent letters from his mother. And it is not sufficiently known, whether at the town of Nola he found Augustus still breathing or dead. For Livia had closed off the house and the roads with strict guards, and in the meantime was publishing optimistic announcements, until, having looked ahead to what the times required, the same statement reported that at the same time Augustus had departed and Nero was in charge of affairs (*simul excessisse Augustum et rerum potiri Neronem fama eadem tulit*). (1.5)

This passage is deeply layered with attributed and unattributed narratives: public suspicion of Livia; a rumour which takes up half the chapter; a woman heard lamenting at her husband's funeral; letters from Livia to her son; public announcements; and the final statement, the *fama*.

Explanation is here avoided in favour of narrative juxtaposition; the story of Augustus' reconciliation with his grandson is set beside the suspicion about Livia, and we are left to draw out the implications. The same sort of narrative juxtaposition accounts for the 'strange story'[15] of Maximus and Marcia. Immediately after Tacitus has recalled Marcia's accusation of herself he returns to the narrative of Augustus' demise, leaving the words 'that she was the cause of her husband's death' as both the conclusion to the strange story and an oblique commentary on what comes after. In this way Tacitus alleges Livia's crimes not only by recording the suspicion of others (thereby avoiding responsibility for the allegation) but also by including an accusation made about a completely different character and leaving it to the reader to judge its applicability by proximity.

Narrative juxtaposition also plays a crucial role in the statement which ends the passage. The same statement (*fama eadem*) tells of two events, Augustus' death and Tiberius' assumption of power. The power of this narrative juxtaposition is first hinted at by the floating adverb *simul*, 'at the same time', which can be applied to the narrative of the events or the events themselves, and which points up that these events happen at the same time *because* they are told of in the same statement. The statement further implicates Livia in suspicion. Because her husband has died when she says that he has died, she is in effect made responsible for what she narrates. By juxtaposing his death with her son's assumption of power, Livia creates a statement which brings about the first accession to the new principate, thereby bringing within her narrative control a highly problematic transition of power.

As I remarked above, Tacitus devolves responsibility for the allegations about Livia to other voices in the text: the people of Rome; Marcia; perhaps Livia herself. It can be seen from the end of the passage that he also surrenders the report of Augustus' death to Livia's *fama*. But the strength and power of this *fama* threatens to subsume Tacitus' own narrative, which is entitled 'from the death (*excessu*) of the god Augustus'.[16] When Tacitus' narrative surrenders its own starting-point to the indirect speech of the empress, it raises again the question of whose voice one chooses to hear in the text. Livia's *fama* not only subsumes the starting-point of the *Annals*, but can also be extended to cover the later books. By naming Tiberius here as 'Nero', her *fama* potentially refers to the final

---

[15] Goodyear (1972) 131.
[16] For further discussion of this point see O'Gorman (1995b).

Julio-Claudian accession as well as the first. The application of the term *eadem*, 'the same', thus shifts: *fama eadem* embraces two events (the death and the accession), two narratives (Livia's and Tacitus') and two emperors (Tiberius 'Nero' and 'Domitius' Nero). The narrator's voice, therefore, competes with that of the empress.

While the better-known allegations about the younger Agrippina can be seen to have shaped the more nebulous suspicions of Livia's role in her husband's death, the more elaborate narrative control which Livia exercises over her son's accession could be said to colour our reading of Agrippina's manipulations. Like Livia, Agrippina uses arts to deal with the rival to her son, but, whereas Livia's arts resulted in the banishment of Agrippa Postumus, Agrippina uses her arts for the confinement of Britannicus: 'by various arts (*artibus*) she held him back, so that he could not leave the bedroom' (12.68.3).[17] When some of the soldiers hesitate in proclaiming Nero emperor, they ask for Britannicus, but lack an 'authority/author (*auctor*)' to back their request: 'soon, with no author for a different statement (*nullo in diversum auctore*), they followed what was on offer' (12.69.1). If we read these traces in conjunction with the strong precedent of Livia, they can be read as signs of the empress's narrative control, particularly when they are followed by the reference to Agrippina's emulation of Livia at Claudius' funeral.

The empresses' power depends not only on their control of narrative but also on their manipulation of themselves as signs of the dynasty. This recalls the self-display of Messalina and of Agrippina the elder, who point to themselves as bearers of the dynastic future and of ancestral nobility. The elder Agrippina's pre-eminence in nobility and fertility is compared with that of the younger Livia, wife of Drusus Caesar, in Tacitus' examination of the rival adherents of Drusus and Germanicus. As with the play on the name 'Nero' at the beginning of the *Annals*, the names 'Agrippina' and 'Livia' here for a moment blur their referents, suggesting the more powerful bearers of the same names.

> Germanicus' spouse Agrippina outstripped in fecundity and in fame Livia, the wife of Drusus.

---

[17] At the betrothal of Nero to Octavia Tacitus assigns the 'art' of promoting Nero to the freedmen, and terms Agrippina's machinations 'enthusiasms' (*studia*) (12.9.2). The mother's *studia* are coloured here by proximity to the literary *studia* of Seneca (12.8.2). We might also note that Agrippina's first choice for the elimination of Claudius is Locusta the *artifex* (12.66.2).

et coniunx Germanici Agrippina fecunditate ac fama Liviam, uxorem Drusi, praecellebat. (2.43.6)

This juxtaposition of the names Agrippina and Livia can be read as a commentary on the younger Agrippina's emulation of the elder Livia at her husband's funeral: 'with Agrippina emulating the magnificence of her great-grandmother Livia' (12.69.3). Given the strong narrative control that Livia maintained over the script of her husband's death, this comparison of Agrippina and Livia suggests that Agrippina the younger emulates and surpasses Livia in self-display as a conscious form of history-writing.

The extent to which Agrippina surpasses Livia is reflected in the parallel passages which record their assumption of the name 'Augusta'.

> Livia was taken into (*adsumebatur*) the Julian family and the Augustan name (*nomenque Augustum*). (1.8.1)

> And Agrippina was increased (*augetur*) by the name of Augusta (*cognomento Augustae*). (12.26.1)

Whereas Livia is presented as the object of the name change, being absorbed by both the name and the family, Agrippina is portrayed as an autonomous entity to which the name is added. One reason for this is that Agrippina is already in the family of the Julio-Claudians, as the daughter of Tiberius' adopted son and the niece of Claudius (who is head of the Claudian family after the adoption of Germanicus into the Julian family), whereas Livia is from the Claudian family but not the Julian. The contrast between Livia and Agrippina is strengthened by the attraction of the name Augusta from name (*cog(nomen)tum*) to the woman herself; Livia is taken into the 'Augustan name (*nomen Augustum*)', while Agrippina receives increased authority from the 'name of Augusta (*cognomento Augustae*)'. In the case of Agrippina, the feminine ending of the name, and the appropriateness of the verb *augetur*, contributes to a stronger sense of her active presence in the distribution of power.

'HISTORY IS LIKE MOTHER'[18]

As I remarked above, the successful empress emplots a reign which has as its culmination the accession of her own son. The empress's success,

---

[18] Gallop (1994).

in living long enough to see this culmination, is also her greatest weakness. Since she continues to exist past the end which she has constructed, she finds herself in a new and invidious position in relation to the ruler. She can hark back to her former actions and remind him of what he owes her, or she can plot a new teleology, to climax in the accession of a new protégé. Both options (even if not taken) make her an object of suspicion to the emperor, who needs a different narrative of his rise to power and is hostile when faced with the question of his successor, whose existence seals his own fate. In this respect the empress is viewed in the same way as is an imperial assassin, as one who facilitates the emperor's accession but who may at any point enact a repetition of their greatest deed.[19] The negotiation of the mother–son relationship after the son assumes supreme position, therefore, requires further examination. Thus Livia must be compared with Agrippina *after* the point at which Agrippina is said to emulate Livia, which is at the point of Nero's accession.[20]

Tiberius' resistance to his mother's narrative control begins early with his reluctance to grant her certain titles and monuments.

> There was much adulation towards Augusta also from the senators . . . many proposed that to the name of Caesar should be added (*adscriberetur*) the title 'son of Julia'. Tiberius . . . anxious with envy (*anxius invidia*) and interpreting a woman's dignity as a diminution of his own (*muliebre fastigium in deminutionem sui*) . . . prohibited an altar in honour of her adoption and other things of this kind. (1.14.1–2)

Later in the hexad a rift occurs between mother and son, the cause of which is Livia's inscription of her son's name after, or under, her own.

> When Julia dedicated a statue to the god Augustus not far from Marcellus' theatre, she wrote the name of Tiberius underneath her own (*postscripserat*), and he was believed, regarding it as beneath the majesty of the princeps (*inferius maiestate principis*), to have hidden it in deep and disguised resentment. (3.64.2)

---

[19] Agrippina's attempted incest with her son, which I will examine later in this chapter, plays on this fear; by offering sex to her son she puts herself in the same relationship to him as she had with her late husband. This position can only be interpreted by the emperor as a threat.

[20] Consequently I shall not discuss Agrippina's striking displays of power in book 12, during the reign of Claudius, such as, for example, Caratacus' homage to her at 12.37.4 or her entering the Capitol in a chariot at 12.42.2.

These two instances are clearly in parallel, both referring to Livia as 'Julia' (stressing her adoption by Augustus' will[21]) and both involving a 'subscription' (*adscriberetur/postscripserat*) of the emperor which he interprets as a lessening or lowering (*diminutionem/inferius*) of his authority. The earliest indication of Tiberius' anxiety to construct his authority independently of his mother's arts is given as one explanation for his reluctance openly to act as princeps in senate.

> He conceded also to *fama*, so that he would seem to have been called upon and chosen by the state rather than to have crept in by means of a woman's ambition and through an old man's adoption.

> *dabat et famae, ut vocatus electusque potius a re publica videretur quam per uxorium ambitum et senili adoptione inrepsisse.* (1.7.7)

Tiberius' concern is for his *fama*, the second occurrence of the term in the *Annals*, and it is in one sense the same as the first *fama*, the one that states 'that Nero was in power' (1.5.4). The second *fama* elaborates on the first, detailing how Tiberius/Nero came to power. According to the second *fama*, Tiberius either reaches the principate 'called upon and chosen by the state' (his preferred version) or 'by means of a woman's ambition and through an old man's adoption'. It is clear that this second *fama* echoes the arts of Livia at the beginning of book 1: 'by the obscure arts of his mother ... for she had bound the aged Augustus'. Again we can see that the *fama* which conveys (in both senses of the verb) imperial power is a construction of Livia's art. Livia's narrative, now that she has achieved her aim, becomes retrospective. Her attempts to remind her son of what he owes her can be refigured as another form of dissident history: not one which memorialises the oppressed but one which commemorates an unacceptable narrative of how the emperor came to power. Tacitus repeats and validates Livia's narrative when he suggests that Tiberius withdrew to Capri to escape from his mother.

> For it is passed on that he was driven out by his mother's lack of self-control, a woman he spurned as a partner in domination (*dominationis sociam*), but could not remove, since he had received that domination as her gift (*dominationem ipsam donum eius*). For Augustus had hesitated over whether he should not place Germanicus, his grand-nephew, praised by all, in charge of the Roman state, but overcome by the

---

[21] The only other time, apart from these two instances, that Livia is called 'Iulia' is at her death in 5.1.1.

prayers of his wife (*precibus uxoris evictus*) he had Tiberius adopt Germanicus, and he himself adopted Tiberius; and Augusta would reproach Tiberius with this and demand return for it (*exprobrabat, reposcebat*). (4.57.3)

The suggestion inherent in this repetition *dominationis sociam . . . dominationem . . . donum* is that the very definition of Tiberius' power is bound up in its status as a gift. Livia's version of events here in book 4 echoes Tacitus' narrative early in book 1, where Livia 'had bound (*devinxerat*) the aged Augustus'. The echo with Augustus being 'overcome' (*evictus*) here suggests that Livia's narrative remains consistent and is upheld by Tacitus' narrative. But the status of her history as a reproach to her son is an indicator of how far the empress's narrative has diverged from the emperor's: here there is no univocal *fama*.

Yet the power of Livia's narrative continues later in the *Annals* when Claudius is persuaded to adopt his stepson. His freedman Pallas, at Agrippina's bidding, uses Augustan precedent to achieve the adoption.

> Thus under the god Augustus, although supported by his grandsons, his stepsons had flourished; Germanicus had been taken up by Tiberius over his own offspring . . . overcome (*evictus*) by these arguments Claudius placed Domitius, who was three years older, over his own son. (12.25.1–2)

When Claudius is said to be *overcome* by these precedents we are reminded by the term *evictus* of Livia's claim in book 4 to be responsible for this order of adoptions: 'overcome (*evictus*) by her prayers Augustus had Tiberius adopt Germanicus, and he himself adopted Tiberius'. The arguments of Pallas turn out to be the *fama* of Livia again (what Livia suggests, what Augustus adopts, what Pallas cites as precedent), and it is thus the same *fama* which ensures Nero's adoption, the first step to his accession. In that respect Livia's *fama* is again responsible for what it narrates: 'the same *fama* reported that Nero was in power'.

Livia's words to Tiberius in book 4 correspond to one of the empress's options which I outlined above: to remind her son of what he owes her and thereby to maintain her influence over him.[22] The unpopularity with the emperor of this explicit claim to gratitude is conveyed by the strength of the term *exprobrabat* 'reproach openly', which is repeated in a

---

[22] Dixon (1988) 168–209 discusses the general type of influence a mother would have over her adult son.

similar exchange between Nero and Agrippina.[23] This is Agrippina's defence against a charge of plotting against her son, an accusation jointly made by Junia Silana and Domitia Lepida, the aunt of Nero. In this latter case Tacitus states that Agrippina does *not* remind Nero of what she has done for him: 'she discussed nothing about her innocence, as she would seem to lack confidence, nor about her benefits, as she would seem to reproach him (*quasi exprobraret*)' (13.21.6). But at this point Agrippina need not recapitulate, since in her preceding defence speech she has drawn a contrast between herself and Domitia which harps on her efforts for her son.

> 'She was improving her fishponds at Baiae, when by my planning (*meis consiliis*) adoption and proconsular power and designation to consulship and the other ways to attain power were in preparation.' (13.21.3)[24]

Nero's adoption, proconsular power and designation as consul, the preliminaries to imperial succession, are attributed by Agrippina to her planning, which corresponds to Livia's arts by which Tiberius becomes son, colleague in proconsular power[25] and holder of tribunician power at the beginning of the *Annals*. Agrippina's planning also corresponds to Livia's prayers in book 4, which determine the order of adoption under Augustus. This correspondence brings Livia's reproach (*exprobrabat*) into close alignment with Agrippina's speech, and indicates that Agrippina's subsequent avoidance of reproach owes nothing to diffidence but rather derives from the fact that the reproach has already been made in direct speech.[26] Indeed the general increase in explicitness which makes a difference between Livia and Agrippina may account for the fact that Livia reproaches in indirect and Agrippina in direct speech,[27] or the fact

---

[23] The term also occurs, indicating a continuous practice of upbraiding, in book 13, where the subject of Agrippina's reproach is Nero's affair with the freedwoman Acte: 'and the more foully she reproached him, the more eagerly he was fired up' (13.13.1).

[24] The contrast between the two women's activities here is sarcastically pointed up by the repeating syllables of the frivolous fishponds (*piscinas*) and the attaining of imperial power (*apiscendo imperio*). [25] Goodyear (1972) 112–13.

[26] Agrippina's avoidance of *seeming* to reproach sets her son on a path of reading reproach into more innocent acts, such as Montanus' apology: 'he apologised and, as if he had reproached Nero (*quasi exprobrasset*), was driven to death' (13.25.2); Anicetus' assistance: 'ministers of evil deeds were looked upon as if reproaching him (*quasi exprobrantes*)' (14.62.2); and the continued existence of Lucius Vetus, his mother-in-law and his daughter: 'as if by living they reproached him (*tamquam vivendo exprobrarent*) with the death of Rubellius Plautus' (16.10.1).

[27] Note also that while Livia frequently uses the traditionally approved prayers (*preces*) to

that Agrippina is directly called upon in the narrative to defend her attitude to her son, while Livia's relationship with Tiberius is only the
subject of popular murmurs.

The term *exprobrare* in the context of the mother's reproach conveys
the matter for reproach as a benefit, or rather a reminder of past
benefits.[28] But the term also suggests that the matter of reproach is a
shameful act or the accusation of a shameful act, a *probrum*.[29] The mother
forcefully recalls her former influence, which to both her and her son can
be a source of shame, as evidenced particularly by Tiberius' attempt to
re-narrate his rise to power and write his mother out of imperial history.
But the reproach also marks as shameful this attempted obliteration of
the mother. *Exprobrare*, the revelation of a mark concealed by the
emperor, reveals also a conflict of representation between mother and
son.

When the women reproach they uncover a mark which the emperor
would have passed over. It is interesting to compare the gestures of the
mutinous soldiers in book 1, who uncover their bodies to display as a
reproach the marks of former wounds.

> Some displayed reproachfully (*exprobrantes*) the marks of the lash,
> others their grey hair, most their worn clothes and naked bodies.
> (1.18.1)

> They all bared their bodies and displayed reproachfully (*exprobrant*) the
> scars from wounds, the marks of the lash. (1.35.1)

The signs on the soldiers' bodies stand for military service: the scars of
battle, the marks of discipline, and the length of service, signified by their
greying hair. When the soldiers display these marks as a reproach, they are
pointing to their fulfilment of military service, but at the same time
remonstrating at the lack of any return for their labours. Thus the marks
of the lash indicate the harshness to which they are subjected, and their
hair marks a complaint of the excessive number of years which they must
serve. The worn-out clothes and nakedness serve as unambiguous accusations about lack of pay. Even the battle scars, which serve as signs of

---

influence her husband and son (1.13.6; 3.15.1; 3.17.1; 3.17.4; 4.57.3; 6.26.3), Agrippina
resorts to threats (*minae*): 'the sentence was changed by Agrippina using threats rather
than prayers (*minis magis quam precibus*) (12.42.3); 12.64.3 (*minax*); 13.14.2; 13.15.3.
[28] For this sense of *exprobrare* see *TLL* v[II] 1802.15–55.
[29] Caper in Keil, *Gramm. Lat.* 7.100, 19: 'he reproaches (*exprobrat*) who reminds you of
what he has offered, he taunts (*obprobrat*) who casts your disgrace in your face'.

courage, are shamefully juxtaposed with the marks of the lash in order to emphasise the difference, according to the soldiers, between their labour and their reward. We have already seen in the preceding chapter how a similar form of self-revelation is exploited by the actor Mnester, who attempts to use his body to evoke memory in the emperor Claudius. Although Mnester's plea to the emperor is not in terms of a reproach, his invocation of memory and display of the marks of the lash can be read as an injunction *to the reader* to recall the earlier displays of the soldiers. These earlier displays, which are termed reproaches, are also implicitly designed to evoke memory: the marks on the soldiers' bodies are meant to provide a record of their military service.

If we return to the empresses' reproaches we find that in both cases there is no indication of self-display; both women use words alone to evoke the memory of their services to their sons.[30] This is particularly striking given that both women are elsewhere noted for their *magnificentia*, their self-display. The reproach, then, is in purely narrative form; in this way the reproach can be seen as another aspect of the *fama* through which the empress negotiates her way to the position of mother to an emperor. Unlike the *fama*, which is promulgated through report and display, the reproach is enacted privately between mother and son, and simultaneously marks the divergence of narratives in this conflict of power. The aspect of the narrative has also changed. Whereas the *fama* put about by the empress is concerned more with present and future, the reproach has to do with the past.

VENTREM FERI

The effect of both Livia's and Agrippina's reproach is far from what either woman intended. They utter their commemorative narratives in order to gain more influence over their sons. Tiberius, however, withdraws to Capri in response, and Nero grants his mother's requests on the specific occasion of the reproach, but shows no more signs of being influenced by her. More dramatically, the reproach in both cases marks the final appearance in the narrative of the living empresses. Agrippina makes her speech at 13.21 and disappears for the rest of the book, re-

---

[30] It is worth noting that Mnester's speech, which accompanies his self-display, contains an argument reused by Agrippina in her defence: 'nor would anyone else have perished before him, if Silius had come to power' (11.36.1); '"would I have been able to survive with Britannicus in power?"' (13.21.5).

emerging for the extended narrative of her murder at the start of book 14. Livia's reproach occurs at 4.57, and her obituary begins book 5. In the interim she is mentioned only once, at the death of the younger Julia, which foreshadows Livia's own death by the similarity in language: 'at the same time Julia met her death (*Iulia mortem obiit*)' (4.71.4); 'Julia Augusta met her death (*Iulia Augusta mortem obiit*)' (5.1.1).[31] Thus it seems that the narrative which the empress produces to memorialise her own actions causes her effectively to disappear from Tacitus' own narrative. If we turn to the account of Agrippina's murder, we can see how *fama* and the narrative arts turn to her son's advantage and her own destruction.

The motivating force behind Nero's crime is at first Poppaea, who assails the princeps with her own verbal rendering of the situation: 'with freqent recriminations, sometimes by mockery accusing the princeps and calling him a minor, dependent on another's commands, who lacked not only power, but even freedom' (14.1.1). Poppaea's complaints take up most of the opening chapter and are accompanied, as Tacitus concludes, by art: 'these and suchlike, effective by means of tears and the art (*arte*) of an adulteress' (14.1.3). In the second chapter the historical tradition joins in with the account of Agrippina's attempted incest with her son. Tacitus records first Cluvius' version, where Agrippina takes the initiative, then mentions (only to refute) Fabius Rusticus, who maintained that Nero desired the incestuous union. Cluvius, according to Tacitus, is backed up by other authors, and furthermore '*fama* tended towards this version' (14.2.2). *Fama* here is inclined to condemn Agrippina; the argument in its favour is one of plausibility in the light of her past history.

> ... or whether the consideration of a new passion seemed more credible (*credibilior*) in a woman who as a girl had allowed debauchery with Marcus Lepidus in hope of domination, who with equal desire had lowered herself to the lusts of Pallas, and had experienced every crime in her marriage to her uncle. (14.2.2)

Incest with her son would coincide with her previous sexual behaviour, which culminates in incest with her uncle, the subject of the beginning of book 12. There Agrippina also takes advantage of the family relationship in order to have regular and intimate access to the emperor (12.3.1).

---

[31] Goodyear (1972) 110–11 remarks on the relative frequency of this term for death, but notes also the variety of terms used by Tacitus. As I have mentioned above, Tacitus' choice of name for Livia at different points in the text is of particular significance.

Moreover, in book 12 *fama* of the incest strengthens her position ('the marriage settled between Claudius and Agrippina was confirmed now by *fama*, now by illicit love' (12.5.1)) whereas the *fama* of book 14 brings about her downfall. At the same time, this latter *fama* depends for its existence upon the former, the *fama* of her incest with Claudius, which is cited as a reason for believing that she desired incest with her son. The consistency of this narrative works against Agrippina rather than in her favour.

The *fama* of Agrippina, in the sense of her reputation, her past history, works against her by its very consistency. At the end of Agrippina's life, however, her voice is heard in both direct and indirect speech, commenting on her own downfall in such a way as to link her own destruction to that of historical narrative and historical memory. When she first sees her assassin, Anicetus, her remarks are rendered in indirect speech.

> Well, if he had come to visit, let him report back that she was recovered, if he was about to carry out a crime, she would not believe it of her son (*nihil se de filio credere*); parricide was not commanded (*non imperatum parricidium*). (14.8.4)

This refusal to recognise her son's part in the murder can be read as an attempted act of self-preservation; Agrippina had earlier considered that 'the one remedy was if she did not (seem to) understand' (14.6.1). But her words to Anicetus are undercut by her final words in Tacitus' narrative, quoted from the tradition that she had foreseen her death.

> Agrippina had believed that this was her end for many years previously, and had defied it. For astrologers had replied to her consultation about Nero with the prophecy that he would have command and would kill his mother; and she said 'let him kill, so long as he commands'.

> *hunc sui finem multos ante annos crediderat Agrippina contempseratque. nam consulenti super Nerone responderunt Chaldaei fore ut imperaret matremque occideret; atque illa 'occidat' inquit, 'dum imperet'.* (14.9.3)

The words of Agrippina answer and refute themselves, from 'she would not believe it (*nihil . . . credere*)' to 'she believed it (*crediderat*) and defied it' and from 'parricide was not commanded (*imperatum*)' to 'let him kill, so long as he commands (*imperet*)'. In these final moments the *fama* of Agrippina reveals its inner tensions, showing that the univocal *fama* initiated by Livia has become an internecine *fama*, which enacts in Agrippina's self-contradictory words the conflict which those words represent. Agrippina's final self-contradictory narrative brings out the tensions of a history which veers between complicity with and dissent from power. Her famous last words to her executioner represent the final destruction of an imperial history begun by her mother and great-grand-mother.

> To the centurion drawing his sword for the fatal blow she stuck out her womb and shouted 'strike my belly' (*protendens uterum 'ventrem feri'* *exclamavit*), and with many wounds she was finished off. (14.8.5)

While in her preceding words she refused to ascribe any blame to her son, Agrippina in this last gesture enacts her final reproach. As I remarked above, both empresses reproach their sons in purely verbal terms, in contrast to the mutinous soldiers who display their bodies. Here, in the place of the scar, Agrippina displays her womb and seeks death by Caesarean section. Her actions point, once more, to memory; when she shows her womb she reminds all onlookers of her role as mother of the emperor, displaying the famed fecundity with which she was recommended to Claudius. She reminds the reader, too, of her mother, whose womb was displayed to various onlookers, as I discussed in chapter 3. I remarked, too, at the beginning of this chapter on how the elder Agrippina might be seen to be commenting on her own iconic role when she draws a contrast between herself and the mute statue before which the emperor sacrifices. Her daughter's commentary is far more iconoclastic; having internalised memory within her own body she asks that the site of memory be torn apart. This form of protest at her own removal paradox-ically constitutes another sort of narrative which contends with domi-nant imperial history. The destruction of memory becomes itself a memorable act.[32] By asking the centurion to strike at her womb, more-over, Agrippina delivers a symbolic blow to the future of the Julio-Claudian family. This could be said to be fulfilled when Nero's wife Poppaea dies in her second pregnancy: 'by a chance rage of her husband, by whom she was struck with a kick while pregnant' (16.6.1). Agrippina's words, read as a curse against the dynastic succession, could also be said to point up the extent to which tradition and repetition subsume individual characters into narrative tropes.

---

[32] Like Messalina, Agrippina has a pet Mnester, who commits suicide at her funeral. The refusal of this second Mnester to protest in memory of his mistress perhaps mirrors Agrippina's destruction of memory. Cf. Henderson (1989) 207 n. 140.

The book which starts with Agrippina's death ends with Octavia's, as a sort of pale pendant to the highly coloured murder of her stepmother. Octavia's plight in the story and in the narrative could be seen to demonstate the useless burden of tradition, since memory in this instance operates as a source of destruction. Octavia's ancestry is presented as the main cause of Nero's hostility to her: 'although she conducted herself with modesty, she was a burden (*gravem*) because of the name of her father and the favour of the people' (14.59.3). When Octavia is finally banished to Pandateria, her plight evokes pity and recollection in the Roman people, an effect which is by now familiar to the reader from the various poses of Agrippina the elder[33] and of Messalina. The place of Octavia's exile evokes the reader's recollection of Julia the elder, whose exile to Pandateria is mentioned by Tacitus in her obituary (1.53.1). The pitying onlookers supply further recollections of other unfortunate Julio-Claudian women.

> No other exiled woman had affected the eyes of the onlookers with greater pity. Some still remembered Agrippina exiled by Tiberius, and a fresher memory of Julia, driven out by Claudius, hovered before their eyes.

> *non alia exul visentium oculos maiore misericordia adfecit. meminerant adhuc quidam Agrippinae a Tiberio, recentior Iuliae memoria obversabatur a Claudio pulsae.* (14.63.2)[34]

The pattern of Julio-Claudians evoking both memory and pity through their misfortunes and the similarity of their misfortunes to those of the relatives has been evident throughout the *Annals*. The number of precedents for this sort of scene within the narrative occur to Tacitus' reader just as memory is evoked by the onlookers. Octavia would thus seem to represent the survival of a history of oppression. Yet this sort of history survives only in its perpetuation; Octavia evokes the memory of the other Julio-Claudian women because she too is to be exiled and put to

---

[33] 'Hence there was shame and pity (*miseratio*) and the memory (*memoria*) of her father Agrippa' (1.41.2); 2.75.1; 3.1; 4.52.3. See the discussion in chapter three.

[34] We know from Suetonius that the elder Agrippina was exiled to the same island (*Tib.* 53.2); Furneaux (1884) 312 conjectures that Julia the daughter of Germanicus also was sent there, and adds '[t]he banishment of Julia, daughter of Augustus (1, 53, 1) is omitted, probably as having faded out of memory'. It is not known whether Tacitus specified the place of exile for either Agrippina or the daughter of Germanicus, since these both occur in the lost books, but it is likely that he did take the opportunity to evoke that site of memory and unfortunate family precedent.

death. This is poignantly highlighted when the moment of Octavia's execution arrives, and she invokes family tradition, calling on her own and Nero's ancestors.

Octavia is ordered to die and calls in vain on the names of her own, and Nero's family.

> She called them to witness that she was a widow and now only a sister and she called on the Germanici they had in common and finally the name of Agrippina. (14.64.1)

The specific names which Octavia calls out, however, tell a history of family murder, from the proto-victims Germanicus[35] and the elder Agrippina to Octavia's and Nero's common (step)parents Claudius (Germanicus) and Agrippina the younger.[36]

History, at this stage in the principate, provides so many precedents for tyranny and oppression that the very process of narrating seems to make the possibilities for the redemption of liberty in the future ever more unimaginable. Tacitus returns us to the question of what future there might be to which his history can be meaningfully addressed. More despairingly, his outburst which (almost) concludes book 14 suggests that tyranny may well have irrevocably altered the language of his history.

> To what end will I commemorate (*que<m> ad finem memorabimus*) the gifts decreed to the temples on this account? Whoever examines the calamities of these times in my writings or that of other authors, let him take this for granted, that however many times the princeps ordered exiles and killings, so many times thanks was given to the gods, and what was once a sign of prosperous affairs was at this time a sign of public disaster. But still I shall not be silent if any decree represents a novelty in adulation or an extreme in submissiveness. (14.64.3)

---

[35] Or even further: the father of Germanicus and Claudius was Drusus Germanicus, who also died under allegedly suspicious circumstances.

[36] Octavia's final cry of Agrippina's name recalls also the last woman to make that name her final word, the imprudent maid Acerronia in the collapsing-boat scene, who calls out 'that she is Agrippina' and is immediately killed (14.5.3).

Ghostwriting the emperor Nero

> The 'sense of an ending', which links a terminus of a process with its origin in such a way as to endow whatever happened in between with a significance that can only be gained by 'retrospection', is achieved by the peculiarly human capacity of what Heidegger called 'repetition'.
>
> Hayden White, *The Content of the Form*

> Repetition, witting and unwitting, characterizes imperial Roman history as much as it does an imitative literary tradition.
>
> Philip Hardie, *The Epic Successors of Virgil*

In the previous chapter I suggested that the voice of the imperial woman constituted a historical narrative which at times subverted or controlled not only Julio-Claudian history but perhaps also Tacitus' own *Annals*. The dissent from imperial narrative is therefore voiced from within the imperial family itself, diverting the reader's attention away from the senatorial voice of the narrator. Hence I remarked at the end of the last chapter on how Tacitus questions his own narrative with the words 'to what end will I commemorate?' (*quem ad finem memorabimus*). The question, couched in terms which evoke the end of memory, reminds us not only of the future to which the history is addressed, but also of the end of (the) history itself. Tacitus' fear is expressed here that the imperial strain on republican language will replace 'true' meaning, that the reader will have to internalise and gradually consent to this change of meaning.

> Whoever examines the calamities of these times in my writings or that of other authors, let him take this for granted, that however many times the princeps ordered exiles and killings, so many times thanks was given to the gods, and what was once a sign of prosperous affairs was at this time a sign of public disaster.
>
> *quicumque casus temporum illorum nobis vel aliis auctoribus noscent, prae-sumptum habeant, quotiens fugas et caedes iussit princeps, totiens grates deis*

actas, quaeque rerum secundarum olim, tum publicae cladis insignia fuisse. (14.64.3)

Tacitus continues to protest at the shift in meaning over time; the signs (*signa*) which indicated prosperity in the past (*olim*) are signs of disaster in the present (*tum*). Recalling their earlier significance is a way of ensuring that their misuse does not settle into established meaning. Yet the future which Tacitus imagines here, the time of the reader, is one in which this misuse is to be taken for granted, an assumption which anticipates the narrative. The reader is enjoined, moreover, to anticipate misuse: '*let* him take this for granted'. This future reader can thus be read by us in two ways: either he anticipates the misuse of signs because his reading practice is already ironised; or he has internalised and colluded with the misuse of signs and has accepted the imperial narrative. Both potentialities for the future exist in the present, so that the choice of which possibility should dominate our interpretation of the passage becomes another Tacitean challenge. His injunction to a future reader, 'whoever he may be (*quicumque*)' invites us to assess what kind of reader he might be and how much he might be one of us.

One possible future reader has internalised the narrative of the princeps. Tacitus could be seen to guard against the creation of this future by his portrayal of the last Julio-Claudian emperor, the (provisional) end of dynastic history. We can see one aspect of this portrayal in the passage quoted above. While a sharp distinction is drawn between past and present (*olim, tum*), the present, the time of Nero, is characterised in terms of monotonous repetition. Tacitus makes the same sort of claim during his narrative of Tiberius' reign in book 4, and later in Nero's reign in book 16.

> I am presenting in succession cruel commands, continuous accusations, false friendships, the ruin of innocent men and the same causes of death, being faced with sameness and weariness of events.

> *nos saeva iussa, continuas accusationes, fallaces amicitias, perniciem innocentium et easdem exitii causas coniungimus, obvia rerum similitudine et satietate.* (4.33.3)

> Even if I were commemorating foreign wars and deaths encountered for the state with such a sameness of destruction, weariness would have taken hold even of me, and I would expect disgust from others, turning away from the unhappy and continuous deaths of citizens however

noble in themselves: but now the servile submissiveness and so much bloodshed in domestic life tire the mind and paralyse it with grief.

etiam si bella externa et obitas pro re publica mortes tanta casuum similitudine memorarem, meque ipsum satias cepisset aliorumque taedium exspectarem, quamvis honestos civium exitus, tristes tamen et continuos aspernantium: at nunc patientia servilis tantumque sanguinis domi perditum fatigant animum et maestitia restringunt. (16.16.1)

Although the monotony of destruction works against historical memory, Tacitus mobilises his narrative against the contraction of memory into one eternally repeating event. He makes this explicit in book 16, immediately after the passage quoted above, by asserting that this disaster to the Roman state cannot be narrated in a single mention (*non semel edito transire licet*) and that illustrious men should receive individual commemoration (*propriam memoriam*) so as not to be confused in a common burial (*promisca sepultura*).[1] Tacitus' narrative, therefore, expands the monotonous repetition, asserting the individuality of the principate's victims but also highlighting the destructive nature of the regime as a repetitive one. It could be said that Tacitus rescues the senatorial victim from a memory-destroying repetition which he turns upon the princeps himself. It could also be said that the sort of repetition within which he entraps the princeps (and especially Nero) is an ironically negative version of tradition. Tacitus represents Nero as engaging with a tradition which has become so burdensome that it imposes on the princeps roles and gestures which deny him any sort of autonomy. In particular, Tacitus achieves this effect through a loaded use of literary allusion.[2] The narrative of the *Annals* is densely allusive throughout, but in the Neronian books it can be seen to be directed towards a portrayal of the emperor as effectively voiceless. The silencing of the imperial voice towards the end of the *Annals*, as well as the entrapment of Nero in repetition,[3] allows the possibility to emerge of a future for the senatorial voice and senatorial autonomy.

---

[1] There are echoes here of Cicero's story about the origins of mnemonics (*ars memoriae*) in the *De Oratore* 2.351–3, where Simonides recalls the seating arrangement of the guests who have been crushed in the collapse of the palace (which echoes also the collapse of the amphitheatre at Fidenae). The result is individual burial for the guests (*uniuscuiusque sepeliendi fuisse*). [2] Cf. in particular Hinds (1998).
[3] See especially the examination of filiative and affiliative repetition (and their interactions) in Said (1976). Quint (1993) 50–96 is of considerable importance.

VOX PRINCIPIS

Allusion is, as I have remarked, prevalent throughout the *Annals,* but it appears to interact most self-consciously with the story in the Neronian books. This could be seen to be an effect of the prominence in these books of Lucius Annaeus Seneca, contemporary author and teacher of Nero. Seneca's prominence brings the minor roles played by two other contemporary authors, Lucan and Petronius, into this comparison between the imitative and silent Nero and the autonomous poets.

Seneca appears early in book 12, when he is recalled from exile, and commits suicide towards the end of book 15.[4] His role as teacher to Nero is introduced as part of Agrippina's plotting on behalf of her son; Seneca's teaching is supposed to help Nero along the path to power.

> Agrippina, lest she be known (*ne notesceret*) only for her evil deeds entreated pardon from exile and the praetorship for Annaeus Seneca, thinking that it would be a popular act on account of the fame of his studies and so that the boyhood of Domitius could mature with such a teacher (*tali magistro*) and so that they could make use of his advice in their hope for domination, since he was believed to be loyal to Agrippina in memory of her help (*memoria beneficii*) and hostile to Claudius from the distress of his wrongs. (12.8.2)

The introduction of Seneca's political role is part of a sentence where double motives are adduced for Seneca's recall. The first motive is to enhance Agrippina's own image; 'lest she be known only for her evil deeds'. Her calculated act of leniency is explained by Seneca's supposed popularity 'on account of the fame of his studies'. The second motive is then sketched (Seneca's role in Nero's development as rival to the throne) and, to balance the explanation of the first motive, the sentence ends with another supposition about Seneca, 'since he was believed to be loyal to Agrippina'. The two motives here do not rule each other out but rather enhance and strengthen each other. Seneca's studies (*studia*), in particular, are demonstrated to have considerable political uses, not only making him a pawn for Agrippina to win popular favour (the first motive for his recall) but also making him a suitable teacher (*magister*) for the future emperor (the second motive). At the start of the Neronian reign Seneca's magisterial role is again brought to our attention, when he and

---

[4] Seneca presumably also appeared in *Ann.* 7–10. For references to his experiences under Caligula, see Dio 59.19.7–8, and under Claudius, see Dio 60.8.5.

Afranius Burrus, the praetorian prefect, are characterised as 'the guides (*rectores*) of the emperor's youth' (13.2.1). The strength of their political position is evoked by the term *rectores*, which recalls the introduction of Tiberius' praetorian commander Aelius Sejanus near the beginning of book 1: 'a guide (*rector*) to the young Drusus and the demonstrator of dangers and rewards to the others' (1.24.2). This serves to insinuate that Seneca and Burrus almost threaten to supersede their pupil, since Sejanus' later relationship to Drusus, the son of Tiberius, was not as a guide but as a rival. The identity of 'the others' to whom Sejanus demonstrates dangers and rewards could be read retrospectively from book 13 as Burrus and Seneca, to whom Sejanus' fate serves as a warning not to employ their arts against the house of Caesar.[5] The arts of Seneca, used to guide the young princeps, are 'lessons of eloquence and respectable affability' (13.2.1), making explicit the association between Senecan studies and his magisterial power, implicitly drawn in book 12. Syme states that '[t]he author of the *Annales* would be primarily concerned with the character, policy, and actions of Annaeus Seneca as a minister of state; but he could not fail to essay somewhere or other an appreciation of his style and talent'.[6] But it is rather the case that Seneca's 'primary' status in the *Annals* as a minister of state is articulated through his magisterial, literary status both within and outside the text of Tacitus.

Nero's first public appearance as princeps in book 13[7] is at the funeral of Claudius, where he delivers the oration.[8] This appearance, already self-consciously concerned with firsts, is ironically undercut by the remark that Nero is the first emperor to use 'borrowed eloquence', since the funeral speech has been written by Seneca.

> ... although the speech, composed by Seneca, displayed much culture, as that man had a talent which was pleasant and adapted to the ears of the modern audience.

> ... *quamquam oratio a Seneca composita multum cultus praeferret, ut fuit illi viro ingenium amoenum et temporis eius auribus accommodatum.* (13.3.1)

---

[5] Sejanus' arts are introduced at the beginning of book 4, while the arts of Burrus and Seneca appear just after their characterisation as *rectores*.   [6] Syme (1958) 333.

[7] It is arguable that his ceremonial exit from the palace at 12.69.1 (his exit from the Claudian books and into his own) is also his first appearance as princeps.

[8] The other first for Nero is his adoption into the Claudian family, which, like this scripted speech, is noted through the focalisation of perceptive contemporaries: 'the learned remarked (*adnotabant periti*) that there had been no adoption before this' (12.25.2); 'the elders remarked (*adnotabant seniores*) that Nero was the first ...' (13.3.2).

Thus it is not the case that, as Shadi Bartsch has put it, 'in a very real sense, (Nero's) audience is compelled to follow a script over which the emperor has total control',[9] since the audience in this crucial performance (Nero's appearance as the heir to Claudius) are fully aware of its scripting by Seneca. The speech displays much culture, which is designated as a fair reflection of the man himself (pleasant and adapted to his times) and which echoes also the recent reference to his 'respectable affability' (13.2.1). There is a strong sense that Nero's funeral oration is so Senecan that it could not possibly be mistaken for Nero's own voice. Later in the same chapter, after a review of the oratorical skills of each preceding emperor, Tacitus returns to Nero and enumerates the activities which he pursues in preference to rhetoric.

> Nero from boyhood had turned his lively mind to other pursuits: sculpture, painting, singing and horse-training; and in his composition of poetry he sometimes demonstrated that he had the elements of learning.

> *Nero puerilibus statim annis vividum animum in alia detorsit: caelare pingere, cantus aut regimen equorum exercere; et aliquando carminibus pangendis inesse sibi elementa doctrinae ostendebat.* (13.3.3)

The third section of the sentence elaborates on one particular art, poetic composition, but what the poems of Nero display is 'the elements of learning', a phrase with a dominant pedagogical sense. This may be read in parallel with the sentence about Seneca's speech quoted above, where 'displayed (*praeferret*)' echoes the use in this passage of the term 'demonstrated (*ostendebat*)'. But whereas Seneca's speech displays Seneca's qualities, Nero's poetry displays the beginnings of learning – as inculcated by Seneca himself. In both cases the literary production (the funeral oration and the poetry) is seen as transparent, unproblematically revealing its creator. In both cases, however, the creator is not the poet Nero but his teacher. Nero's voice proves in this case to be non-existent. Other episodes in which Seneca is seen as a writer also pick up on the way Nero does not speak, but is spoken through.

The next instance shows a series of speeches on clemency put about by Seneca on Nero's behalf.

> . . . harping on his clemency in frequent speeches, which Seneca published through the voice of the princeps, in order to give witness

[9] Bartsch (1994) 22.

to how respectably he had taught Nero, or to boast of his own talent.

clementiam suam obstringens crebris orationibus, quas Seneca testificando, quam honesta praeciperet, vel iactandi ingenii voce principis vulgabat. (13.11.2)

The topic is clearly an allusion to Seneca's *De Clementia*,[10] and these speeches serve the same purpose as both the funeral oration and the poetry of 13.3, which displayed respectively Seneca's talent and Nero's education. Here education is again displayed ('how respectably (*honesta*) he had taught (*praeciperet*) Nero'), making explicit the source of the emperor's learning, and evoking both the arts of Seneca mentioned at 13.2.1: 'lessons (*praeceptis*) of eloquence and respectable (*honesta*) affability'. Once more, as at the funeral oration, the literary and pedagogical talent of Seneca is displayed, while the mediation of display is this time made explicit: 'the voice of the princeps'.

The extent to which Seneca's scripting of the Neronian reign is recognised by contemporary Romans (as we have seen at the funeral of Claudius, examined above) is evident in the next reading of a Neronian piece of writing, a letter to the senate explaining the circumstances of his mother's death. After listing the accusations made against Agrippina as justification for her murder, Tacitus remarks on the implausibility of Nero's story (in terms which ironically recall the earlier words of Anicetus asserting the plausibility of this same version of events).[11] He concludes with the popular response to this story, which indicts not Nero but Seneca.

> But rumour was inimical not to Nero, whose monstrosity exceeded all complaint, but to Seneca, on the grounds that he had written a confession in such a speech.
>
> *ergo non iam Nero, cuius immanitas omnium questus anteibat, sed Seneca adverso rumore erat, quod oratione tali confessionem scripsisset.* (14.11.3)

---

[10] See Syme (1958) 334–6. A reference to Nero's age at *De Clementia* 1.9.1 dates this treatise to around AD 55; Tacitus' allusion to the work here comes at the beginning of his account of that year.

[11] Thus Anicetus argues against anyone regarding the shipwreck as contrived: 'nothing was so open to chance as the sea: and if she were caught in a shipwreck who would be so unjust as to (*quem adeo iniquum ut*) assign to criminal intentions what is committed by the wind and the waves?' (14.3.3). When Nero narrates the shipwreck, Tacitus adds a disbelieving question in response: 'and he told the story of the shipwreck: where could a person so obtuse be found who (*quis adeo hebes inveniretur ut*) would believe that it was chance?' (14.11.2).

The speech here becomes a confession; the lie is so implausible that it unmasks the truth. But, interestingly, rumour as a result of this turns upon Seneca, not Nero, as if Seneca's speech is a confession of his own actions, not of Nero's. This goes beyond reference to Seneca's implication in the murder of Agrippina (14.7.3) and suggests not only that the voiceless Nero requires Seneca to render him in speech, but also that when Seneca scripts Nero, he renders him speechless, that Seneca's speeches are always evidently emanating from Seneca. Thus Seneca displays Nero as an absence (of voice) in these moments of ghostwriting.[12]

The pivotal scene for this is the rhetorical confrontation between Seneca and Nero towards the end of book 14. This is the sole instance of paired speeches in the *Annals* as they come down to us; Martin comments that '[t]here is intended irony in the fact that the device, so loved of rhetorical historians, is used by Tacitus only when the artificiality of the occasion is apparent'.[13] But there is a further irony apparent in the choice of speakers for this dialogue, since the style of these speeches is discernibly Senecan,[14] suggesting that this confrontation too is scripted by the minister. This is interesting given that Nero is often interpreted as emerging victorious from the debate, having denied Seneca's request and represented denial as favour. His speech is thus seen as rhetorically more adept than that of Seneca.[15] This display of Nero as surpassing Seneca, written in self-consciously Senecan language, appears as another instance where Nero's achievements are grounded in an education which he owes to his teacher. Nero's opening words make this explicit.

> I consider this to be primarily your gift, that I can answer immediately your premeditated speech, you who taught me (*docuisti*) how to give an account not only prepared in advance, but also on the spur of the moment. (14.55.1)

Seneca initiates this crucial exchange because he is aware of what is being said to Nero behind his back. His detractors bring a number of 'charges'

---

[12] 'The most literary of emperors is the one who is most often ghosted or parodied by his own contemporaries. He provides the inspiration, the context, for their own prolific output, just as they write the script': Gowers (1994) 132.

[13] Martin (1981) 177.

[14] Syme (1958) 335–6. Griffin (1976) usefully traces specific Senecan allusions in these Tacitean speeches, 442–3.

[15] Syme (1958) 335: 'the pupil even surpassed the master'; Too (1994) 213: 'the teacher has empowered the student, even to the extent of giving the student authority over the teacher'.

against him (14.52.2–4): that he is excessively wealthy (and thereby attracting too great a following); that he claims precedence in eloquence and challenges the emperor's versifications with his own output; that he derides the emperor's own accomplishments. The list of accusations ends with the rhetorical question from the detractors: 'to what end (*quem ad finem*) will nothing be famous in the state which is not believed to have been devised by Seneca himself?' I will return to the suggestive terms of the question below, but for now I want to concentrate on the way in which Seneca meets some of these accusations (14.53.1–3). Immediately after the indirect speech of the detractors Tacitus writes 'but Seneca was not unaware of the recriminations', and indeed the pointedness of some of Seneca's arguments bears this out. It is important to note that he responds to most of the accusations by giving in to them, thus putting Nero in a position where he has to protest against his concessions.[16] The detractors want Nero to give up being a pupil ('let him shed his teacher'); Seneca's response is to offer to retire. The detractors consider his wealth excessive; Seneca offers to surrender his possessions to the emperor. Most suggestively, the detractors point out to Nero that he has no further need of 'tutors (*doctores*)' while he has ancestral precedent to guide him.[17] Seneca meets this by pointing to ancestral precedent for allowing him to retire ('I shall use the mighty example . . . your great-grandfather Augustus'),[18] leaving Nero to cite the same example supporting the opposing argument. In short, Seneca puts Nero in the position of refuting the nameless detractors of the preceding chapter. It could be said indeed that the speeches themselves counter the accusation made by these detractors that Seneca outshines Nero in eloquence; by requesting this exchange Seneca attempts to 'demonstrate' Nero's superiority in rhetoric, although that superiority, as I have argued, can only redound to Seneca's credit as a teacher.

The rhetorical question uttered by Seneca's detractors sarcastically comments on his position of literary supremacy, which threatens to subsume all literature at Rome. The question, with its repetition of *quem*

---

[16] The usual Tacitean/imperial disjunction between word and act occurs here. Seneca requests and Nero denies what Nero *seems* to want, and what subsequently takes place almost as if the speech had never been uttered (14.56.3).

[17] Koestermann (1968) 126 points out that the use of the term *doctor* is confined in the *Annals* to the Neronian books.

[18] Syme (1958) 335 n. 3 calls this Senecan/Tacitean example 'bad history'. Clearly Seneca is setting up an easy target for Nero's rebuttal.

ad finem, resonates with Tacitus' own question later in the same book, which I have already examined in detail.[19] The earlier question of end in relation to Seneca seems to be answered by the conclusion to the speeches episode, a conclusion which is couched in the most explicitly Senecan terms: 'Seneca gave thanks (*grates agit*), which is the end (*finis*) of all conversations with men in power' (14.56.3). This seems to answer the question in terms which grant supremacy to Nero, and which may be echoed in Seneca's earlier words '"but you have surrounded me with immeasurable thanks" (*gratiam immensam*)' (14.53.5). If *gratia* is the end of all, that end seems to be set by Nero and to circumscribe Seneca. But the authority for setting *gratia* as the end again reverts to Seneca, since the conclusion to the episode recalls a passage from his work, the *De Ira*.

> A most remarkable speech was made by a man who had grown old in the courts of kings: when someone asked him how he had achieved that thing most rare in a palace, old age, he said 'by accepting wrongs and giving thanks'.
>
> *notissima vox eius qui in cultu regum consenuerat: cum illum quidam interroga- ret quomodo rarissimam rem in aula consecutus esset, senectutem, 'iniurias' inquit, 'accipiendo et gratias agendo.' (De Ira 2.33.2)*[20]

The narrative voice of Tacitus here chimes with the 'remarkable speech' of Seneca's old man in the *De Ira*. Moreover, by making Seneca claim that he has reached old age (given as one of the reasons for his wish to retire), Tacitus further aligns Seneca with the unnamed old man in the text to which he alludes.[21] The Senecan authorisation of this conclusion to the exchange, therefore, answers the *quem ad finem* question in full: nothing in the state is celebrated unless it has been devised by Seneca, just as the exchange of speeches has been initiated and summed up by him. Seneca, despite or even by means of his disclaimers, continues to assert literary dominance over his emperor.

The narrative's epigrammatic and Senecan conclusion to the episode

---

[19] These are the only two instances of the construction *quem ad finem* in the *Annals*.

[20] As Griffin (1976) 442 and Ogilvie and Richmond (1967) 296 remark, this passage of Seneca is also recalled in the *Agricola*.

[21] So Tacitus' Seneca says '"therefore in this journey of life I am an old man (*senex*), unequal even to the lightest cares"' (14.54.2) and '"we elder (*seniores*) companions can request retirement"' (14.54.3), while Seneca's old man 'had grown old (*consenuerat*) in the courts' and 'had achieved old age (*senectutem*)'. There might also be a hint that Seneca, by virtue of his name, inevitably recalls the *senex* (perhaps even the *annosus senex*).

reintroduces the possibility that Tacitus himself may succumb to the burden of literary precedent. The pervasive sameness of historical events, which problematises narrative memory, is the subject of the second *quem ad finem* question, which I have already examined in detail. The monotony of sameness in this second passage, however, has implications for the Seneca–Nero exchange, since the later interjection of Tacitus is clearly informed by the earlier episode. Tacitus exhorts the reader to take it as read that 'however many times the princeps ordered exiles and killings, so many times thanks was given (*grates . . . actas*) to the gods' (14.64.3). As in the exchange between Seneca and Nero, thanks (*grates*) is the term evoked for every imperial act, however inappropriate. Indeed we can see that Tacitus' statement at the end of book 14 bears even closer similarity to the epigram from the *De Ira* 'by accepting wrongs and giving thanks'. The thanksgiving of the senate by its shift in meaning creates a distinction between past and present at the same time as it evokes an absence of distinction between good and bad throughout Nero's reign. If it is brought together with Seneca's thanksgiving, and read with the epigram from the *De Ira*, there is a suggestion that thanksgivings are also blurring the distinction between different narrative voices. Hence the reader must take the pervasiveness of thanksgiving as read throughout the narrative of Tacitus or *of any other author*; Tacitus addresses 'whoever examines the calamities of these times in my writings or that of other authors (*nobis vel aliis auctoribus*)' (14.64.3). The thanksgivings, then, flatten out differences, moral, historical, or authorial.

As I have remarked above, Nero's poetic efforts, mentioned in the catalogue of his cultivated skills at the start of his reign, serve only to display the training given to the emperor by his teacher Seneca. The next mention of Nero's poems again puts forward the view that Nero's writing can only reproduce the voices of his stronger contemporaries. After an account of Nero's theatrical activities, Tacitus mentions Nero's literary and philosophical dinner parties.

> But lest only the theatrical arts of the emperor be known, he took on an enthusiasm for poetry too, gathering together those who had a certain ease of composition and were not yet well established in critical opinion. They would sit down with him, and join up verses brought to the gathering or devised on the spur of the moment, and thus fill up the words of the emperor, which were brought out in whatever mode/manner. The appearance of the poems itself shows this, since they do not flow with force, inspiration or with one voice.

ne tamen ludicrae tantum imperatoris artes notescerent, carminum quoque studium adfectavit, contractis quibus aliqua pangendi facultas necdum insignis aestimatio. hi considere simul, et adlatos vel ibidem repertos versus conectere atque ipsius verba quoquo modo prolata supplere. quod species ipsa carminum docet, non impetu et instinctu nec ore uno fluens. (14.16.1)

Here again, as in book 13, the poetry transparently displays its creator, or in this case creators, and thereby renders Nero speechless. This passage goes further even than the earlier episodes of Seneca's ghostwriting, where Nero merely delivered the words written by another. Here Nero himself is written into the poetry, as his guests take up his occasional words, 'brought out in whatever manner or mode' and turn his random 'manner (*modus*)' into metrical verse (*modus*). The two actions of the poets, 'to join up (*conectere*)' and 'to fill up (*supplere*)', implicitly ascribe to Nero's words the qualities of disconnectedness and insufficiency. The poetry of the guests is either premeditated or thought up on the spot: the result, coming from such a number of sources, is a babble of themes and voices, perfectly reflecting the convivial scene from which it arose.[22]

Although the poets who attend these dinner parties are not named, a later reference would seem to indicate that one of Nero's ghostwriters is the poet Lucan. Lucan is first named at the beginning of Tacitus' account of the Pisonian conspiracy (15.49.2). Tacitus begins the chapter with an assertion of the difficulty of recording the origins of this conspiracy: 'but I cannot easily record who was the first author (*primus auctor*), by whose inspiration (*instinctu*) was aroused that event which would destroy so many'. The presence of the term *auctor* pre-sensitises the reader to the following term *instinctus*, the same term used for the poetic inspiration of Nero's writing in book 14. Like the poetry composed at the dinner parties, the conspiracy seems to come from a variety of authorial sources, such that it is impossible to identify a *primus auctor*, an original, or a

[22] Suetonius interprets Nero's poetry differently: 'his writing tablets and notebooks passed through my hands, and in them were some remarkable verses, written in his own handwriting, and it is easy to see that they were not transcribed or taken down to someone else's dictation, but are clearly penned by the one who thought them up and created them; since there are many things crossed out and written over and above the words' (Suet. *Nero* 52). It is interesting that both writers ground their assertions on the appearance of the poems; Tacitus' reference to their appearance, however, seems to reflect a judgement 'founded on a critical study of the extant poems' (Furneaux (1884) 253), while Suetonius approaches the problem as a manuscript scholar. See also Bardon (1940) 201–2.

preeminent author.[23] It is interesting that Tacitus immediately goes on to delineate a hostility between Lucan and Nero which is derived precisely from the question of who is poetically pre-eminent.

> Personal reasons were firing up Lucan, because Nero was suppressing the fame of his poems and, being vain in his assimilation (*vanus adsimulatione*), had prohibited him from displaying them. (15.49.3)

As in the exchange between Seneca and Nero, after which Seneca is effectively removed from a public position, Nero here seems to have the upper hand by virtue of his ability to silence his rival. But his motive for repression undercuts his apparent position of dominance, when he is said to be *vanus adsimulatione*. This phrase can be read in a number of ways. Furneaux interpreted it as '"vainglorious in his comparison" (of himself to Lucan)'.[24] The meaning of *vanus* here, as 'full of foolish or empty pride' (*OLD* 6b), is an extension of its more common meanings, 'insubstantial, a phantom, devoid, lacking significance' (*OLD* 1 & 2). The comparison between the two poets renders Nero insignificant or meaningless. Moreover the term *adsimulatio* (the only use by Tacitus of this noun) suggests that Nero becomes meaningless because of excessive similarity with Lucan (*OLD* *adsimulatio* 1), a process mirroring the destruction of signification charted and played out by the text as a whole. This reading of *vanus adsimulatione* also contributes to the representation of Nero as voiceless, as spoken through others; he is in effect a phantom in comparison to Lucan because Lucan is one of his ghostwriters.[25]

Nero's assimilation to Lucan can also be seen to empty the princeps of meaning at the moment of his suppression of the poet. Thus the phrase represents a circular process: Nero attempts to be like Lucan, to replace Lucan; in order to do this he suppresses Lucan's voice, thereby leaving a space for his own voice; but precisely because he *is* like Lucan, his silencing of Lucan effectively silences himself.[26] This process could be seen to

---

[23] Woodman (1993) has analysed the account of this conspiracy in terms of theatrical metaphors, but does not comment on this particular section of the narrative.

[24] Furneaux (1884) 382.

[25] The rarity of *adsimulatio* prompted an alternative reading of this phrase as *vanus aemulatione* by Lipsius and Ursinus, followed by Nipperdey (cf. Furneaux (1884) 382 and Koestermann (1968) 269). This could be translated as 'made foolish by jealousy' (Furneaux) or 'vainglorious in his imitation'. *Aemulatio*, although it cannot be sustained here, would strengthen the phantom imagery of this phrase, by making Nero into an *imago*.

[26] Bloom (1973) 87–91 figures repetition in relation to 'kenosis', the emptying or

underpin the death-utterances of the three authors of Nero's reign, all of whom strongly assert their authorial voices in the final moments of their lives. All three (Seneca, Lucan and Petronius) are assuming the position of pre-eminent author or 'strong poet' (*primus auctor*) by creating text *within*, *about*, and *by* their ends.[27]

Lucan's response to Nero's suppression of his poetry is, first, participation in the theatrical undertaking of the Pisonian conspiracy,[28] and, secondly, a final defiant recitation at the moment of his enforced suicide.[29]

> With his blood flowing out, when he realised that his feet and hands were getting cold, and that gradually the life was leaving his extremities, with his heart still warm and still in control of his mind, he recalled a poem composed by himself, in which he had given an account of a wounded soldier dying the image of a death of this sort, and he recited the very verses, and this was his final speech.

> *is profluente sanguine ubi frigescere pedes manusque et paulatim ab extremis cedere spiritum fervido adhuc et compote mentis pectore intellegit, recordatus carmen a se compositum, quo vulneratum militem per eius modi mortis imaginem obisse tradiderat, versus ipsos rettulit, eaque illi suprema vox fuit.* (15.70.1)

Ordering the poet to die seems to repeat Nero's attempted suppression, but Lucan, by quoting his own words as his final or supreme speech (*suprema vox*), achieves poetic supremacy over the emperor. In the first place he composes his own death by reciting a composed poem (*carmen compositum*; clearly there is word-play here between his poetic composition and his state of being *compos mentis*). By reciting a poem about dying he reasserts his poetic control over the emperor's artwork (his subject's death); Lucan makes Nero's command into an image or 'mere' semblance of death (*imago mortis*), emptying it of poetic autonomy. His final words re-appropriate the death which is under Nero's control and refigure it as

undoing of the precursor, but stresses the danger that the poet would undo himself by the same process. My argument throughout this chapter is that Nero fails to attain the status of strong poet, remaining always an ephebe, which is how Henderson (1989) 181 and *passim* characterises him. Consequently his relations to precursors or contemporaries *always* result in the emptying of Nero. Later in the *Annals* an attempted *forgery* of Lucan's writing is termed *adsimilatis Lucani litteris* (16.17.4), retrospectively suggesting that Nero's role in relation to Lucan is that of copyist or replica.
[27] Bloom (1973) 79: '[d]eath . . . properly befriends all strong poets'.
[28] This has been examined in detail by Woodman (1993).
[29] Tucker (1987) and Wilson (1990) review the accounts of Lucan's death to consider whether it was suicide or an execution.

an *imago*. Most explicitly, Lucan reasserts his literary supremacy in his final words, an action also adopted by Seneca and Petronius, whose final moments of life are devoted to acts of creation.[30] Seneca dictates a final work which is subsequently published.

> His eloquence remaining adequate even in that last moment, having called for secretaries he dictated much which I will refrain from rendering, since it was published in his own words.

> *et novissimo quoque momento suppeditante eloquentia advocatis scriptoribus pleraque tradidit, quae in vulgus edita eius verbis invertere supersedeo.* (15.63.3)

Petronius writes a narrative of the emperor's sexual indiscretions and sends it to Nero under seal (16.19.3). Petronius' death is often seen as a parody of Seneca's self-consciously Socratic suicide, but it is important to note of all three deaths that they are *generic*;[31] these final scenes are congruent with the literary output of each author, so congruent that in the case of Lucan he is moved to sum up his situation with his own verses.[32]

Lucan's status as a strong poet in his death scene, however, is more problematic than is represented above. Lucan quotes his own words in a new context, that of his own death, in much the way that Nero sang of the fall of Troy when Rome was burning.[33] The assimilation of these two acts of quotation threatens to empty *Lucan* of signification. This effect is enhanced by Tacitus' use of a *Virgilian* allusion to convey Lucan's quotation of his *own* poem; 'the image of a death (*mortis imago*)' clearly recalls Virgil's summing-up of the generalised scene of chaos at the fall of Troy: 'on all sides there was terror and many an image of death (*plurima mortis imago*)' (*Aen.* 2.369). This choice of allusion brings Lucan's moment of quotation into closer alignment with Nero's singing of the fall of Troy, and relegates Lucan, along with Nero, to the ranks of failed poets, those who only *repeat* the words of their predecessors. The question then arises as to why Tacitus characterises this mere quotation with

---

[30] See Bertrand-Dagenbach (1992) 604 for an analysis of Petronius' death scene as a means of characterisation by paradox: 'the art of living (*ars vivendi*) culminates in an art of dying (*ars moriendi*)'.

[31] Connors (1994) 228–9 on Petronius' death as a parody; 230 on the genres of these authors and of their deaths.

[32] Suetonius tells us that Lucan's final moments were spent in poetic revision: 'but when free choice of death was obtained he wrote notes to his father with the corrections for some of his verses' (Suet. *Vita Lucani*).

[33] I will examine the Troy song of Nero in the next section.

the words 'final speech' or 'final voice' (*suprema vox*), a term which carries overtones of supremacy.[34] Is the supremacy *exclusively* Virgilian, or does the voice also belong to Lucan? The allusion itself offers some illumination here; Virgil's phrase denotes many different types of death (*plurima mortis imago*) while Lucan's choice of *one* specific instance from his own poem (a poem which could be said to *constitute* many an image of death) narrows Virgilian plurality down to one, singular death. The 'supreme voice' of his allusive quotation, from this perspective, re-enacts the striving for supremacy enacted by epic heroes and epic poets, who expansively incorporate a multitude of predecessors.[35] But this allusion still retains a plurality of voices. The Virgilian phrase is appropriated by another civil war writer, by Tacitus himself in his account of the second battle of Cremona in AD 69: 'diverse forms of dying men and every image of deaths (*omni imagine mortium*)' (*Hist.* 3.28.1). This allusion on the part of Tacitus thus brings out the civil war latent in Virgil's fall of Troy, as well as recovering the original Greek context for the phrase, which is also from a civil-war narrative, Thucydides' account of *stasis* at Corcyra: 'and there existed every image of death (πᾶσα ἰδέα θανάτου)' (Thuc. 3.81.5). Tacitus thereby suggests that this phrase is the poetic property of a civil-war writer; by making Lucan in effect quote Tacitus he is re-asserting the civil-war context of the phrase; although a Virgilian allusion it is in a sense more Lucan's than Virgil's, but only by means of Tacitus' pre-existing text.[36]

The authorial death scene can be read as the final assertion of strong poets over the imperial ephebe. Each author in turn stresses his literary stature by scripting his last moments. Nero is left in a position where imitation of his strong predecessors takes him to the point of a structured death scene, where literary rivalry has fatal consequences. What Tacitus would have done with the death of Nero is a matter for conjecture. In both Dio's and Suetonius' accounts we hear of Nero's lament 'what an

---

[34] *Supremus* is always used in the *Annals* in a funereal context. The majority of these occurrences, moreover, are in the context of an imperial death, and in the few non-imperial occasions it is applied to the death of a character closely implicated in the dynasty (Varus, Germanicus' Piso, Nero's Piso). Its use here for the final utterance of Lucan, therefore, suggests that the death has a closer connection with the emperor than is made explicit; I would argue that the connection is a literary one.

[35] See also Hardie (1993) 3–11 ('The One and the Many').

[36] There is a sense in which Tacitus asserts poetic autonomy over Lucan too, by making the poet quote his successor. For the relationship between Tacitus and Lucan as played out in the *Histories*, see O'Gorman (1995a).

artist dies in me!' (qualis artifex pereo! (Suet. Nero 49.1) οἶος τεχνίτης παραπόλλυμαι! (Dio 63.29.2)) but the emperor's claim to be an artist (artifex, τεχνίτης) is not backed up by any demonstration of his art to rival those of Lucan, Seneca and Petronius.[37] Suetonius' detailed narrative of Nero's death merits closer examination. His most quoted utterance, designating himself artist, is not the last word.

> Periodically he would inveigh against his own sluggishness with these words: 'It is a disgrace, a shame that I live – this does not befit Nero, it does not befit – in these moments one ought to be sober – come, rouse yourself.' Now the horsemen were approaching, who had been ordered to bring him back alive. When he heard this, he said quaveringly: 'The thunder is beating against my ears of fast running horses.'[38]

> *interdum segnitiem suam his verbis increpabat:* 'vivo deformiter, turpiter – οὐ πρέπει Νέρονι, οὐ πρέπει – νήφειν δεῖ ἐν τοῖς τοιούτοις – ἄγε ἔγειρε, σεαυτόν.' *iamque equites appropinquabant, quibus praeceptum erat ut vivum eum adtraherent. quod ut sensit, trepidanter effatus:* "Ἵππων μ' ὠκυπόδων ἀμφὶ κτύπος οὔατα βάλλει.' (Suet. Nero 49.3 (Hom. Il. 10.535))

As his disconnected reproaches attest, Nero is not in the composed state of the authors who die in his reign. Instead his actions are marked by sluggishness from which he attempts to awaken ('rouse yourself') and by a lack of shape (deformiter) and direction. This is reflected in the shapelessness of his phrases. In the final crisis Nero resorts to the first author, Homer, to sum up (although even then he speaks quaveringly). The quotation, though apt, is not recontextualised by Nero to such an extent that it could be termed creative imitation. Nero is left at the end ready with a suitable tag, like any well-educated Roman, but in poetic terms voiceless, spoken by others.

The final words are spoken after the death blow has been dealt.

> He drove a sword into his throat, helped by Epaphroditus the private secretary (a libellis). And when the centurion burst in and placed a cloak on the wound, pretending he had come to help, Nero, still half alive, made no response except 'too late' (sero) and 'this is fidelity' (haec est fides). And with that speech he died (in ea voce defecit). (Suet. Nero. 49.3–4)

---

[37] Connors (1994) 230: 'the Suetonian emphasis on Nero's hesitation and fumbling in his attempts to control his destiny by committing suicide (Nero 47–9) undercuts Nero's pose as an artist who artistically contrives the script of his final moments'.

[38] Richmond Lattimore's translation of the Iliad, Chicago 1951.

Nero's reproach to the centurion can be read as a reproach to himself, for having waited until too late, and with too little fidelity, to make an exemplary death. The death utterance, which is meant to sum up and suitably conclude the life, only reproaches Nero with the problem he has suffered all along, the problem of being 'too late' on the authorial scene, of having too many predecessors to incorporate. With this speech or voice he dies (*in ea voce defecit*) in sharp contrast to Tacitus' Lucan, whose final words are termed his *suprema vox* (15.70.1). The Suetonian Nero's death is framed in terms of failure, deficiency (*defecit*) and incompleteness; his suicide forms an unsatisfactory epilogue rather than an end in itself.

There is no way of telling how Tacitus would have framed Nero's death, though certainly the quotation and disjointed Greek phrases of the Suetonian passage would not have been replicated by the historian, who tends to minimise the intrusion of alien utterance into his text, and who never uses Greek. Clearly the ever increasing density of death scenes in the Neronian narrative as we have it is leading up to the moment when the dynasty ends. We can with a reasonable amount of certitude state that Tacitus would have produced a death which 'summed up' Nero.[39] His weakness and indecision at the point of suicide, which is alluded to by Dio and drawn out by Suetonius, could perhaps have also been a feature of the Tacitean version. Perhaps, too, Nero's death in the *Annals* could have been adumbrated by Messalina's cowardice at 11.38.1, where 'wavering (*trepidatio*)' is the term used by Tacitus for her hesitant and fumbling attempt at suicide.[40] What we can assume is that Nero's death was also characterised as a failure to achieve a final, decisive act: either by a strong utterance or by an emblematic gesture. The aid Nero requires to make the imperfect end in Suetonius' version is predominantly literary; Homer is called up to voice the emperor's predicament, and the final blow is thrust home by the imperial secretary 'in charge of petitions/documents (*libellis*)'. Given that Tacitus throughout the narrative has stressed Nero's literary voicelessness, perhaps we can conjecture that his scripting of Nero's suicide represented (in a more allusive manner than that of Suetonius) a 'death in quotation marks'.[41]

---

[39] On the death as a final clause see Connors (1994) 227–8.

[40] There are many parallels between Tacitus' setting of Messalina's death and the Suetonian passage on Nero's death: the presence of companions who urge the central figure to avoid indignity by suicide; the time wasted in useless laments; the arrival of assassins which in one case hastens and in another pre-empts the suicide.

[41] The title of a book by S. Boym, cited in Connors (1994).

THE GAME OF TROY

The Tacitean Nero, then, is an emperor who quotes rather than speaks. But the historian himself, as I have already remarked, prefers allusion to quotation in his own text (in order to avoid being another Nero). Furthermore, Tacitean allusion mobilises pre-existing texts against Nero, rendering him doubly voiceless. I have already demonstrated how, by making Lucan quote Tacitus, the historian invokes tradition from two chronological perspectives at the same time, elevating both himself at Lucan's expense and Lucan at Nero's. The literary tradition through which Tacitus demonstrates the strength and autonomy of his own work is at the same time refigured as a burdensome and sterile repetition which renders Nero historically weak. This is evident from Nero's earliest appearance in the *Annals*, participating in the game called Troy at Claudius' secular games.

> While Claudius was present at the circus games, when the boys of the aristocracy on horseback embarked on the game of Troy, among whom were Britannicus the emperor's son and Lucius Domitius, soon after admitted by adoption to power and the name of Nero, the more eager favour of the plebs for Domitius was taken as a prediction.
>
> *sedente Claudio circensibus ludis, cum pueri nobiles equis ludicrum Troiae inirent interque eos Britannicus imperatore genitus et L. Domitius adoptione mox in imperium et cognomentum Neronis adscitus, favor plebis acrior i<n> Domitium loco praesagii acceptus est.* (11.11.2)

Nero's mention here (probably the first in the text) is accompanied by a number of features designed to enhance the significance of the moment. The first is a temporal highlighting; Nero emerges at the beginning of the new era, 800 years after Rome's founding. His popularity at the games is seen to presage his future reign, and is linked in the following chapter to popular support for the descendants of Germanicus. The significance of the Troy game itself in relation to Rome's foundation and to the Julio-Claudian appropriation of legend operates also in these chapters. The game appears to have become popular from the time of Julius Caesar,[42] and features in Suetonius' lives of all the Julio-Claudian emperors, usually in the context of the various spectacles put on by each

---

[42] Although Sulla also exhibited the game (Plutarch, *Cat. Min.* 3.760).

emperor,[43] but in the cases of Tiberius and Nero mentioning their performance in the game itself as young children.[44] Either as exhibitors or participators the emperors gain credit from the Troy game; Augustus is said by Suetonius to have thought it a worthy way to display young nobles to popular view.

> Besides he gave frequent performances of the game of Troy by older and younger boys, thinking it a time-honoured and worthy custom for the flower of the nobility to become known in this way (*clarae stirpis indolem sic notescere*). (*Aug.* 43.2)

The particular relevance of the Troy game to the Julio-Claudian dynasty (because of their claimed descent from Aeneas' son Iulus) is, of course, mediated through the *Aeneid* of Virgil. There the Troy game is the culmination of Anchises' funeral games in book 5 and thus combines honour for one's predecessors with the joyful display of one's successors: 'the Trojans gazed upon them, shaken by the applause, and recognised in their faces the faces of their ancestors (*veterumque agnoscunt ora parentum*)' (*Aen.* 5.575–6).[45] Similarly Nero's appearance at Claudius' games is seen to be connected to the memory of his grandfather Germanicus, and recalls the earlier, unsuccessful Nero (the emperor Nero's uncle) who seemed by recent memory (*recenti memoria Germanici*) to be an image of his father (4.15.3). In this sense one can see Nero's presence in the Troy game as an appearance in honour of his grandfather, a point to which I will return.

Virgil, in his narrative of the game, has an eye to the wider span of history, evoked in microcosm by the resemblance across generations. He concludes his description of the game by an account of how it is handed on as a tradition by Ascanius to the Latins, and hence to Rome.

> This tradition of manœuvre and these battles Ascanius first brought back, when he was building his walls round Alba Longa, and he taught the early Latins to celebrate it. In the same manner as he had done as a boy, and the Trojan youths had done with him, this the Albans taught their sons to do; in the end mighty Rome received the tradition from Alba and preserved the honour of their ancestors; now the boys are called 'Troy' and their troop is called 'the Trojan Troop'. (*Aen.* 5.596–602)

---

[43] *Iul.* 39.2; *Aug.* 43.2; *Cal.* 18.3; *Claud.* 21.3.   [44] *Tib.* 6.4; *Ner.* 7.1.

[45] Aeneas sends instructions to Ascanius: 'Let him lead out the ranks for his grandfather and display himself in arms' (*Aen.* 5.550).

The young boy who leads the troop in his grandfather's honour becomes in turn one of the ancestors who is honoured by the Romans in performing the game. The sense of the game showing us history in the making is intensified by the foreshadowing (both explicit and implicit) in Virgil's mention of the three young leaders. Young Priam, grandson of Troy's king, is set in the context of both past and future, 'bringing back the name of his grandfather' (*nomen avi referens* (*Aen.* 5.564)) and 'a noble descendant soon to increase (*auctura*) the Italian race' (5.564–5). The second leader, Atys, is named as the founder of the *gens Atia*, the family of Augustus' mother. The friendship between Atys and Iulus (5.569) has dynastic significance, while Iulus' pre-eminence in the game points up his destiny as the ancestor of the pre-eminent Julian family. This stress on the youths, who together hold the future of Rome and of the imperial dynasty, is in contrast to the theme running through the *Aeneid* of young men meeting a premature end, only hinted at here in the mention of young Priam's father Polites, who is killed at Troy in book 2.[46] This undercurrent of pathos is present also in Tacitus' text, where the popular favour shown to Nero has sinister repercussions for Britannicus, also present at the games.[47] Unlike Iulus and Atys, whose friendship symbolises the future union of their descendants, Nero and Britannicus are destined to enact the discord, not the unity of brothers. Nero thus represents a variation of Iulus; whereas Iulus goes on to found a family, Nero marks its end.[48]

Beyond the significance of who participates in the game of Troy, there is the significance of the game itself within the text of the *Aeneid*. The game enacts a battle (*pugnae simulacra* (5.585)) and thus serves to memorialise the Trojan war. As an enactment of war it at first seems to entail the kind of empty repetition (*simulacra*) which locks the participant into a regressive pattern of the past, which indeed is how David Quint sees the first half of the *Aeneid*.

> The Trojans' successive unsuccessful attempts to settle outside of Italy in the first six books of the epic constitute a pattern of repetition that

---

[46] See Heinze (1993) 157–9. Putnam (1965) 86 remarks on the recurrence of the *ora parentum* between the game scene and the death of Polites, reminding us that the son was killed before his father's eyes.

[47] The favour shown to Nero will result in his prevailing over Britannicus for the succession, and Britannicus, too, dies in front of his family.

[48] Dio, in his obituary of Nero, remarks that he was 'the last (ἔσχατος) of the descendants of Aeneas and of Augustus' (Dio 63.29.3).

threatens to keep them in continual wandering and blocks their progress to their destined future. . . . The first half of the *Aeneid* describes the experience of the losers of the Trojan War who must rid themselves of their past, of their sense of loss and victimization. . . . But in the second six books of the epic, Aeneas and the Trojans find themselves caught precisely in a repetition of the Trojan War – the war against the native Latins that seems uncannily to evoke and reproduce the events of the fighting before Troy. . . . Thus the new *Iliad* of the second half of the *Aeneid* forces the Trojans to repeat their past struggle, but they will repeat it *with a difference*: this time they will be the winners.[49]

The two similes which Virgil introduces at this point in the poem bear out this repetition element in the Troy game and link it to the pervasive repetitions of Aeneas' travel and of Virgil's text. The first simile likens the patterned interweaving of the Troy players to the labyrinth at Crete.

> Just as once the labyrinth in lofty Crete is said to have had a passage weaving between blind walls and dubious riddle in a thousand paths, where the undetected and irretraceable wandering would break the signs of the trail: thus the sons of the Trojans entangled the traces of their manœuvres and wove flight and battle in their game.

> *ut quondam Creta fertur Labyrinthus in alta*
> *parietibus textum caecis iter ancipitemque*
> *mille viis habuisse dolum, qua signa sequendi*
> *frangeret indeprensus et inremeabilis error:*
> *haud alio Teucrum nati vestigia cursu*
> *impediunt texuntque fugas et proelia ludo.* (5.588–93)

The implications conveyed by this simile have important consequences for the status of the Troy game. The labyrinth is a type of art, and it is the artistry of the labyrinth which is recalled by the interweaving of the Troy players. It is tempting to read the description of both game and labyrinth as self-reflexive, mirroring the pattern of flight and battle in the poem itself. This is particularly suggestive given the use of the labyrinth elsewhere in the *Aeneid*, in the ecphrasis at the opening of book 6, and the usual interpretation of this as a mirror of Aeneas' own wanderings. The labyrinth is both like Aeneas' travels and like the Troy game, conjoining the first half of the book as repetition of the destruction of the city,

---

[49] Quint (1993) 50.

according to David Quint's formulation.[50] The labyrinth itself exists through repetition; by doubling its routes it achieves its purpose. When Virgil describes the labyrinth in book 5 he also describes the process of the simile. The labyrinth confuses by a multiplicity of sameness; the simile weaves significance through the text by producing likeness between different events. Both the labyrinth and the game of Troy seem to produce text by their interweaving: 'a passage weaving (*textum*) between blind walls'; 'they wove (*texunt*) flight and battle in their game'. But the suggestion of the labyrinth simile is that this constant drawing of likeness threatens to collapse into an undifferentiated mass. In the subsequent ecphrasis at book 6 the artist offers a way out of his own work of art[51] but here in book 5 the labyrinth still functions as a 'perverted architecture'[52] by destroying signification within its pattern of sameness.

The second simile also alludes to a later ecphrasis; the Trojan players are like dolphins, who reappear on the shield of Aeneas in the representation of the battle of Actium.

> In the middle of this ran the golden image of the wide swelling sea . . .
> and around it in silver bright dolphins in a circle were sweeping through the sea and cutting the waves with their tails. In the middle the bronze fleet, the battle at Actium, was to be seen.

> *haec inter tumidi late maris ibat imago*
> *aurea . . .*
> *et circum argento clari delphines in orbem*
> *aequora verrebant caudis aestumque secabant.*
> *in medio classis aeratas, Actia bella,*
> *cernere erat.* (8.671–6)

On both occasions the dolphins are portrayed as cutting through the mass of the sea (in book 5 'they cut (*secant*) through the Carpathian and Libyan seas with their swimming' (5.594–5)). In the ecphrasis at book 8 they divide the sea just as the sea divides the shield into upper and lower halves. The dolphins thus seem to operate as a symbol of some dividing characteristic (operating on the supreme symbol of formlessness, the water) without which meaning would be impossible. Since the boys who play

---

[50] See also Hardie (1993) 1–18.
[51] 'Here was the labour, that house and the inextricable wandering (*inextricabilis error*) . . . Daedalus himself secretly solved the riddle and the doubt (*dolos . . . ambagesque resolvit*)' (*Aen.* 6.27–9). [52] Barchiesi (1994) 443.

the Troy game are likened to dolphins it is clear that this characteristic of difference may be applied to them also. As the labyrinth simile suggests that the pattern of the game is a repetition (a potential dangerous entrapment) of the past, so the dolphin simile reminds us that the participants have the potentiality to create difference, to break out of the repetition. Since the players all foreshadow both Rome's foundation and the subsequent dynasty, there is a sense in which that difference is realised. Tacitus' evocation of Virgil, however, highlights the constant threat of regressive repetition which Nero's enactment of the Troy theme will demonstrate.

The game and its similes as set up by Virgil thus provide a series of perspectives on past and future events, operating as a site for evoking memory and prophecy. It also connects the major ecphrases of the epic in one moment. The significance of Virgil's Troy game has resonances in Tacitus' text when the young Nero makes his first appearance. As I have already pointed out, the game in Tacitus evokes both prophecy and memory in the onlookers. The memory of Germanicus aroused by the presence of Nero recalls Germanicus' own 'epic' presence, which the Troy game enhances. Between the account of the game and reference to Germanicus' memory Tacitus records a rumour about Nero's childhood, 'that serpents as guards had attended him in infancy'. This is clearly derived from tales about Alexander, which were also told of Scipio Africanus and Julius Caesar. As is noted by various scholars[53] Tacitus' portrayal of Germanicus is overlaid with textual traces of these heroes. It is possible that when Nero states that there was only one snake in his room, Tacitus' immediate transition to the memory of Germanicus (Nero's grandfather) is informed by the funeral games of *Aeneid* 5, which take place in the presence of the snake curled around Anchises' (Iulus' grandfather's) tomb (*Aen.* 5.84–6).

The relationship of Nero to Germanicus, at least as important as his relationship to Augustus and Tiberius, is mediated through *both* the Roman ideology of ancestry *and* the epic tradition of heroic and literary predecessors. When Nero is termed 'that one remaining male descendant (*illa reliqua suboles virilis*) of Germanicus' (11.12.1) the concern is not only with the transmission of a noble line but also with the poetic motif of remnants as formulated by Virgil's epic.[54]

---

[53] Baxter (1972); Bews (1972); Malissard (1990); Pelling (1993) 74.
[54] For an examination of *reliquus* in the opening chapters of the *Annals*, see O'Gorman (1995b).

The presence of Nero at the game of Troy, therefore, positions him at the centre of a web of historical signification which is reflected in the patterning of Tacitus' own narrative. It is also important that Nero appears first in a game which, in the influential epic portrayal of its performance, displays both the self-reflexivity of artifice and the potential destructiveness of repetition. Tacitus' introduction of Nero at the game of Troy exemplifies this repetition, when he recounts the fabulous story about Nero's serpent guards.

> And it was commonly said that serpents as guards had attended him in infancy, a mythical story likened to foreign wonders; for Nero himself, not at all inclined to be self-deprecating, was wont to tell that only one snake had been seen in the bedroom.

> *vulgabaturque adfuisse infantiae eius dracones in modum custodum, fabulosa et externis miraculis adsimilata; nam ipse, haudquaquam sui detractor, unam omnino anguem in cubiculo visam narrare solitus est.* (11.11.3)

Once more we can see the relationship between fable and miracle on the one hand and truth on the other, which is nevertheless made difficult by Nero's own version of the story. This serpent, as I have already remarked, could be seen to point to Nero's grandfather Germanicus, both through narrative juxtaposition and through the Virgilian model of the Troy game and the serpent-Anchises. The serpent story could also be seen to assimilate Nero to his grandfather through the heroic figure of Scipio Africanus, as mediated through Livy's account of the same miracle.[55]

> For Scipio was not only remarkable for his real abilities, but thanks to a certain art had also from his youth composed himself for their display . . . This custom, which he maintained throughout his lifetime, confirmed in some men the belief made common knowledge, whether deliberately or by chance, that he was a man of divine race. And it revived the tale commonly told in the past of Alexander the Great, equally vain and mythical, that he was conceived by intercourse with an immense serpent, and that the appearance of the monster had very often been seen in his mother's bedroom, and that, when people came in, it had suddenly glided away and disappeared from sight. Belief in these wonders was never mocked by him; on the contrary it was rather

[55] The tombs of ancestors recur also in Livy, just before the passage quoted in the text above, where the Romans reflect on the implications of sending Scipio to campaign in provinces where his father and uncle are entombed (*AUC* 26.18.11).

increased by a certain art of neither denying such a thing nor openly affirming it. Many other things of the same sort, some true, some pretended, had passed the limits of admiration for a mere man in the case of this youth.

fuit enim Scipio non veris tantum virtutibus mirabilis sed arte quoque quadam ab iuventa in ostentationem earum compositus . . . hic mos, quem per omnem vitam servabat, seu consulto seu temere volgatae opinioni fidem apud quosdam fecit, stirpis eum divinae virum esse, rettulitque famam in Alexandro Magno prius volgatam, et vanitate et fabula parem, anguis immanis concubitu conceptum, et in cubiculo matris eius visam persaepe prodigii eius speciem, interventuque hominum evolutam repente atque ex oculis elapsam. his miraculis nunquam ab ipso elusa fides est; quin potius aucta arte quadam nec abnuendi tale quicquam nec palam adfirmandi. multa alia eiusdem generis, alia vera alia adsimulata, admirationis humanae in eo iuvene excesserant modum. (AUC 26.19.3–4, 6–9)

Livy's Scipio is positioned across the changing spectrum of narrative truth and fiction. Tacitus' account of the serpent story as applied to Nero clearly makes gestures towards the Livian version. Thus what is 'commonly said (*vulgabantur*)' about Nero echoes what is 'common knowledge (*volgatae opinioni*)' about Scipio and what is 'commonly told (*famam volgatam*)' about Alexander. In addition, what Tacitus says is 'a mythical story likened to foreign wonders (*fabulosa et externis miraculis adsimilata*)' occupies the same position as Livy's assessment of a story as 'equally vain and mythical (*fabula*)', but clearly points also to his reference to 'these wonders (*his miraculis*)' and 'some things true, some pretended (*alia vera alia adsimulata*)'. This compression into individual words and phrases in Tacitus of what was more disparate (although carefully structured) in Livy is contrasted by the doubling (or more) of the serpent; what was one 'immense serpent (*anguis immanis*)' in Livy has become multiple serpents (*dracones*) in Tacitus. Nero's reaction to the story thus is of major significance, since his firm assertion returns the story to the Livian version: 'he was wont to tell that only one snake (*unam omnino anguem*) had been seen in his bedroom'. The prevailing version is likened to foreign miracles (*externis miraculis*) but Nero's version, by strongly echoing Livy (both Nero and Livy call the beast an *anguis* while Tacitus calls them *dracones*), likens his story to that of his countryman Scipio. It is interesting too that the tradition of more than one snake is marked as 'mythical (*fabulosus*)' because of (*nam*) Nero's version, which is strongly based on the account (*fama*) in Livy, an account which Livy characterises

as a myth (*fabula*).[56] Nero's Livian story diminishes his creative autonomy, especially when juxtaposed with Tacitus' rendering of the popular
version. Tacitus manages to evoke Livy's story by creative imitation,
through compression of several elements into one phrase and elaboration
of another element (the number of snakes). Nero, on the other hand,
breaks in with a virtually unchanged bit of Livy, that the snake 'had been
seen in the bedroom (of his mother) (*in cubiculo* (*matris eius*) *visam*)', thus
failing to create a version which can break free of its predecessor. The
imperial version of Nero's history is thereby subordinated to the narrative of the senatorial historian.

Nero's story of the snake is presented in terms of the mythical or fabulous: 'a mythical story likened to foreign wonders (*fabulosa et externis
miraculis adsimilata*)'. In Livy's account the proximity of the story to myth
(*fabula*) is also represented, and there the term *adsimulata* is used in the
sense of 'pretended', as opposition to truth: 'some things true, some pretended (*alia vera alia adsimulata*)' (*AUC* 26.19.9). Tacitus' text alludes to
Livy's in part by echoing *adsimulata* in a phrase which points to the act of
allusion itself; Nero's story is 'likened to' or 'assimilated from' foreign
wonders.[57] More importantly, by directing the reader to the presence of
Livy's text behind his own, Tacitus insinuates both his own and Livy's
meaning into the one term, describing the practice of falsehood, or simulation, (*adsimulata*) and the drawing of likeness, or absorption, through
assimilation (*adsimilata*). If we return to Nero in the Troy game, we see
that the process of assimilation, operating within and between the
various texts, begins with the drawing of parallels by remarking on similarities, between two characters, two events and two texts. So in the Troy
game Nero is like his grandfather Germanicus within the *Annals*. Then,
moving between texts, he is like Virgil's Iulus (and Germanicus is like
Anchises). Later in the chapter he is like Livy's Scipio. There are further

---

56 Tacitus characterises Nero as 'not at all inclined to be self-deprecating (*haudquaquam
    sui detractor*)' in the course of this account. The point of this, according to most inter-
    pretations, is that since Nero is not likely to belittle his own prestige in the usual course
    of events his reduction in the number of serpents in the story has particular force. We
    can read Nero's version of the story as being in no way a belittling of his reputation,
    but rather a drawing of a direct parallel between himself and Scipio.
57 Hinds (1995) has usefully coined a term which seems to me to apply in this case:
    '[c]ertain allusions are so constructed as to carry a kind of built-in commentary, a kind
    of *reflexive annotation*, which underlines or intensifies their demand to be interpreted *as*
    allusions' 41 (Hinds' italics). Woodman and Martin (1996) 298 refer to '"encoding" . . .
    alerting readers to decode an intertextual reference'.

likenesses to be drawn, but the danger, represented by Virgil's representation of the Troy game as a labyrinth, is that pervasive similarity threatens to collapse into meaninglessness. Nero is sufficiently late in history to bear the burden of being like all his ancestors and all their heroic role-models. As well as running the risk of becoming meaningless, Nero is in danger of being assimilated into the past rather than assimilating the past into himself: the trope of regressive, rather than progressive repetition.

> Conceptually the central problem for the latecomer necessarily is *repetition*, for repetition dialectically raised to re-creation is the ephebe's road of excess, leading away from the horror of finding himself to be only a copy or a replica.[58]

Nero's excess as represented in the *Annals*, however, only serves to emphasise his status as a copy or a copyist. This dynamic is clearly apparent in Nero's most famous allusion to Troy, his singing at the burning of Rome. This account opens the second half of book 15, preceding the long narrative of the Pisonian conspiracy. It is itself preceded by Tacitus' description of Nero's projected (and cancelled) Grand Tour, and of his further excesses at Rome. This section culminates in the representation of a 'typical' party of the time[59] after which Nero engages in a mock marriage and public sex with a character named Pythagoras. The fire at Rome is represented almost as a consequence of the myriad transgressions depicted, opening with the words 'a disaster ensued' (15.38.1).[60] In more than a symbolic sense Nero is seen as the incendiary agent, since the possibility that he has started the fire is introduced at the outset: 'a disaster ensued, whether by chance or by the treachery of the princeps it is uncertain (for authors (*auctores*) hand down both traditions)'.[61] Later in the account a further piece of evidence incriminates Nero: the activities of arsonists witnessed during the disaster. 'Others were openly throwing torches and were shouting (*vociferabantur*) that they had authority (*auctorem*) to do so, either so that they could loot more freely or because of an

---

[58] Bloom (1973) 80.
[59] Tacitus introduces the event with the words 'I will recount this as an example' (15.37.1).
[60] Compare the death of Seneca, which is seen as a *consequent* as well as a *subsequent* event to the Pisonian conspiracy: 'the killing of Annaeus Seneca ensued (*sequitur caedes*)' (15.60.2). Koestermann at 15.38.1 sees both these transitions as very abrupt.
[61] It is worth remarking that Tacitus is the only extant author to introduce doubt about the start of the fire (compare Suet. *Nero* 38; Dio 62.16.1; Pliny, *NH* 17.1.1). We could conjecture that he projects his doubt onto the other authors.

order' (15.38.7). This second use of the term *auctor* in the chapter retains some of the literary signification of the first. The suggestion that Nero might be the author/authority named here is made explicit in the next chapter.

> A rumour had got around that at the same time as the city was burning Nero had gone onto his private stage and had sung of the fall of Troy, assimilating present evils to ancient disasters (*praesentia mala vetustis cladibus adsimulantem*). (15.39.3)

Thus the three passages alluding to Nero's part in the fire, as quoted above, conflate authorship and authorisation, extending the matter of Nero's poem from the words he sings to the city he destroys. The tradition of authors portrayed as *doing* what they are *narrating* contributes to this identification; by singing the fall of a city Nero is enacting it.

When Nero sings of the fall of Troy, Tacitus characterises this action as 'assimilating (*adsimulantem*) present evils to ancient disasters'. As in the snake story, when Nero assimilates a foreign myth to himself, here an existing story is applied to a new situation. As I have already pointed out, the term *adsimilata* in book 11 highlights the text's own assimilation of another text, producing a highly self-conscious allusion. This second occurrence of the term, therefore, again describing Nero's act of allusion, should be read with an awareness of possible further layers. In other words, while *adsimulantem* at 15.39.3 refers primarily to Nero's assimilation of Rome to Troy, the act of assimilation itself may assimilate the speaker to another speaker in another text. The most obvious imitation here is of Virgil, whose epic incorporates the subject of Nero's poem, the fall of Troy. But another reading is suggested by the memory that Nero's telling of the snake story recalled Livy's Scipio Africanus; here (though less explicitly) Nero's allusion could allude to another Scipio, the destroyer of Carthage. Appian (citing Polybius) tells us that when that city was in flames the Roman general wept and quoted Hector's prophecy from the *Iliad*: "'a day will come when sacred Troy shall perish, and Priam, and the people of Priam'" (Hom. *Il.* 6.448–9).

Thereby Scipio, like Nero, assimilated the sack of the city before his eyes with the epic fall of Troy. Scipio then assumes the role of the prophetic warrior, by foretelling the fall of his own city, as Appian records.

> When Polybius asked him freely (since he was his teacher) what this statement meant, they say that without reserve he plainly named his

own country, for which he feared when he looked on human things. (App. 8.19.132 = Polyb. 38.22.3)[62]

Nero's poem at the burning of Rome is no prophecy, but can be seen to be a conflation of Scipio's two acts of assimilation (Troy to Carthage, and Troy/Carthage to Rome), an act of poetic imitation which puts into quotation marks the very action of reciting a poem. It also explains the popular hostility towards Nero aroused by his rumoured recitation, since his re-enactment of Scipio causes him to assume the role of a sacker of cities.[63]

This assumption of Scipio's role also stresses the reductive and potentially destructive nature of assimilation; the three cities (Troy, Carthage and Rome) are alike *only in that* they are destroyed by fire. Destruction adopts the role of excessive assimilation; each undermines signification by flattening out difference. Assimilation of Rome to Troy can therefore be seen as the destruction of Rome (so that Nero's poem is not merely a commentary on the situation but a curse which sets the disaster in motion). The regressive nature of this repetition entraps not only Nero (who replicates Scipio and Virgil) but also the people of Rome. Their inability to escape from the allusive city is recounted at length by Tacitus. A pervasive feature of this passage is the extent to which the city itself, as well as the speed of its catching fire, impedes those fleeing to safety: 'the city was exposed to danger because of the narrow passages winding this way and that and the irregular streets (*artis itineribus hucque et illuc flexis atque enormibus vicis*)' (15.38.3). The shapelessness of the irregular streets and lack of definite direction in the winding and narrow passages make the city a paradigm of the badly-wrought poem. The perverted architecture of the labyrinth is also evoked here. Although the city is not

---

[62] Another Polybian fragment omits the literary reference and has Scipio's 'prophecy' in direct speech: 'and turning away from this and grasping me by the right hand he said "O Polybius, this is a fine sight, but I do not know whether this command will ever be given about my own country"' (Polyb. 38.21.1).

[63] Much of the surrounding narrative makes more explicit reference to Nero as waging war on the city, as argued by Keitel (1984). See also Kraus (1994b) for further implications of Nero's enemy occupation of Rome. Woodman (1992), through examination of the chapters leading up to the great fire, convincingly argues for an assimilation of Nero's Rome to Alexandria, a city which Nero, as a descendant of both Antony and Octavian, must inevitably both decorate and destroy. (Woodman's interpretation could account for the inclusion in Tacitus' account of the destruction of works of literature (15.41.1).) The Neronian city can be seen to resemble the princeps in that there are too many precedents for it to imitate.

a well-constructed work of art, it does achieve the labyrinthine purpose, by confusing those who move through it, bringing them face to face with the disaster they try to elude: 'if they escaped into nearby places (*proxima*), when these too were carried off by fire, even those places which they believed to be far away (*longinqua*) they found in the same destruction (*in eodem casu*)' (15.38.5). Thus, in effect, the *form* of the city exemplifies the excess of assimilation.

The counterpart to this disaster in the Tiberian narrative is the collapse of the amphitheatre at Fidenae, which I have examined in chapter 4. There, an unstable building causes the elision of difference, when even relatives cannot identify the mangled bodies. In the fire at Rome, on the other hand, the elision of difference is a cause rather than an effect. This can be seen as a specific feature of Neronian Rome. When the fire has burnt out, however, and the rebuilding programme is under way, the origin of the labyrinthine city is recounted: 'but that part of the city which was left over from his mansion was rebuilt not, as after the Gallic sack, with no differentiation (*nulla distinctione*) or at random' (15.43.1). As Christina Kraus has recently demonstrated, Tacitus in his description of the old city and the new offers a reading of Livy 5.55.2–5, the account of the rebuilding of Rome after the Gallic invasion, a catastrophe which Livy himself assimilates to the destruction of Troy.[64] Nero's rebuilding, which is represented by Tacitus as the plundering of Rome and Italy, appears as the repetition *both* of the city's sack *and* its refoundation. The new city, moreover, in spatial terms is not simply a replica of the old; in the place of narrow and winding streets Nero builds wide thoroughfares at orderly intervals. The final comment on the new form of Rome, however, returns the reader to the flames that threaten to overwhelm the city.

> But there were those who believed that the ancient form of the city (*veterem illam formam*) had agreed more with their health, since the narrowness of the streets (*angustiae itinerum*) and the height of the roofs had not been penetrated by the rays of the sun: but now the open expanse, protected by no shadow,[65] burned with a greater heat (*graviore aestu ardescere*). (15.43.5)

---

[64] Kraus (1994b) 270–8 for Rome as Troy; 285–7 for Tacitus' reading of Livy.
[65] The lack of shade in Nero's city has literary connotations: most suggestively, the urban glare of some of Calpurnius Siculus' eclogues. See Gowers (1994) 131–2.

This description clearly echoes the earlier representation of the labyrinth which trapped the fleeing Romans: 'the city with its narrow passages (*artis itineribus*) winding this way and that and the irregular streets, such was ancient Rome (*qualis vetus Roma fuit*)' (15.38.3). The new city's non-labyrinthine characteristics, however, leave it open to the risk of the same thing (or worse) happening again: 'it burns with a greater heat'.[66] This too picks up on the opening of the fire episode, where the disaster is characterised as 'greater and more devastating (*gravior atque atrocior*)' (15.38.1). Consequently Nero's reconstruction attempts, but does not achieve, the transformations which show a creative engagement with tradition; his new city, which retains the potential to become another Troy, continues to stand for the burden of repetition.[67]

---

[66] Tacitus uses *ardescere* for flames at 4.67.2: 'Mount Vesuvius burning (*ardescens*) transformed the appearance of the place.'

[67] 'Troy itself is repeatedly presented as having the power to displace Rome, to reclaim its own identity ... And it is the Caesars who have the power to make Rome into Troy or Troy into Rome': Edwards (1996) 64–6.

Conclusion: the end of history

> It was history as a story that knew itself as such; it was politics as storytell-
> ing, the production of a narrative specifically intended to inspire in its
> audience a potential for change and to reclaim some kind of goal for a
> people thrown into confusion by the traumas of the past.
>
> Shadi Bartsch, *Ideology in Cold Blood*

The narrative of the *Annals* breaks off in mid-sentence nearly halfway
through book 16. It is a fortuitous and fitting break, for it emphasises the
death of Thrasea Paetus, the senator whose determined display of
'liberty' has been recorded at various points in Tacitus' narrative.[1] As his
blood spatters on the ground he offers it as a libation to Jove the liberator
and exhorts his son-in-law Helvidius Priscus to follow examples of constancy. The memory of Thrasea Paetus and Helvidius Priscus becomes a
site of contestation between senatorial writers and the emperors (particularly Domitian) at the start of Tacitus' much earlier monograph, the
Agricola.

> We have read (*legimus*) that when Thrasea Paetus was praised by
> Arulenus Rusticus and Helvidius Priscus by Herennius Senecio, it was
> a capital crime, and cruelty was exercised not only against the authors,
> but also against their books, since the triumviral committee was dele-
> gated to ensure that these monuments to the noblest of talents (*monu-
> menta clarissimorum ingeniorum*) were burnt in the comitium and forum.
> (*Agr.* 2.1)

Hence the emperor finds it necessary to suppress these dissident senators
twice, by driving them to suicide and by attempting to obliterate both

---

[1] Thrasea's first appearance in the extant text is at 13.49, where he is immediately
identified with the defence of senatorial liberty. His most memorable action is to walk
out of the senate in the aftermath of Agrippina's death (14.12). The destruction of
Thrasea begins at 16.21.

their memory and the memory of their literary commemoration. Tacitus and other writers counter the attempted obliteration first by recording the lives and deaths of such men and secondly by writing a history which reminds the reader of the (attempted) suppression of their memories: 'we have read this'. These commemorations of violence and suppression become the vehicle of protest at the principate. We have seen Tacitus' defiant confidence in the strength of memory against tyrannical suppression in his account of Cremutius Cordus' trial in book 4, as well as his more pessimistic statements about his own history in books 4, 14 and 16. In the *Agricola*, Tacitus records the near total obliteration of the historical record under Domitian.

> Indeed, in that fire the voice of the Roman people and the liberty of the senate and the conscience of the human race were thought to have been destroyed ... We offered, in short, a great example of submissiveness; and just as antiquity saw the extremes of liberty, so we saw extremes of servitude, having given up throughout the inquisition even the exchange of speaking and listening. We would have lost memory itself along with voice, if it had been in our power to forget as well as to remain silent.

> *scilicet illo igne vocem populi Romani et libertatem senatus et conscientiam generis humani aboleri arbitrabantur ... dedimus profecto grande patientiae documentum; et sicut vetus aetas vidit quid ultimum in libertate esset, ita nos quid in servitute, adempto per inquisitiones etiam loquendi audiendique commercio. memoriam quoque ipsam cum voce perdidissemus, si tam in nostra potestate esset oblivisci quam tacere. (Agr. 2.2–3)*

The fire which destroys the works of Herennius Senecio and Arulenus Rusticus is assumed to destroy the senatorial voice: not only the narrative voice but also the social and political exchanges which bind the senate together as a community. Tacitus sees the partial retention of past freedom in memory, which defies the senators' attempts to forget: 'we *would have* lost memory *if* it had been in our power to forget'. But memory is silent, and therefore has no perpetuation beyond the individual senators; they cannot transmit this memory in the form of history. (Indeed, in the ensuing chapter this residual memory is seen to be useless even in the exercise of liberty under the next regime.) Consequently the memory which senators have no power to lose cannot be addressed to the future, and therefore fails to be a vehicle for some future redemption of liberty. The history which Domitian's senators can perpetuate is a narrative of their own oppression: 'we gave strong proof (*documentum*) of submissiveness'. This proof or testimony can be seen to be addressed to the future as a warning;[2] the senators' submissiveness is presented to the reader who may reconstitute from it a *new* memory of liberty.

The restoration of liberty is claimed by Tacitus to have occurred first under the emperor Nerva and then under Trajan, in whose reign Tacitus is able to write about his own loss of voice under Domitian.

> But I will not be ashamed to compose a record of our previous servitude and a testimony to our present welfare, even if in a disordered and rough voice.
>
> *non tamen pigebit vel incondita ac rudi voce memoriam prioris servitutis ac testimonium praesentium bonorum composuisse. (Agr. 3.3)*

Memory here has been given a voice, to contrast with its consignment to silence in the preceding chapter. But the form of the historical narrative is itself a testimony to the earlier tyranny; the 'disordered and rough' voice of the narrator is a sign of his previous silence. In particular the disordered nature of the narrative voice points to the disjunction of Tacitus' historical writing from its tradition as a result of Domitian's suppression of Tacitus' historical predecessors. Nerva and Trajan, then, make the writing of history possible, but the nature of that writing is determined by the reign of Domitian.

Tacitus makes two claims about the reigns of Nerva and Trajan, one in the *Agricola* and one in the *Histories*. Both claims characterise the reigns in terms of the reconciliation of opposites which have structured (or will structure) Tacitus' representation of the Julio-Claudians: liberty vs. principate; inner thought vs. outward expression. In addition, the two claims in the two texts distinctly echo one another, inviting the reader to set them side by side.

> Now at last our spirit returns; and although in the first dawn of this blessed age Nerva Caesar at once mingled those things once incompatible, principate and liberty, and although Nerva Trajan daily increases the happiness of these times, and public calm has acquired not only hopes and prayers, but the very trust and strength of prayer fulfilled . . .
>
> *nunc demum redit animus; et quamquam primo statim beatissimi saeculi ortu Nerva Caesar res olim dissociabiles miscuerit, principatum ac libertatem,*

---

[2] 'Those things are called *documenta* which give examples in order to teach (*docendi causa*)' (Varro, *Ling. Lat.* 6.62).

augeatque cotidie felicitatem temporum Nerva Traianus, nec spem modo ac votum securitas publica, sed ipsius voti fiduciam ac robur adsumpserit. (Agr. 3.1)

But if life remains, I set aside the principate of the divine Nerva and the rule of Trajan, a richer and safer matter, for my old age, in that rare happiness of times when you are allowed to think what you want and say what you think.

quod si vita suppeditet, principatum divi Nervae et imperium Traiani, uberiorem securioremque materiam, senectuti seposui, rara temporum felicitate, ubi sentire quae velis et quae sentias dicere licet. (Hist. 1.1.4)

A sharp disjunction is drawn between the past (*olim*), when liberty and principate were irreconcilable (*dissociabiles*), and Nerva's present, when the distinction between them collapses and they are mingled (*miscuerit*) into a state of unity. In political terms the intermingling of principate and liberty requires a certain amount of explaining (away); if liberty is understood as the ability to create an utterance, this last passage explains how Tacitus can write about the loss of voice in the reign of Domitian. If the republic represents the extremes of liberty and Domitian's reign the extremes of servitude, Nerva and Trajan can be seen as having established an era of moderation, a balancing of polar opposites. But to suggest that this balance is at all unproblematic is to evade some of the issues of liberty as a condition of historical writing. Chaim Wirszubski has pointed out some of the difficulties of understanding the balance.

> [W]hile the conflict between the Principate and *libertas* under the emperors from Tiberius to Domitian appears to have been a fact, it is by no means clear what was the nature of that conflict. The real issue is somewhat obscured, for the modern student at least, by the ambiguity of the relevant political terms, above all *libertas* itself. *Libertas* means either personal and civic rights, or republicanism, or both, and, while under each of these heads fall several cognate but distinct notions, it is not always easy to ascertain exactly what *libertas* means in each particular instance. Similarly, *principatus* may mean either what the Principate actually became, but never ought to have become, or what it ought to be, but seldom was.[3]

Passing over the ambiguities of the terms 'liberty' and 'principate' for the moment, I would like to concentrate on Wirszubski's opening

---

[3] Wirszubski (1950) 125.

sentence: 'while the conflict between the Principate and libertas under the emperors from Tiberius to Domitian appears to have been a fact, it is by no means clear what was the nature of that conflict'. The conflict between these two concepts is configured by Wirszubski as a 'fact' (presumably a 'historical fact'), hence the task he sets himself is to sketch out definitions of these concepts: a task fraught with difficulty since, as he makes clear in the rest of the paragraph, there is no one hard meaning to either term. I would contend first of all that the meanings of liberty and principate could be seen to reside in their conflict itself, in other words that the question is not 'exactly what does each term entail in itself', but 'what meaning is conveyed by the opposition (or intermingling) of these terms'. My second point is in relation to Wirszubski's reference to this conflict as a 'fact'; another way of configuring the conflict between liberty and principate is offered by Bruno Latour in his discussion of modernity as a mode of understanding contemporary culture. Latour draws an analogy with the way that the idea of revolution shaped an understanding of events in 1789.

> Since the 1970s, French historians have finally understood that the revolutionary reading of the French Revolution had been added to the events of that time, that it had organized historiography since 1789, but that it no longer defines the events themselves. The Revolution as 'modality of historical action' is to be distinguished from the Revolution as 'process'. The events of 1789 were no more revolutionary than the modern world has been modern. The actors and chroniclers of 1789 used the notion of revolution to understand what was happening to them, and to influence their own fate.[4]

In the same way that Latour and the historians of 1789 see the terms 'modernity' and 'revolution' as terms which organise historiography, as 'readings' of the events of a specific time, we can see the conflict between liberty and principate as a modality of historical action figured by the historians and politicians of the Early Principate, and particularly by the senatorial historian Tacitus.

The extent to which the conflict underpins historical action and understanding can also be seen in Tacitus' treatment of the second unity effected by Nerva and Trajan. In the passage from the *Histories* quoted above, the happiness of the Nervan and Trajan era (*temporum felicitas*

---

[4] Latour (1993) 42.

repeated in both passages) is represented by the unity of inner thought and outward expression: 'when you are allowed to think what you want and say what you think (*ubi sentire quae velis et quae sentias dicere licet*)'. This is seen by Michael Sage as 'assuring the possibility of recreating *real* historical writing'.[5] Sage goes on to make it clear that what he means by 'real historical writing' is Republican history. But the characteristic of expression under Nerva and Trajan, as sketched by Tacitus, can also be seen to be the polar opposite of a type of rhetorical expression in *both* Republican *and* Imperial Rome which Tacitus himself has increasingly been seen to represent, namely *ironic* expression. We have already seen in the introduction how the characteristics of irony and dissimulation, according to the rhetorical treatises, have to do with a disjunction between thought and speech. The terms used by Cicero in the *De Oratore* directly echo Tacitus' phrase for historiography under Nerva and Trajan.

> Sophisticated dissimulation is when you think things other than what are said (*cum alia dicuntur ac sentias*), not, in that manner I spoke about earlier, when you say the opposite . . . but when in your whole manner of speaking you are at play seriously, when you think otherwise from what you say (*cum aliter sentias ac loquare*). (Cicero, *De Orat.* 2.269)

Paradoxically, the reigns of Nerva and Trajan make ironic expression impossible by being indescribable in ironic terms. Tacitus' disordered and rough voice, therefore, should fall silent when he comes to speak about the reigns of these emperors.

We can imagine the end of Tacitean history, not when his works end nor when his history is obliterated by a tyrant, but when a political regime elides the oppositions through which his historical understanding is articulated. The imagined unity of appearance and reality creates a state of totality within which the Tacitean expression of alienation has no place. At the same time this imagined totality explicates the alienation which Tacitus expresses throughout his history, the sense of the present as a state that is somehow at odds or out of joint. The condition of alienation thus could be said to be one most often explicated by history. One might even say that alienation brings history, particularly ironic history, into being. The present must be out of joint in relation to another time (or place) that exists in totality or harmony. Totality can be projected to

---

[5] Sage (1990) 877 (my italics).

the ends of the earth or the beginnings of time, so long as it is projected to somewhere *other* than where the speaker is presumed to be. (This other place or time is articulated as the *aliud*, the other meaning which is not entirely manifest in the ironic expression.)

This argument does not require us to believe that a state of totality (political or otherwise) exists or did exist at any time or place. Alienation requires that idealised totality be projected elsewhere; any attempt to approach totality will cause it to recede. So, for example, the republic exists in an idealised past in so far as it exists to guarantee the political alienation of the principate. That is to say, the political alienation of the senatorial historian under the emperors is brought into being by a sense that a state of totality (the oligarchic republic) has been lost. But the republic as it is represented in Tacitus' writings does not necessarily display qualities of idealised totality. Any attempt in the ironic narrative to approach an event in republican history will cause the idealised state of totality to recede.[6] From this it can be seen that the condition of alienation resides *within the narrative itself*, that alienation makes it possible for the narrative to be spoken, and thereby renders the state of totality unspeakable.

Alienation could thus be said to be a condition of language. Yet we have already seen how Tacitus succeeds in claiming this present as an era of totality from which (and about which, briefly) he speaks. But the ironic nature of Tacitean writing works upon these claims too. His postponement of the history of Nerva and Trajan to his old age reads like a variant on a *recusatio*, a writer's rationale for not dealing with a particular subject in the present work. Indeed, when read alongside Tacitus' praise for the two emperors in these two passages, it suggests that Tacitus, like Seneca's old man in the *De Ira*, will attain old age by confining his speech about the present regime to thanksgiving.[7] But above all, Tacitus' historical understanding makes it impossible for his reader to apprehend Nerva's mingling of principate and liberty, and, conversely, such an achievement of political totality makes it impossible for Tacitus to write his sort of history. This disjunction in itself offers a sort of ironic commentary on the new regime *and* on the position of the historian.

In the first chapter I quoted Hayden White's formulation of an ironic writer as one who discloses 'the *contrast* that lies hidden within every

---

[6] Flach (1985) 190–256 argues that the ideal state for Tacitus is a utopia.
[7] Discussed in chapter seven.

resemblance or unity'.[8] Throughout this book we have seen how Tacitus promotes a kind of reading which elicits this sort of disclosure. This suggests that his statement about Nerva's reign in the *Agricola* can be read as another example of ironic history. The resemblance or unity of Nerva's reign resides in the harmonious blending of principate and liberty. Yet Tacitus reminds us of a past in which these two concepts were irreconcilable, and implies that our understanding of principate and liberty is grounded in the tradition of their irreconcilability. Within present unity Tacitus exposes traces of past disjunction, but also privileges disjunction as a form of understanding by means of definition. Even when mingled as concepts, *principatus ac libertas* remain two distinct words, joined by the word *ac* which points up their incompatibility as much as their conjunction.[9]

Even the briefest mention of an era by the ironic historian causes its supposed totality to recede. Totality, moreover, is utilised not only as an ideal which makes alienated expression possible but also as an ironic commentary on the limits of Tacitus' own historical project. Although totality is unattainable, the action of using it to think towards remains a laudable one.

> Whether history is written for accuracy or for expressivity, it is always written against forgetting and perhaps ultimately for either freedom or piety.[10]

[8] White (1978) 128.
[9] Gallop (1982) 1: 'the most strenuous task allotted to "and" might be to connect two substantives that are totally indifferent to each other'.
[10] Roth (1995) 211.

Bibliography

Alexander, W. H. (1952) 'The Tacitean "non liquet" on Seneca', *Calif. Publ. in Class. Phil.* 14.8: 269–386

Allison, J. E. and Cloud, J. D. (1962) 'The Lex Julia Maiestatis', *Latomus* 21: 711–31

André, J. (1981) *Anonyme Latin, Traité de Physiognomonie*, Paris

Archer, L. J., Fischler, S. and Wyke, M. eds. (1994) *Women in Ancient Societies: an Illusion of the Night*, London

Avery, W. T. (1959) 'Roman ghost-writers', *CJ* 54: 167–9

Baldwin, B. (1970) 'Seneca's potentia', *CPh* 65: 187–8

Barchiesi, A. (1994) 'Immovable Delos: *Aeneid* 3.73–98 and the Hymns of Callimachus', *CQ* 44: 438–43

Bardon, H. (1940) *Les empereurs et les lettres latines d'Auguste à Hadrian*, Paris

Barthes, R. (1982) 'Tacitus and the funerary baroque' in Sontag (1982) 162–6

Barton, T. S. (1994a) *Ancient Astrology*, London

(1994b) *Power and Knowledge: Astrology, Physiognomics, and Medicine under the Roman Empire*, Ann Arbor, MI

(1994c) 'The *inventio* of Nero: Suetonius' in Elsner and Masters (1994) 48–63

Bartsch, S. (1994) *Actors in the Audience. Theatricality and Doublespeak from Nero to Hadrian*, Cambridge, MA

(1997) *Ideology in Cold Blood. A Reading of Lucan's Civil War*, Cambridge, MA

Bastomsky, S. J. (1972) 'Tacitus, Annals 14, 53, 2. The pathos of the Tacitean Seneca's request to Nero', *Latomus* 31: 174–8

Baxter, R. T. S. (1972) 'Virgil's influence on Tacitus in books 1 and 2 of the *Annals*', *CP* 67: 246–69

Bennett, A. and Royle, N. (1995) *An Introduction to Literature, Criticism and Theory: Key Critical Concepts*, London

Béranger, J. (1953) *Recherches sur l'aspect idéologique du principat*, Basel

Bérard, F. (1991) 'Tacite et les inscriptions', *ANRW* II 33.4: 3007–50

Bertrand-Dagenbach, C. (1992) 'La mort de Pétrone et l'art de Tacite', *Latomus* 51: 601–5

Betensky, A. (1975) 'Neronian style, Tacitean content: the use of ambiguous confrontations in the *Annals*', *Latomus* 37: 419–35

Bettini, M. (1991) *Anthropology and Roman culture: Kinship, Time, Images of Soul*, Baltimore

Bews, J. (1972) 'Virgil, Tacitus, Tiberius and Germanicus', *PVS* 12: 35–48

Bloom, H. (1973) *The Anxiety of Influence: a Theory of Poetry,* Oxford

Borzsák, St. (1969) 'Das Germanicus-Bild des Tacitus', *Latomus* 28: 588–600
(1970) 'Zum Verständnis der Darstellungskunst des Tacitus. Die
Veränderungen des Germanicus-Bildes', *Acta Antiqua Academiae
Scientiarum Hungaricae* 18: 279–92

Bowie, M. (1987) *Freud, Proust and Lacan: Theory as Fiction,* Cambridge

Bremmer, J. and Roodenburg, H. eds. (1991) *A Cultural History of Gesture.*
Cambridge

Brilliant, R. (1963) *Gesture and Rank in Roman Art. The Use of Gestures to Denote
Status in Roman Sculpture and Coinage* (Mem. Conn. Acad. of Arts and
Sciences XIV), New Haven

Brooks, P. (1984) *Reading for the Plot: Design and Intention in Narrative,*
Cambridge, MA

Cancik-Lindemaier, H. and Cancik, H. (1986) 'Zensur und Gedächtnis. Zu
Tacitus, Annales IV 32–38', *AU* 29: 16–35

Carson, A. (1992) 'Simonides Painter' in R. Hexter and D. Selden eds.,
Innovations of Antiquity, London, 51–64

Charlesworth, M. P. (1923) 'Tiberius and the death of Augustus', *AJPh* 44:
145–57

Christes, J. (1994) 'Tacitus und die Moderatio des Tiberius', *Gymnasium* 101:
112–35

Classen, C.J. (1991) 'Virtutes imperatoriae', *Arctos* 25: 27–8

Connors, C. (1994) 'Famous last words: authorship and death in the *Satyricon*
and Neronian Rome' in Elsner and Masters (1994) 225–35

Conte, G. B. (1986) *The Rhetoric of Imitation: Genre and Poetic Memory in Virgil
and Other Latin Poets,* Ithaca, NY

Croisille, J.-M. ed. (1990) *Alejandro Magno, modelo de los emperadores romanos,*
Brussels

Cruttwell, R.B. (1946) *Virgil's Mind at Work: an Analysis of the Symbolism of the
Aeneid,* Oxford

Dane, J. A. (1991) *The Critical Mythology of Irony,* Athens, GA

Daut, R. (1975) *Imago. Untersuchungen zum Bildbegriff der Römer,* Stuttgart

Dawson, A. (1968) 'Whatever happened to Lady Agrippina?', *CJ* 64: 252–67

Develin, R. (1983) 'Tacitus and techniques of insidious suggestion', *Antichthon*
17: 64–95

Di Cesare, M.A. (1974) *The Altar and the City: a Reading of Vergil's Aeneid,* New
York

Dixon, S. (1988) *The Roman Mother,* London

Doob, P. R. (1990) *The Idea of the Labyrinth from Classical Antiquity through the
Middle Ages,* Ithaca, NY

Dorey, T. A. ed. (1969) *Tacitus,* London

Drucker, J. (1995) *The Alphabetic Labyrinth. The Letters in History and Imagination*, London

Dudley, D. R. (1968) *The World of Tacitus*, London

Dyson, S. L. (1970) 'The portrait of Seneca in Tacitus', *Arethusa* 3: 71–83

Eck, W. (1984) 'Senatorial self-representation: developments in the Augustan period' in Millar and Segal (1984) 129–68

Edmunds, L. (1975) 'Thucydides' ethics as reflected in the description of stasis (3.82–83)', *HSCP* 79: 73–92

Edwards, C. (1993) *The Politics of Immorality in Ancient Rome*, Cambridge
   (1994) 'Beware of imitations: theatre and the subversion of imperial identity' in Elsner and Masters (1994) 83–97
   (1996) *Writing Rome: Textual Approaches to the City*, Cambridge

Elsner, J. and Masters, J. eds. (1994) *Reflections of Nero: Culture, History and Representation*, London

von Erffa, H. and Staley, A. (1986) *The Paintings of Benjamin West*, New Haven

Evans, E. C. (1935) 'Descriptions of personal appearance in Roman history and biography', *Harvard Studies in Class. Phil.* 46: 43–84

Feeney, D. (1998) *Literature and Religion at Rome. Cultures, Contexts, and Beliefs*, Cambridge

Fentress, J. and Wickham, C. (1992) *Social Memory*, Oxford

Fischler, S. (1994) 'Social stereotypes and historical analysis: the case of the imperial women at Rome' in Archer, Fischler and Wyke (1994) 115–33

Flach, D. (1985) *Einführung in die römische Geschichtsschreibung*, Darmstadt

Fletcher, A. (1976) *The Literature of Fact*, New York

Flower, H. I. (1996) *Ancestor Masks and Aristocratic Power in Roman Culture*, Oxford

Furneaux, H. (1884) *The Annals of Tacitus*, Oxford, 2 vols.

Gallop, J. (1982) *Feminism and Psychoanalysis. The Daughter's Seduction*, Basingstoke and London
   (1985) *Reading Lacan*, Ithaca, NY
   (1994) 'History is like mother' in Veeser (1994) 311–41

Genette, G. (1980) *Narrative Discourse. An Essay in Method*, trans. Jane E. Lewin, Ithaca, NY

Gillis, D. (1977) 'Imitatio Alexandri: the license to kill', *Centro Ricerche e Documentazione Sull' Anchita Classica* 9: 45–65

Gilmartin, K. (1975) 'A rhetorical figure in Latin historical style: the imaginary second person singular', *TAPA* 105: 99–121

Ginsburg, J. (1981) *Tradition and Theme in the Annals of Tacitus*, New York

Gleason, M. W. (1995) *Making Men. Sophists and Self-Presentation in Ancient Rome*, Princeton, NJ

Gombrich, E. H. (1982) *The Image and the Eye: Further Studies in the Psychology of Pictorial Representation*, Oxford

Gomme, A. W. (1956) *A Historical Commentary on Thucydides*, vol. 2, Oxford

Goodyear, F. R. D. (1972) *The Annals of Tacitus Books 1–6*, vol 1: *Annals 1.1–54*, Cambridge

(1981) *The Annals of Tacitus Books 1–6*, vol 2: *Annals 1.55–81 and Annals 2*, Cambridge

Gowers, E. (1994) 'Persius and the decoction of Nero' in Elsner and Masters (1994) 131–50

Graf, F. (1991) 'Gestures and conventions: the gestures of Roman orators and actors' in Bremmer and Roodenburg (1991) 36–58

Grant, M. (1956) *Tacitus on Imperial Rome*, Harmondsworth

Gregory, A. P. (1994) '"Powerful images": responses to portraits and the political uses of images in Rome', *JRA* 7: 80–99

Griffin, M. T. (1976) *Seneca: a Philosopher in Politics*, Oxford

(1982) 'The Lyons Tablet and Tacitean hindsight', *CQ* 32: 404–18

Grimal, P. (1967) 'Le discours de Sénèque à Neron dans les "Annales" de Tacite', *GIF* 20: 131–8

Halperin, D., Winkler, J. and Zeitlin F. eds. (1990) *Before Sexuality. The Construction of Erotic Experience in the Ancient Greek World*, Princeton, NJ

Hanson, A.E. (1990) 'The medical writers' woman' in Halperin, Winkler and Zeitlin (1990) 309–37

Hardie, P. (1986) *Virgil's Aeneid: Cosmos and Imperium*, Oxford

(1992) 'Augustan poets and the mutability of Rome' in Powell (1992) 59–82

(1993) *The Epic Successors of Virgil: a Study in the Dynamics of a Tradition*, Cambridge

(1997) 'Closure in Latin epic' in Roberts, Dunn and Fowler (1997) 139–62

Havas, L. (1991) 'Éléments du biologisme dans la conception historique de Tacite', *ANRW* II 33.4: 2949–86

Haverfield, F. (1912) 'Four notes on Tacitus', *JRS* 11: 195–200

Heinze, R. (1993) *Vergil's Epic Technique*, trans. H. Harvey, D. Harvey and F. Robertson, Bristol

Henderson, J. (1989) 'Tacitus/the world in pieces', *Ramus* 18: 167–210

(1997) *Figuring out Roman Nobility: Juvenal's Eighth Satire*, Exeter

Henry, E. (1991) 'Virgilian elements in Tacitus' historical imagination', *ANRW* II 33.4: 2987–3005

Herrmann, L. (1960) 'Le "De clementia" de Sénèque et quelques faits historiques', *StudClas* 2: 243–6

Hinds, S. (1995) 'Reflexive annotation in poetic allusion', *Hermathena* 158: 41–51

(1998) *Allusion and Intertext: Dynamics of Appropriation in Roman Poetry*, Cambridge

Hunt, J.W. (1973) *Forms of Glory: Structure and Sense in Virgil's Aeneid*, Illinois

Hutcheon, L. (1994) *Irony's Edge: the Theory and Politics of Irony*, London

Hutchinson, G.O. (1993) *Latin Literature from Seneca to Juvenal: a Critical Study*, Oxford

Jakobson, R. (1971) 'Two aspects of language and two types of aphasic disturbances' in *Selected Writings*, vol. 2, The Hague, 239–59

Kearney, R. and Rainwater, M. eds. (1996) *The Continental Philosophy Reader*, London

Keitel, E. (1984) 'Principate and civil war in the *Annals* of Tacitus', *AJPh* 105: 306–25

Klingner, F. (1955) 'Beobachtungen über Sprache und Stil des Tacitus am Anfang des 13. Annalenbuches', *Hermes* 83: 187–200

Koestermann, E. (1963) *Cornelius Tacitus, Annalen Band I, Buch 1–3*, Heidelberg
  (1965) *Cornelius Tacitus, Annalen Band II, Buch 4–6*, Heidelberg
  (1967) *Cornelius Tacitus, Annalen Band III, Buch 11–13*, Heidelberg
  (1968) *Cornelius Tacitus, Annalen Band IV, Buch 14–16*, Heidelberg

Kraus, C.S. (1994a) *Livy, Ab Urbe Condita VI*, Cambridge
  (1994b) '"No second Troy": topoi and refoundation in Livy, book V', *TAPA* 124: 267–89

Kraus, C.S. and Woodman, A.J. (1997) *Latin Historians* (Greece & Rome New Surveys in the Classics 27), Oxford

Lana, I. (1989) 'Introspicere in Tacito', *Orpheus* 10: 26–57

Lateiner, D. (1987) 'Nonverbal communication in the *Histories* of Herodotus', *Arethusa* 20: 83–119
  (1995) *Sardonic Smile: Nonverbal Behaviour in Homeric Epic*, Ann Arbor, MI

Latour, B. (1993) *We Have Never Been Modern*, Cambridge, MA

Leach, E.W. (1988) *The Rhetoric of Space: Literary and Artistic Representations of Landscape in Republican and Augustan Rome*, Princeton, NJ

Leeman, A.D. (1978) 'Tacite sur Pétrone. Mort et liberté', *ASNP* III 8: 421–34

Leigh, M. (1997) *Lucan: Spectacle and Engagement*, Oxford

Levick, B.M. (1966) 'Drusus Caesar and the adoptions of AD 4', *Latomus* 25: 227–44
  (1976) *Tiberius the Politician*, London
  (1978a) 'A cry from the heart from Tiberius Caesar?', *Historia* 27: 95–101
  (1978b) 'Antiquarian or revolutionary? Claudius Caesar's conception of his principate', *AJP* 99: 79–105

Lodge, D. (1977) *The Modes of Modern Writing: Metaphor, Metonymy, and the Typology of Modern Literature*, London

Lucas, J. (1974) *Les Obsessions de Tacite*, Leiden

Luce, T.J. and Woodman, A.J. eds. (1993) *Tacitus and the Tacitean Tradition*, Princeton, NJ

Macleod, C. (1983) 'Thucydides on faction (3.82–83)' in *Collected Essays*, Oxford (= *PCPS* 205: 52–68)

McCulloch, H.Y. (1980–1) 'The case of Titius Sabinus (*Ann.* 4.68–70)', *CW* 74: 219–20

(1984) *Narrative Cause in the Annals of Tacitus*, Königstein
(1991) 'Historical process and theory in the "Annals" and "Histories" of Tacitus', *ANRW* II 33.4: 2928–48
Macmillan, D. (1986) *Painting in Scotland. The Golden Age*, Oxford
Malissard, A. (1990) 'Germanicus, Alexandre et le début des *Annales* de Tacite' in Croisille (1990) 328–38
Manetti, G. (1993) *Theories of the Sign in Classical Antiquity*, trans. Christine Richardson, Indiana
Marincola, J. (1997) *Authority and Tradition in Ancient Historiography*, Cambridge
Martin, R.H. (1955) 'Tacitus and the death of Augustus', *CQ* 49: 123–8
(1981) *Tacitus*, London
Martin, R.H. and Woodman, A.J. (1989) *Tacitus Annals Book IV*, Cambridge
Martindale, C.A. (1993) *Redeeming the Text: Latin Poetry and the Hermeneutics of Reception*, Cambridge
Masters, J. (1994) 'Deceiving the reader: the political mission of Lucan *Bellum Civile* 7', in Elsner and Masters (1994) 151–77
Mellor, R. (1993) *Tacitus*, London
Mendell, C.W. (1970) *Tacitus: the Man and his Work*, New Haven
Millar, F. and Segal, E. eds. (1984) *Caesar Augustus: Seven Aspects*, Oxford
Miller, N.P. (1956) 'The Claudian tablet and Tacitus', *RhM* 99: 304–15
(1959) *Tacitus Annals Book I*, London
(1968) 'Tiberius Speaks. An examination of the utterances ascribed to him in the *Annals* of Tacitus', *AJPh* 89: 1–19
Momigliano, A. (1962) 'Osservazioni sulle fonti per la storia di Caligola, Claudio, Nerone', *Rendiconti della R. Accademia dei Lincei* 8
Morford, M.O. (1991) 'How Tacitus defined liberty', *ANRW* II 33.5: 3420–50
Morgan, J.R. (1985) 'Lucian's *True Histories* and *The Wonders beyond Thule* of Antonius Diogenes', *CQ* 35: 475–90
Moxon, I.S., Smart, J.D. and Woodman, A.J. (1986) *Past Perspectives: Studies in Greek and Roman Historical Writing*, Cambridge
Nagy, G. (1983) 'Sema and Noesis: some illustrations', *Arethusa* 16: 35–55
Newbold, R.F. (1979) 'Boundaries and bodies in late antiquity', *Arethusa* 12: 93–114
(1990) 'Nonverbal communication in Tacitus and Ammianus', *AncSoc* 21: 189–99
Nicolet, C. (1991) *Space, Geography, and Politics in the Early Roman Empire*, Ann Arbor, MI
Ogilvie, R.M. and Richmond, I. (1967) *Cornelii Taciti De Vita Agricolae*, Oxford
O'Gorman, E.C. (1993) 'No place like Rome: identity and difference in the *Germania* of Tacitus', *Ramus* 22: 135–54
(1995a) 'Shifting ground: Lucan, Tacitus and the landscape of civil war', *Hermathena* 159: 117–31

(1995b) 'On not writing about Augustus: Tacitus' *Annals* Book 1', *MD* 35: 91–114

Oliver, R.P. (1980) 'Thrasyllus in Tacitus (*Ann.* 6.21)', *ICS* 5: 130–48

Parker, H.M.D. (1928) *The Roman legions*, Oxford

Paul, G.M. (1982) '*Urbs Capta*: sketch of an ancient literary motif', *Phoenix* 36: 144–55

Pelling, C. (1993) 'Tacitus and Germanicus' in Luce and Woodman (1993)

Plass, P. (1988) *Wit and the Writing of History: the Rhetoric of Historiography in Imperial Rome*, Madison, WI

Powell, A. ed. (1992) *Roman Poetry and Propaganda in the Age of Augustus*, Bristol

Purcell, N. (1986) 'Livia and the womanhood of Rome', *PCPS* 212: 78–105

Putnam, M. (1965) *The Poetry of the Aeneid*, Cambridge, MA

Quint, D. (1993) *Epic and Empire: Politics and Generic Form from Virgil to Milton*, Princeton, NJ

Rich, J. and Shipley, G. eds. (1993) *War and Society in the Roman World*, London

Ricoeur, P. (1996) 'On interpretation' in Kearney and Rainwater (1996) 138–55

Roberts, D.H., Dunn, F.M. and Fowler, D.P. eds. (1997) *Classical Closure. Reading the End in Greek and Latin Literature*, Princeton, NJ

Romm, J.S. (1992) *The Edges of the Earth in Ancient Thought*, Princeton, NJ

Roth, M.S. (1995) *The Ironist's Cage. Memory, Trauma and the Construction of History*, Chichester, NY

Rouveret, A. (1991) 'Tacite et les monuments', *ANRW* II 33.4: 3051–99

Rutland, L.W. (1987) 'The Tacitean Germanicus. Suggestions for a re-evaluation', *RhM* 130: 153–64

Ryberg, I.S. (1942) 'Tacitus' art of innuendo', *TAPA* 73: 383–404

Sage, M. (1990) 'Tacitus' historical works: a survey and appraisal', *ANRW* II 33.2: 851–1030

Said, E. (1976) 'On repetition' in Fletcher (1976) 135–58

Seager, R. (1972) *Tiberius*, London

Shatzman, I. (1974) 'Tacitean rumours', *Latomus* 33: 549–78

Shotter, D.C.A. (1966) '*Ea simulacra libertatis*', *Latomus* 25: 265–71

(1969) 'Two notes on Nero', *CPh* 64: 109–11

Sinclair, P. (1991) 'Rhetorical generalizations in *Annales* 1–6. A review of the problem of innuendo and Tacitus' integrity', *ANRW* II 33.4: 2795–832

(1995) *Tacitus the Sententious Historian: a Sociology of Rhetoric in Annales 1–6*, Pennsylvania

Sontag, S. (1978) *Illness as Metaphor*, Harmondsworth

ed. (1982) *A Barthes Reader*, New York

Spratt, A.W. (1896) *Thucydides Book 3*, Cambridge

Suolahti, J. (1963) *The Roman Censors. A Study on Social Structure*, Helsinki

Syme, R. R. (1958) *Tacitus*, Oxford, 2 vols.

(1964) *Sallust*, Berkeley–Los Angeles

(1970) *Ten Studies in Tacitus*, Oxford

(1986) *The Augustan Aristocracy*, Oxford

Tanner, R. G. (1991) 'The development of thought and style in Tacitus', *ANRW* II 33.4: 2689–751

Thomas, R. F. (1982) *Lands and Peoples in Roman Poetry. The Ethnographic Tradition.* Cambridge

Too, Y. L. (1994) 'Educating Nero: a reading of Seneca's *Moral Epistles*' in Elsner and Masters (1994) 211–24

Townend, G. (1962) 'Claudius and the digressions in Tacitus', *RhM* 105: 358–68

Tucker, R. A. (1987) 'Tacitus and the death of Lucan', *Latomus* 46: 330–7

Tuplin, C. J. (1987) 'The false Drusus of AD 31 and the fall of Sejanus', *Latomus* 46: 781–805

Vasaly, A. (1993) *Representations: Images of the World in Ciceronian Oratory,* Berkeley–Los Angeles

Veeser, H. A. ed. (1994) *The New Historicism Reader,* London

Versnel, H. S. (1980) 'Destruction, devotio and despair in a situation of anomy. The mourning for Germanicus in triple perspective' in *Perennitas. Studi in onore di A. Brelich,* Rome, 541–648

Walker, B. (1968) *The Annals of Tacitus. A Study in the Writing of History,* Manchester

Wallace-Hadrill, A. (1982) '*Civilis Princeps*: between citizen and king', *JRS* 72: 32–48

(1991) 'Reading Tacitus: Rome observed', *AU* 34: 76–82

Watson, G. R. (1969) *The Roman Soldier,* London

Wellesley, K. (1954) 'Can you trust Tacitus?', *G&R* II Ser. I: 13–35

(1969) 'Tacitus as a military historian' in Dorey (1969) 63–97

West, D. and Woodman, A. J. eds. (1979) *Creative Imitation and Latin Literature,* Cambridge

White, H. (1978) *Tropics of Discourse: Essays in Cultural Criticism,* Baltimore

(1987) *The Content of the Form. Narrative Discourse and Historical Representation,* Baltimore

Wiedemann, T. E. J. (1992) *Emperors and Gladiators,* London

Wilson, J. (1982) '"The customary meanings of words were changed" – or were they? A note on Thucydides 3.82.4', *CQ* 32: 18–20

Wilson, J. P. (1990) 'The death of Lucan: suicide and execution in Tacitus', *Latomus* 49: 458–63

Winkes, R. (1979) 'Pliny's chapter on Roman funeral customs in the light of the *Clipeatae Imagines*', *AJA* 83: 481–4

Wirszubski, C. (1950) *Libertas as a Political Idea at Rome during the Late Republic and Early Principate,* Cambridge

Wiseman, T. P. (1979) *Clio's Cosmetics: Three Studies in Greco-Roman Literature,* Leicester

(1986) 'Monuments and the Roman annalists' in Moxon, Smart and Woodman (1986) 87–100

(1987) 'Conspicui postes tectaque digna deo: the public image of aristocratic and imperial houses in the late Republic and early Empire' in L'Urbs: espace urbain et histoire, Collection de l'école française de Rome 98: 393–413

Wood, S. (1988) 'Memoriae Agrippinae: Agrippina the Elder in Julio-Claudian art and propaganda', AJA 92: 409–26

Woodcock, E.C. (1939) Tacitus, Annals, Book XIV, London

Woodman, A.J. (1979) 'Self-imitation and the substance of history: Tacitus Annals 1.61–5 and Histories 2.70, 5.14–15' in West and Woodman (1979) 143–55

(1988) Rhetoric in Classical Historiography, London

(1989) 'Tacitus' obituary of Tiberius', CQ 39: 197–205

(1992) 'Nero's alien capital: Tacitus as paradoxographer (Annals 15.36–7)' in Woodman and Powell (1992) 173–88

(1993) 'Amateur dramatics at the court of Nero: Annals 15.48–74' in Luce and Woodman (1993) 104–28

Woodman, A.J. and Martin, R.H. (1996) The Annals of Tacitus, Book 3, Cambridge

Woodman, A.J. and Powell, J. eds. (1992) Author and Audience in Latin Literature, Cambridge

Young, R. (1990) White Mythologies: Writing History and the West, London

Ziolkowski, A. (1993) 'Urbs direpta, or how the Romans sacked cities' in Rich and Shipley (1993) 69–91

Zizek, S. (1992) Enjoy your Symptom: Jacques Lacan in Hollywood and out, London

General Index

actors 24, 39–42
Aemilia Lepida 60, 69
Agrippina the elder 47, 56, 117, 131;
  compared with the younger Livia 74,
  131–2; compared with Sejanus 91–2;
  on display 69–77; echoed by
  daughter 69, 131; as fugitive 70–2; in
  mourning 74–7; read by Tiberius
  80–1, 92–3; verbal protests 123, 141
Agrippina the younger 106, 109, 121 n.
  18, 122–41, 147, 150; her *commentarii*
  123–7; compared with the elder Livia
  126–7; on display 131–2, 141
alienation and totality 181–3
allusion 146–7, 150, 153–4, 158–9, 162,
  168–70, 171–3
alphabet 109–12
ambiguity 1, 81, 92–95
appearance and reality 3–10, 42–4, 72,
  78, 89, 102–3, 180–1
Arminius 54; his wife (Thusnelda) 72–3
Arria the elder 124–6
Arria the younger 124–6
Asinius Gallus 41–5
assimilation 45, 105, 156–7, 170, 172–4
astrologers 13, 103–5
Augustus 38, 62; compared with
  Germanicus 48; death 128; imitated
  by Claudius 107–9; indulgence to
  actors 24–5, 39; introducing trials for
  maiestas 85; restoration of republic 3,
  8–9, 10, 12, 19–20

Britannicus 109, 118–19, 131, 164

Caecina, Aulus 36–7, 54

Caligula 46, 70–1, 72, 106
Cassius the tyrannicide 59–60
censorship 107, 115
Claudius 106–21, 127, 135, 140, 148, 162;
  as anti-historian 109, 121; imitation
  of Augustus 107–9
continuity 23–5, 39–40, 47–9, 51, 56, 57,
  68–9, 107–9
Cremutius Cordus 81, 97, 100–2, 177
curses 141, 173

definition 16–17, 20–2, 23, 26–7, 32–3,
  35–9, 40–1, 64–5, 85, 103
digression 81, 97–103
disorder 23, 25–6, 34–41
dissimulation 78–81, 86–7, 90–5, 96
Drusus, father of Germanicus: adopted
  by Augustus 109; compared with
  Germanicus 47–9, 56, 61, 66–8;
  evoked by Agrippina 71
Drusus, son of Tiberius: accompanied
  by Sejanus 148; compared with
  Germanicus 26, 74; in mutiny
  episode 33–4, 82

eclipse 31–3, 38

Fannia 124–6
focalisation 55–6, 69 n. 41, 74–5, 114

Haterius Agrippa 41–5
Helvidius Priscus 124–6, 176
Herennius Senecio 124–5, 177
historical understanding 2–5, 27, 179–83
Homeric quotation 160, 161, 172–3
Hortensius Hortalus, M. 60–1, 82

Index Locorum

196